Using Observation in Early Childhood Education

Marian Marion
School of Education
University of Wisconsin–Stout

PEARSON
Merrill
Prentice Hall

Upper Saddle River, New Jersey
Columbus, Ohio

Library of Congress Cataloging-in-Publication Data

Marion, Marian
    Using observation in early childhood education / Marian Marion.—1st ed.
        p. cm.
Includes bibliographical references and index.
    ISBN 0-13-888496-X
    1. Observation (Educational method)   2. Early childhood education.   I. Title.
LB1027.28 .M37 2004
372.21'07'23—dc21

                                                    2003010710

Vice President and Executive Publisher: **Photo Coordinator:** Valerie Schultz
   Jeffery W. Johnston   **Cover Designer:** Rod Harris
Publisher: Kevin M. Davis   **Cover photo:** Corbis
Editorial Assistant: Autumn Crisp   **Production Manager:** Laura Messerly
Production Editor: Sheryl Glicker Langner   **Director of Marketing:** Ann Castel Davis
Production Coordination: Penny Walker,   **Marketing Manager:** Amy June
   The GTS Companies/York, PA Campus   **Marketing Coordinator:** Tyra Poole
Design Coordinator: Diane C. Lorenzo

This book was set in Novarese Bk BT by *The GTS Companies*/York, PA Campus. It was printed and
bound by R. R. Donnelley & Sons Company. The cover was printed by Phoenix Color Corp.

Photo Credits: Scott Cunningham/Merrill, pp. 2, 109, 130, 135, 196, 218; Jeff Greenberg/Image Stock
Imagery, p. 5; Dan Floss/Merrill, p. 8; Jo Hall/Merrill, p. 199; KS Studios/Merrill, p. 238; Anthony
Magnacca/Merrill, pp. 25, 87, 97, 105, 112, 214, 243; Merrill, pp. 159, 182; Pearson Learning, p. 53;
Barbara Schwartz/Merrill, pp. 20, 67, 84; Teri Stratford/PH College, p. 139; David Strickler/StrixPix,
p. 150; Anne Vega/Merrill, pp. 10, 44, 49, 64, 102; Todd Yarrington/Merrill, pp. 27, 163, 232

Pearson Education Ltd.   Pearson Education Australia Pty. Limited
Pearson Education Singapore Pte. Ltd. Pearson Education North Asia Ltd.
Pearson Education Canada, Ltd.   Pearson Educación de Mexico, S.A. de C.V.
Pearson Education—Japan   Pearson Education Malaysia Pte. Ltd.

10 9 8 7 6 5 4 3 2 1
ISBN: 0-13-888496-X

For Roxie Jane and Bekka Jean, my canine companions of 11 years and my writing buddies, now waiting for me at the "Rainbow Bridge"

For three of my professors, in whose classes I first learned about the value and process of observing:
Alice P. Eyman, University of Delaware
Kathy R. Thornburg, University of Missouri–Columbia
In memory of Virginia Fisher, University of Missouri–Columbia

Preface

Welcome to *Using Observation in Early Childhood Education*. My purpose in writing this text was to give students a book that will help them understand the process of observation. I want students to be able to observe, document, and assess children's development and progress. I want students to know just how powerful a tool ethical and responsible observation can be in their professional life.

I have constructed this textbook so that it, like my other textbook, *Guidance of Young Children*, reflects my beliefs about children.

📖 **I believe that protecting children is a teacher's most important role.** Students reading this text should understand that we teach and protect children most effectively by making active conscious choices about our practices, including how we assess and observe children. We protect children when we refuse to use inappropriate assessment strategies that are potentially harmful. We protect children by observing ethically and responsibly and by protecting children's privacy.

  The National Association for the Education of Young Children (NAEYC), in its Code of Ethical Conduct, notes that the most important part of the code is that early childhood professionals never engage in any practice that hurts or degrades a child. I take this advice seriously. Students who use this textbook will learn *only* responsible, ethical strategies and a respectful approach to observing and assessing young children.

📖 **I believe that observation is a powerful tool.** Students who read this book should come away convinced that they can use observation to increase their effectiveness as professionals. Students will learn how to observe children and document their development and progress. They will also learn to use observation to observe children's behavior, to become reflective practitioners, to prevent or solve problems, and to work with parents.

📖 **I believe that we have a choice about how we observe and use observation.** Students have a choice about how they responsibly observe and assess children. Students should know that the methods they choose *do* matter, and should know how to choose informal and formal observation and assessment strategies. They should also know how to embed the observations in the daily life of a classroom.

📖 **I believe that there is no one right way to observe and assess children's development and progress, but that there are many good ways.** This textbook will give students a clear and precise picture of major observation strategies. It will urge them to use a single developmentally appropriate observational strategy, or a combination of these, to get the information that they need. My hope is that they will value the opportunity to use a variety of observational strategies.

SPECIAL FEATURES OF THIS TEXT

📖 Students will see how these teachers have woven observation into the fabric of their teaching: Mrs. Vargas (preschool), Mr. Claiborne (first grade), Mr. Nellis (K–2), and Mr. Lee (third grade).

📖 An emphasis on observation as a part of authentic assessment of young children.

📖 Discussion of problems associated with standardized testing of young children.

📖 A discussion of the ethics of observation.

📖 Practical and specific help in doing observations in a time-efficient way.

📖 Clear descriptions of specific major observational methods.

📖 Many examples of observational methods—examples from real classrooms. If running records are under discussion, then several running records are presented. They are not just described. Students see real examples.

📖 Case studies for many of the chapters.

📖 Helpful figures throughout the text, such as a timeline for observing, checklists, and rating scales.

📖 Real-life examples of observations from primary, kindergarten, and preschool classrooms.

📖 Terms that are clearly defined.

📖 Student-friendly writing style.

📖 Web sites for each chapter.

📖 Two appendices (Appendix A and B) providing an outline for writing observation reports and suggestions of what to look for when observing a play material or activity.

📖 An appendix (appendix C) with reproducible forms for different observational methods.

STRUCTURE OF THIS TEXT

This book is organized by chapters within three parts.

Part I: The Power, Process, and Ethics of Observation in Early Childhood

Part I of this text consists of two chapters, designed to do two things. First, I want students to understand how powerful a tool observation is for early childhood professionals. Second, I want students to understand that they have a professional obligation to observe ethically.

Chapter 1, "The Power of Observation in Early Childhood," emphasizes that there is real power in observation. One of the things that is emphasized is that observation is an essential element in authentic assessment of young children. Students will see that they can use observation to prevent or solve many of the problems that they will face as professionals.

Chapter 2, "The Ethics and Process of Observing," explains ethical observation. Students will learn how to protect children's privacy while observing. They will also learn how to protect their observations. This chapter will introduce two major categories of observation—narrative and nonnarrative—and also several of the major practical strategies for observing nested within each of these categories.

Part II: Methods of Observing and Documenting Progress and Development in Early Childhood

When students are finished with Part II, they will have a good start in understanding several of the major methods for observing and documenting young children's development and progress. They will read a sound rationale as well as specific, detailed, and usable information about each strategy.

Chapter 3, "Anecdotal Records: A Short Narrative Method of Observation," will show students how to write good and useful anecdotal records. They will quickly learn the value of using anecdotal records to observe almost any aspect of a child's development or progress.

Chapter 4, "Running Records: A Longer Narrative Method of Observation," will help students learn to record an event in more detail. They will discover the power of running records in authentic assessment, will learn how to write about a child or an activity without giving their opinions, and will learn how to reflect on the data that they collect.

Chapter 5, "Checklists and Rating Scales: Nonnarrative Methods for Observing Development and Progress," describes two shortcut observation strategies. Students will learn that both checklists and rating scales are useful strategies to use when they need to gather specific types of information quickly. They will also learn how to develop different types of checklists and rating scales.

Chapter 6, "Documenting and Reporting Development and Progress: Children's Products, Observation Reports, and Portfolios," shows students several different ways to document and report children's development and progress: with children's products and work samples, with documentary displays, and with observation reports. This chapter also describes portfolios as a way of documenting and reporting. Students will learn practical strategies for using children's portfolios in their classrooms.

Part III: Using Observation

This section of the text will help students put observation to work for them.

Chapter 7, "Observing Behavior: Cracking the Code," facilitates student learning about observing children's behavior. They will quickly see the value of observation in dealing with challenging behaviors, for example.

Chapter 8, "Using the Eclectic Approach to Observe Motor and Cognitive Development," challenges students to discover and build on children's strengths through systematic observation. It shows students how to use an eclectic approach to observe both cognitive and large motor development.

Chapter 9, "Using the Eclectic Approach to Observe Emotional and Social Development," like chapter 8, focuses on using a combination of wisely chosen observation instruments. Such a combination enables students and teachers to get the most helpful information about children's feelings and relationships. They will see a teacher use the ready-made and easily obtainable Social Attributes Checklist as well as several teacher-made observation tools.

Chapter 10, "Using Observation to Prevent and Solve Problems," urges students to adopt a problem-solving approach, an attitude that says, "This is a problem and I am willing to try to solve it." It demonstrates how ethical and reflective teachers value observation as a valuable skill in preventing or solving problems.

Chapter 11, "Using Observation to Become a Reflective Practitioner," will help students use observation to become reflective practitioners. They will have an opportunity to assess their own ability to reflect on their practices.

ACKNOWLEDGMENTS

Many thanks to Ann Davis, the editor at Merrill/Prentice Hall, and now the Director of Marketing, who urged me to write this book. Over the years, I have been amazed at her remarkably good knowledge base in early childhood, her ability to predict trends in our field, and her powers of persuasion.

I hope that you will join me in acknowledging our colleagues who laid the foundation for observation in the early years of our profession. Their work lives in our current knowledge base and skills.

I value the review process for a manuscript, especially the first edition of a textbook such as this one. All of the chapters of this text have been reviewed twice. The reviewers' comments on each round of reviews were insightful, helpfully given, cogently written, and helped me to refine the chapters. For instance, one reviewer suggested adding a timeline for observing in a real classroom so teachers could manage their time well for observing. You will see such a timeline in two separate chapters. Another reviewer suggested emphasizing the child's role in developing his or her portfolio. For these and many other excellent suggestions, I thank the following reviewers of this textbook: Barbara Foulks Boyd, Radford University; Carrie Beth Brouse, Marian College; Phyllis Cuevas, McNeese State University; Pamela O. Fleege, University of South Florida; Barbara G. Graham, Norfolk State University; Berta Harris, San Diego City College; Adrienne L. Herrell, California State University, Fresno; Patricia Hofbauer, Northwest State Community College; Lillian Oxtoby, Borough of Manhattan Community College, CUNY; and Wayne Reinhardt, Edmonds Community College.

The chancellor of my university, Charles Sorensen, has been steadfast in supporting an expanded sabbatical leave policy. On a practical level, this has given faculty with full teaching loads an opportunity to engage more fully in scholarly pursuits. I am grateful to him for his continued support of sabbatical leaves and of scholarly activity in general.

Finally, I want to acknowledge my child development and early childhood colleagues here at UW–Stout: Judy Herr (with whom I've worked for 25 years), Don Platz, Robin Muza, Bert Fox, Julia Lorenz, Kathy Preusse, Jamie Lynch, and adjunct staff. I like working with you and value your knowledge and skills.

Marian Marion
E-mail: Marionm@uwstout.edu

Discover the Companion Website Accompanying This Book

THE PRENTICE HALL COMPANION WEBSITE: A VIRTUAL LEARNING ENVIRONMENT

Technology is a constantly growing and changing aspect of our field that is creating a need for content and resources. To address this emerging need, Prentice Hall has developed an online learning environment for students and professors alike—Companion Websites—to support our textbooks.

In creating a Companion Website, our goal is to build on and enhance what the textbook already offers. For this reason, the content for each user-friendly Website is organized by topic and provides the professor and student with a variety of meaningful resources. Common features of a Companion Website include:

FOR THE PROFESSOR—

Every Companion Website integrates **Syllabus Manager**™, an online syllabus creation and management utility.

- **Syllabus Manager**™ provides you, the instructor, with an easy, step-by-step process to create and revise syllabi, with direct links into Companion Website and other online content without having to learn HTML.
- Students may log on to your syllabus during any study session. All they need to know is the Web address for the Companion Website and the password you've assigned to your syllabus.
- After you have created a syllabus using **Syllabus Manager**™, students may enter the syllabus for their course section from any point in the Companion Website.
- Clicking on a date, the student is shown the list of activities for the assignment. The activities for each assignment are linked directly to actual content, saving time for students.

- Adding assignments consists of clicking on the desired due date, then filling in the details of the assignment—name of the assignment, instructions, and whether or not it is a one-time or repeating assignment.
- In addition, links to other activities can be created easily. If the activity is online, a URL can be entered in the space provided, and it will be linked automatically in the final syllabus.
- Your completed syllabus is hosted on our servers, allowing convenient updates from any computer on the Internet. Changes you make to your syllabus are immediately available to your students at their next logon.

FOR THE STUDENT—

- **Introduction**—General information about the topic and how it will be covered in the Website.
- **Web Links**—A variety of Websites related to topic areas.
- **Timely Articles**—Links to online articles that enable you to become more aware of important issues in early childhood.
- **Learn by Doing**—Put concepts into action, participate in activities, examine strategies, and more.
- **Visit a School**—Visit a school's Website to see concepts, theories, and strategies in action.
- **For Teachers/Practitioners**—Access information you will need to know as an educator, including information on materials, activities, and lessons.
- **Current Policies and Standards**—Find out the latest early childhood policies from the government and various organizations, and view state, federal, and curriculum standards.
- **Resources and Organizations**—Discover tools to help you plan your classroom or center and organizations to provide current information and standards for each topic.
- **Electronic Bluebook**—Paperless method of completing homework or essays assigned by a professor. Finished work can be sent to the professor via e-mail.
- **Message Board**—Virtual bulletin board to post and respond to questions and comments from a national audience.

To take advantage of these and other resources, please visit the *Using Observation in Early Childhood Education* Companion Website at

www.prenhall.com/marion

Educator Learning Center: An Invaluable Online Resource

Merrill Education and the Association for Supervision and Curriculum Development (ASCD) invite you to take advantage of a new online resource, one that provides access to the top research and proven strategies associated with ASCD and Merrill—the Educator Learning Center. At **www.EducatorLearningCenter.com** you will find resources that will enhance your students' understanding of course topics and of current educational issues, in addition to being invaluable for further research.

HOW THE EDUCATOR LEARNING CENTER WILL HELP YOUR STUDENTS BECOME BETTER TEACHERS

With the combined resources of Merrill Education and ASCD, you and your students will find a wealth of tools and materials to better prepare them for the classroom.

Research

- More than 600 articles from the ASCD journal *Educational Leadership* discuss everyday issues faced by practicing teachers.
- A direct link on the site to Research Navigator™ gives students access to many of the leading education journals, as well as extensive content detailing the research process.
- Excerpts from Merrill Education texts give your students insights on important topics of instructional methods, diverse populations, assessment, classroom management, technology, and refining classroom practice.

Classroom Practice

- Hundreds of lesson plans and teaching strategies are categorized by content area and age range.
- Case studies and classroom video footage provide virtual field experience for student reflection.
- Computer simulations and other electronic tools keep your students abreast of today's classrooms and current technologies.

LOOK INTO THE VALUE OF EDUCATOR LEARNING CENTER YOURSELF

Preview the value of this educational environment by visiting **www.EducatorLearningCenter.com** and clicking on "Demo." For a free 4-month subscription to the Educator Learning Center in conjunction with this text, simply contact your Merrill/Prentice Hall sales representative.

Brief Contents

Contents

PART II
Methods of Observing and Documenting Progress and Development in Early Childhood   41

CHAPTER 3
Anecdotal Records: A Short Narrative Method of Observation   45

CHAPTER 4
Running Records: A Longer Narrative Method of Observation   65

CHAPTER 5
Checklists and Rating Scales: Nonnarrative Methods for Observing Development and Progress   85

CHAPTER 6
Documenting and Reporting Development and Progress: Children's Products, Observation Reports, and Portfolios   103

PART III
Using Observation   127

CHAPTER 7
Observing Behavior: Cracking the Code   131

CHAPTER 8
Using the Eclectic Approach to Observe Motor and Cognitive Development   151

CHAPTER 9
Using the Eclectic Approach to Observe Emotional and Social Development   183

CHAPTER 10
Using Observation to Prevent and Solve Problems   215

CHAPTER 11
Using Observation to Become a Reflective Practitioner   233

APPENDIX A

APPENDIX B

APPENDIX C

Name Index   279

Subject Index   283

Note: We have made every effort to provide accurate and current Internet information in this book. However, the Internet and information posted on it are constantly changing, so it is inevitable that some of the Internet addresses listed in this textbook will change.

PART I

The Power, Process, and Ethics of Observation in Early Childhood

Chapter 1 The Power of Observation in Early Childhood.   Observation is a powerful tool. This chapter will help you understand its power and potential in your professional life. Observation can help you learn about child development. Observation can help you to engage in authentic assessment of children's development and progress. Observation can also help you to develop appropriate curriculum and instructional methods. It can assist you in making wise decisions about guiding children and can help you become a reflective teacher. On a very practical level, observation will be one of your best tools for preventing or solving many of the problems that you will undoubtedly face as a professional.

Chapter 2 The Ethics and Process of Observing.   "First of all, do no harm." This is the guiding force in NAEYC's Code of Ethical Conduct, and it applies to early childhood teachers who observe young children. You will learn about ethical observation, that is, how to protect children's privacy while you observe, and about developing policies that make sure that your observations are protected. This chapter should also help you understand two major categories of observation—narrative and nonnarrative. You will learn about several of the major practical strategies for observing nested within each of these categories.

CHAPTER 1

The Power of Observation in Early Childhood

Observe: to see, to inspect, and to take note of; to see through directed careful analytic attention
Observation: a record of the act noted

Chapter objectives

1. *List* several key purposes or functions that ***observation*** serves for early childhood professionals.
2. *Explain* each of these functions.
3. *Give examples* of each of the functions of observation.

THERE IS POWER IN OBSERVATION

This textbook focuses on the powerful skill of **observation** for early childhood profes-sionals. Observing well (taking note of and recording what is noted) is one of the most powerful skills that a teacher can develop and use (Bracken, 2000; Cohen & Stern, 1983; Cohen, Stern, & Balaban, 1996; Hemmeter, Maxwell, Ault, & Schuster, 2001). Teachers gather the information that they need before they can begin, for example, to learn about children, to plan for curriculum, to deal with guidance or discipline dilem-mas, or to prevent or solve a variety of problems (Figure 1.1).

Observation Facilitates Learning About Child Development

Do babies have emotions when they are born? Can we expect a toddler to be able to play cooperatively with another toddler? How much empathy would an abused toddler likely show to other toddlers? What are the sorts of things that arouse anger in preschool children and how do preschool children typically react to anger-arousing situations? Are first-grade children capable of sustained attention? When are children capable of self-control? How do young children understand the concept of friendship?

Observation is a time-honored way for parents, students, teachers, and researchers to learn about children's development and answer such questions. Piaget, for example, observed his own three children when they were babies. He observed how they approached and investigated situations and how they dealt with problems that he set for them (Piaget, 1951).

For several decades now, students have observed children as a way to learn about child development. Researchers have also used observation as an important part of their effort to document and explain children's growth and development. Here are just a few examples.

    📖 We know about emotions in infants and young children because researchers have observed and documented several aspects of emotional development (Fabes & Eisenberg, 1992; Izard, 1982; Malatesta, Culver, Tesman, & Shepard, 1989).

Use Observation

- To learn about child development
- To authentically assess children's progress
- To develop appropriate curriculum and instructional methods
- To make wise child guidance decisions
- To reflect on your own practices
- To prevent or solve problems

Figure 1.1

⊞ We know about several different aspects of children's play because of the observational work of researchers such as Harper and Huie (1985), Howes and Matheson (1992), and Parten (1932).

⊞ We know about individual differences in the quality of attachment between infants and caregivers from the work of Ainsworth, Blehar, Waters, and Wall (1978).

Observation Is Preferable to Formal Testing of Young Children

Mr. Nellis is a K-2 teacher, that is, the children in his class are in kindergarten, first, and second grades. He and other kindergarten and primary grade teachers in his district and state are worried about a proposed change. The district is considering formal standardized testing of all early childhood children (preschool, kindergarten, first-, second-, and third-grade children). The teachers have been assessing children's development and progress primarily through observation and recording at regular intervals (Bredekamp, 1987). They, along with many other early childhood professionals and researchers, regard most forms of formal testing of young children as *in*appropriate. They oppose using formal testing for early childhood children (Genishi, 1992; Kamii, 1990; Katz, 1997; Meisels, 1993).

Observation helps us to learn about child development.

Concerns About Standardized Testing.   The concerns about standardized tests with children in the early childhood years center on three things (Meisels, 1995):

- The nature of standardized tests and the testing situation
- The negative effect that standardized tests are likely to have on early childhood curriculum
- The potential misuse of results of standardized tests

First, the very **nature of standardized tests and the testing situation** are a major problem and make them *in*appropriate for young children. Most young children have never encountered anything like a standardized test. Testers administer a standardized test in the same way to all children taking it. During a standardized test, a child usually has to sit at a table and mark or circle items on a sheet of paper. There is a time limit for such a test.

Additionally, standardized tests are quite passive and the content is generally abstract, making them quite *in*appropriate for children younger than 8 years. Standardized tests require a child to follow many verbal directions, something that is very difficult for young children to do.

Mr. Nellis and the other teachers in his district are especially concerned that the proposed standardized testing might be extremely stressful for the children. Other children, they think, might treat the standardized testing situation as a game, completely unaware that important decisions are based on results of such a test.

Second, **standardized tests can have a negative effect on early childhood curriculum.** Teachers who design developmentally appropriate early childhood curriculum rely on *observing* the needs, interests, and abilities of children in specific curriculum areas as the first step in curriculum development. A major concern of professionals opposed to standardized testing for young children is that teachers who know that their children will take a standardized test might design the curriculum so that it prepares children for the standardized tests. Such a curriculum will not likely be based on the teachers' observations of the needs, interests, or abilities of the children.

Third, **some people have misused the results of standardized tests.** The concern here is that the test results might be used to make decisions that would be harmful to children. Suppose, for example, that a school screened all applicants for their preschool, kindergarten, and primary grades. They gave each child a standardized test and required that a child achieve a certain level on the test before the school would admit the child. This is a potentially harmful practice.

Some parents of children denied entrance to the school because of a single test score might well think that their child does not "measure up" in some way. This attitude might then be reflected to the child, affecting her sense of worth and competence, two of the three building blocks of self-esteem. Second, such tests might favor children from affluent, well-educated families. The playing field, to use a sports analogy, is not a level one for children from poor, less educated families.

Another scenario: a child has to score at a specific level to participate in specific enrichment programs in her current school. This is called *high-stakes* testing: that is, the stakes (child's admission to a school or participating in an enrichment program) are high.

In reality, the score obtained from a standardized test for young children is not very helpful because so little is learned from such a score. It tells the tester only that a child has a percentile ranking. The standardized test score, then, gives only one small piece of information. It often leaves teachers and parents with more questions than answers. Standardized test scores fail to take into account several things and tell us little about a specific child's capabilities.

Example: Ned, a third grader, is very impulsive and has difficulty concentrating. Consequently, he did not score very high on a standardized test because of his difficulty concentrating during the test.

Example: Charlie is in kindergarten. One of the things that his teacher has noticed is that he has a problem following directions. Charlie became agitated during the standardized test because he could not follow the directions.

Example: A second-grade teacher announced every day for 2 weeks that the standardized test was coming up. She told the children how important the test would be, and that they should get lots of sleep the night before the test. The announcements created great stress for several of the children, affecting their scores in a negative way.

Appropriate Assessment of Young Children.   *Authentic assessment* with young children is a developmentally appropriate way to assess children's progress (Genishi, 1992). Teachers who use authentic assessment involve children as much as possible in evaluating their own achievement. Teachers who use authentic assessment systematically observe and document children's development and learning. Authentic assessment is performance based. Teachers who use authentic assessment tend to favor observing and documenting a child's actual performance in a specific area (Clay, 1993). A teacher who believes in developmentally appropriate and authentic assessment in early childhood, then, likes to collect documentation about how children deal with many different types of real-life tasks (Hill & Ruptic, 1994; Snow, 1989).

There are many specific ways to do authentic assessment in early childhood (Genishi, 1992). These methods are the essential and core elements in studying children. The methods include the variety of ways of observing children and taking notes during observations.[1] The methods also include documenting children's development and performance with summaries of observations, portfolios[2] with children's work, and any audio or video recording of a child's performance or classroom activity.

---

[1]Chapters 3, 4, 5, and 6 describe and explain several major methods for observing.

[2]Chapter 6 explains the use of **observation summaries** and **portfolios**.

Authentic assessment. This teacher will be able to document how these boys deal with the real-life task of interacting.

Example: M. Clay (1990, 1993) developed the "Reading Recovery" program. This program depends on a teacher's ability to observe. The teachers in this program observe by writing daily running records[3] of what children can read and write. The teacher uses what she learns through this assessment to guide children to acquire strategies for reading and writing that successful readers use to make sense of print.

Teachers who use this or other similar systems observe to help them decide on what to include in the curriculum for the children. For the teacher, observation is an essential part of the process of deciding the content of the curriculum and how the curriculum is carried out (Genishi, 1992).

Observation Is the First Step in Constructing Developmentally Appropriate Curriculum and Instructional Methods

Genishi's (1992) main concern is with how a teacher and children carry out the curriculum in realistic or lifelike ways. She further states that in a constructivist curriculum, teachers must be trusted to decide which experiences are truly purposeful and developmentally

[3]Chapter 4 describes and explains the **running record** method of observation.

appropriate. Teachers base their best curriculum decisions on what they know about the children—their experiences, what they already know, and their social history. The best way for the teacher to get this information is through observing.

Example: Mr. Lee is a third- and fourth-grade teacher (same school as Mr. Nellis). Mr. Lee talked with Mr. Caristi, a second-grade teacher. Mr. Caristi complained that two boys in his class regularly disrupt large-group times. Both boys have trouble with math worksheets and act out every time that they have to do a math worksheet. He had been placing the boys in time-out when they were disruptive. He said that things had gotten worse with the time-outs.

Mr. Lee listened carefully and then asked his colleague to describe the second grade's schedule for a typical day. Mr. Caristi:

- Arrival/large group (25 minutes)
- Reading/small groups (30 minutes)
- Music, art specialist, guidance counselor, or physical education/large group (30 minutes)
- Workbook sheets for specific curriculum areas/individual work (20 minutes)
- Third large group (30 minutes)

Mr. Caristi: "What does my schedule have to do with this problem?"

Mr. Lee: "I'm not sure, but it's a place to start. Something is bothering the boys and it's probably smart to look at (observe) something as simple as the schedule or what you're expecting them to do. Let's look at how long the children are in some kind of group or are doing individual seat work." Mr. Lee is encouraging his friend to examine his own practices (Kohn, 1996).

Mr. Caristi added the minutes and quickly discovered that he was requiring his children to sit quietly for the entire morning, 2½ hours. He said, "That's the way I've always done my schedule. Is there some kind of problem with that?"

Mr. Lee: "Well, I've found out the hard way that I need to allow my children to be actively involved in their work and to let them move around the classroom—within limits. Do you think that your children might just be reacting to having to be quiet and pay attention for nearly 2½ hours?" Mr. Lee knows the research that tells us that it is very difficult for 7-year-old children to maintain attention for that long a time (Shaffer, 1996).

The way that Mr. Caristi carried out the curriculum with worksheets and so many large groups was a major part of the problem, and it was highly **in**appropriate to punish the boys for disrupting. He also needs to get a better picture of what each boy *can* do in math. The teacher should consider planning his curriculum and his schedule so that they are both developmentally appropriate. For example, he should consider figuring out how to help them learn the math concepts in a more active approach and even eliminating the worksheets for the time being.

Pelander (1997) described the changes that he has made in his instructional methods and schedule in his third-grade classroom. Formerly, he used a traditional or conventional approach to carrying out the curriculum. For example, all the children in the class did the same thing at the same time. Children had little or no choice about where they sat when they worked. They had little or no choice about the order in which they did their work. The teacher took responsibility for keeping children on track.

He described his journey to a more developmentally appropriate way of carrying out the curriculum. In the new schedule, Mr. Pelander's children have a certain time in which to complete specific curriculum work. Children still do all the normal curriculum areas, but they make choices about the order in which they tackle curriculum areas, when they will work on an area, and, within limits, even where they will work. Children are free to move about the classroom and have taken a lot more responsibility for keeping themselves on track.

Observation Is the First Step in Making Wise Child Guidance Decisions

Example: Ms. Vargas is a preschool teacher and Mrs. Lyndon is the assistant teacher in the same classroom. Last week, Mrs. Lyndon noticed that Ralph, 4 years old, was tapping on the wire mesh cover of the gerbil's house, a large aquarium. It looked to her as if he was quietly drumming and scraping the wire mesh with his hands and fingernails. He was not looking at or talking to the gerbils, and he had closed his eyes. As he drummed, he verbalized a drumbeat. The gerbils seemed frightened and ran to hide inside their smaller house in the aquarium.

Observation is the first step in making wise child guidance decisions.

This is a ***discipline encounter,*** which is one part of the whole process of socialization. A discipline encounter is any interaction between an adult and child in which the adult attempts to help a child alter her behavior in some way. There are many types of discipline encounters. One example includes stopping a child from doing something harmful or destructive. Other examples are teaching and encouraging a child to treat a person or animal with respect (for example, being respectfully quiet around the gerbils) and helping children take responsibility for such things as cleaning up or putting things away.

Discipline encounters occur frequently during the early childhood period, even in classrooms and homes where adults are warm and supportive. Teachers face discipline encounters as they help children learn to respect the rights of others and as they help children comply with legitimate authority. Some discipline encounters deal with everyday concerns (such as leaving sand toys strewn about on the trike path, or taking turns). Others center on more serious and harmful problems (such as hurting other people or mean-spirited treatment of animals). All, however, are discipline encounters (Baumrind, 1996; Marion, 2003).

The ***decision-making model of child guidance*** is a way of arriving at decisions about how to handle a variety of discipline encounters with children in a developmentally appropriate way. There are several specific steps that a teacher takes when using this model, and systematic observation is at the heart of the whole process (Figure 1.2).

Step 1: Observe.   Focus on the encounter as a problem to solve. Some adults take the punishment approach to a discipline encounter and view a discipline encounter as a time to simply administer some sort of punishment in an effort to stop the child's behavior (Kohn, 1996). Mrs. Lyndon would have done this if, for example, she had used a time-out with Ralph. All she would have accomplished with time-out would have been to punish Ralph.

A better approach is for a teacher to look at a discipline encounter as a problem to solve and not to blame the child (Kohn, 1996). One of the first things that a teacher has to do when deciding how to deal with a discipline encounter is to *identify the problem*. The teacher must be extremely clear in describing the problem. Then, the teacher has to decide who "owns" the problem. Does the child or the teacher own the problem? To do both of these things, a teacher must be a good observer.

Example: Mrs. Lyndon had quickly observed the situation and did not simply rush to judgment about what Ralph was doing. She saw that the gerbils seemed to be afraid and that Ralph did not seem to be aware of their fear. Mrs. Lyndon, as well as the head teacher, was concerned about the gerbils and was concerned about helping Ralph abide by the classroom rule of fair and respectful treatment of everyone, including classroom pets. This was the problem. Then, the teachers decided that the teacher "owned" the problem because she, not Ralph, was upset by the incident and she would have to help Ralph understand and accept the classroom limit.

When you observe, you will also examine the context of the problem. What in the context might be affecting a child's behavior? The problem that a teacher observes

Four Steps in the Decision-Making Model of Child Guidance

✓ **OBSERVE**

Observe the child's behavior.

Focus on the encounter as a problem to be solved.

Clearly identify the problem. Decide whether the child or the adult "owns the problem." Focus on solving a problem, not on blaming a child.

Examine the context of the problem.

Ask yourself how the child's age might be affecting her behavior. Ask how the child's family, culture, or the classroom physical environment, activities, or materials have contributed to the problem. The idea is not to place blame but simply to get a better picture of the context or setting in which the behavior has evolved.

✓ **DECIDE**

Your observation will tell you what to change. For example, you might need to:

Choose a guidance strategy.

Use *only* developmentally appropriate strategies, not punishment. Consult Marion (2003), chapter 4 and Appendix. Say why the chosen strategy is appropriate for this child at this time

Change the context.

You might decide that you have to change the classroom physical environment or the time schedule. You might decide that you should choose more DAP activities, or that materials need to be organized better.

Change your own practices.

You might decide that you want to change something that you are doing. For instance, you decide that you want to talk with children about playground rules after you realize that you have never done this.

✓ **TAKE ACTION**

Carry out the guidance strategy, make the contextual change, or change the practice that you want to change.

✓ **REFLECT**

Think about how things went after you made a change. What went well and why? Are there some things that you still need to change? Why? If you want to make another change, then go through this 4-step process again to refine your approach.

Figure 1.2

Source: Marion, M. (2003). *Guidance of young children* (6th ed.). Upper Saddle River, NJ: Merrill/Prentice Hall. Used with permission.

and describes unfolded in a specific setting or *context*. Consequently, a teacher has to observe and pay attention to the context of a problem as well as the problem itself. The teacher should observe and take note of how a child's age, interests, and family or the classroom physical environment, activities, or materials might have contributed to the problem. The idea is not to place blame but simply to get a better picture of the context or setting in which the behavior has evolved.

Example: Mrs. Lyndon and Ms. Vargas have already discovered by observing that Ralph has a special interest in music. They had used a checklist[4] of each child's interests. In addition, the teachers documented Ralph's interest in music by placing a song that he had written in his portfolio. They have also seen how gently Ralph always treats classroom animals, which explained their surprise when he drummed on the roof of their house. They have never seen him be intentionally hurtful toward the animals. Therefore, they concluded that Ralph was probably not even aware that he was bothering the animals. They concluded that Ralph was not acting in a mean-spirited way.

Step 2: Decide.   A teacher might decide to choose a specific guidance strategy. In the decision-making model, teachers use strategies that focus on teaching and not on punishment (Marion, 2003). The guidance strategies that they use are appropriate for a particular child at the time of the discipline encounter. Again, it is essential that the teacher carefully observe in order to judge the effectiveness of the chosen strategy.

Example: Mrs. Lyndon decided to do two things to try to help Ralph. She would restate a classroom limit (restating the limit is the guidance strategy). She would also ask him to think about another way to drum.

A teacher might decide instead to change the context or to change his own practices (Figure 1.2).

Step 3: Take action.   Mrs. Lyndon took action.

Example: First, she restated the classroom limit of respectful treatment of the animals. She told Ralph firmly but kindly that he had to stop drumming on the gerbil house lid because the drumming seemed to be scaring the gerbils. Together, they observed the gerbils' reaction. Then she asked him to think of a more appropriate thing to use for drumming. He said, "I can use the real drum but I like the sound that this (the screen) makes."
Mrs. Lyndon: "What if we look for some screen and make it into a drum so that you can make the same sound?"
A nice thing happened immediately after their talk. Mrs. Lyndon had already walked away and Ralph was alone with the gerbils. The teacher turned and observed Ralph leaning over to talk to the gerbils. She heard him say softly, "I'm sorry that I scared you, Weezer and Happy. Please come out to play. I promise not to play on your roof any more."

Step 4: Reflect.   A teacher would evaluate the effectiveness of the guidance strategy, the contextual change, or the effectiveness of changing his own practice. Again, observe to judge the effectiveness of any of these. Mrs. Lyndon thought, from Ralph's comment to the gerbils, that he was beginning to understand that he had frightened them. She also kept an eye on the gerbil house and observed that Ralph did not use the roof as a drum either that day or any other day. After they made a wire mesh drum, she also observed that Ralph used the new drum.

[4]Chapter 5 explains the **checklist** method for observing.

Observation Enables Teachers to Reflect on Their Own Practices

Mrs. LeBlanc, the principal of the Oaklawn School, observed each of her teachers to see whether teachers distributed attention equitably among children in classrooms (Kontos & Wilcox-Herzog, 1997). She **observed** Mr. Nellis (the K–2 teacher) three times as he led science and math lessons. The principal considered Mr. Nellis fair to both boys and girls. She found, though, that the teacher consistently asked more questions of the boys during science as well as math. Mr. Nellis merely nodded when a girl answered a question during math but was much more enthusiastic when boys responded.

The principal talked with Mr. Nellis, who was surprised that he treated boys and girls so differently in these curriculum areas. He was not defensive but, instead, *reflected* on the principal's observations. The next time that he led a math or science activity, he made a note in his lesson plan: "Make sure that I ask questions of both girls and boys. Be sure to acknowledge girls' responses in much the same way that I have acknowledged boys' responses and questions."

He asked the principal to observe again. The principal quickly observed the good questioning directed at both genders. Mr. Nellis's actions had changed as a direct result of how he reflected on and questioned his practices (Kohn, 1996).

Observation, then, is critical to improving teaching effectiveness. Reflective teachers use their observations to examine their own practices. We become even better teachers if we reflect on our own practices and then actively decide whether and how to change things. The essential step in improving our practices is to reflect on our own practices. Observation is crucial to reflecting on practices.

Observation Is the Key to Preventing or Solving Many Problems

Teachers have to make decisions about many issues and not just about guiding children. Here are just a few examples. Teachers must make decisions about problems related to managing the physical space and time schedule as well as the curriculum of their classroom, two major categories of classroom management.

Teachers often face challenges in helping parents understand the program and reasons for different activities. They occasionally have to deal with an angry parent. Teachers must solve classroom problems that seem to begin with stress—stress experienced by a child or the child's family (chapter 10 deals with this issue). Teachers also have to figure out how to deal with workplace problems.

Observation is the key to mapping out strategies for solving problems. Observation is also the key to preventing many problems.

Example: Mrs. Vargas, the preschool teacher at Oaklawn, is a consultant who helps other teachers examine problems that they have with classroom management. Recently, she worked with a kindergarten teacher who was having problems at cleanup with material and equipment that did not work and with disorganization in general. The teacher complained that the children refused to put things away at cleanup or when they were done using things.

As Mrs. Vargas observed the classroom, she focused her attention on the materials in the classroom. She was particularly interested in how the teacher managed materials, which Mrs. Vargas suspected was the root of many of the teacher's problems. Mrs. Vargas evaluated the teacher's management of materials by using a rating scale (Marion, 2003). See Figure 1.3 for her ratings.

Activities to Help You Construct Knowledge and Skills in Observing

ACTIVITY 1

Panel discussion. Invite three early childhood teachers to participate in a panel in your class. Write questions for the panel that gets at how the teachers use observation. Here are three suggested questions. Please consider writing at least two other questions. Give the teachers the questions beforehand so that they have time to think about their responses.

1. Please describe a time when you noticed a discipline problem or encounter and observed carefully to get more information before you made a decision about what to do.

2. Please tell us about a time when you made your curriculum even more appropriate after *observing* that something in a lesson or how you taught it had affected or might affect a child's participation.

3. Have you ever done something like change your schedule or room arrangement after you noticed that they might be affecting a child's behavior? If you have, would you please tell us about it?

ACTIVITY 2

Go to the Web sites at the end of the chapter. Search for information on assessment during early childhood. Look for position papers, publications (books, articles, booklets, pamphlets), videos, or posters. Summarize the view of each organization on assessment during early childhood.

Do some real-world research. Find out what your state's department of public instruction believes and does about standardized testing of very young children. Find out whether and how your local school district uses standardized testing with early childhood children. What does Head Start do about standardized tests? Which tests are used? Ask how schools use results and how the school communicates results to parents. What decisions are made using the scores? Alternatively, ask each source about methods other than standardized tests that they use to assess children's development and progress.

ACTIVITY 3

✓ **SUPPLEMENTAL CASE STUDY: ROB.** Please use the following case study to practice the four steps in the decision-making model of child guidance (Figure 1.2).

Rating Scale: Classroom Management of Materials

Use this rating scale to evaluate classroom management of materials and equipment in this early childhood classroom. Rate each item with the scale. The numeral 1 indicates the lowest rating you can give. The numeral 5 is the highest rating you can give. A space is provided for comments.

The teacher has taken leadership in gathering materials.	1	2	③	4	5
All materials needed for an activity are there.	1	2	③	4	5
Materials appear to have been gathered well in advance of the activity.	1	②	3	4	5
Equipment is correctly sized for children using it.	1	2	③	4	5
Equipment works well.	1	2	③	4	5
Children will be able to use the materials without a lot of adult help.	1	2	③	4	5
Equipment is clean.	①	2	3	4	5
Materials are organized logically.	1	②	3	4	5
Items within centers are stored so that they are easy for children to get to and then to put away.	1	②	3	4	5
If children are expected to clean after any activity, then this teacher appears to have thought through and has provided necessary items.	1	②	3	4	5
If children are expected to set up an activity, then necessary materials are available.	①	2	3	4	5
Materials not intended for children's use are stored out of their reach.	1	2	3	④	5

Comments and suggestions: Has gathered many interesting and useful materials. Problem with gathering things just before an activity. Appears to be concerned about safety. A major problem lies in organizing and cleaning materials. Needs to organize more logically and make it easier for children to put things away. Help children with everyday activities and with cleanup by thinking through activities beforehand and gathering necessary materials. Put all this on a lesson plan. Clean equipment regularly.

Figure 1.3

Source: Marion, M. (2003). *Guidance of Young Children* (6th ed.). Upper Saddle River, NJ: Merrill/Prentice Hall. Used/adapted with permission.

Note: The rating scale has been "filled in" for this book.

Rob is 4 years old. His preschool teacher observed that Rob cursed quite frequently. He cursed in a frustrated tone when the blocks fell over. He cursed enthusiastically when he said how good the raisin bread tasted, "This bread is xxxxed good!" He cursed softly when he splashed water from the water table onto his new shoes. He cursed when angry. The teacher was puzzled about Rob's behavior, and then had a chance meeting with Rob's father and mother in a fast food restaurant. After they chatted briefly, the teacher sat two booths away from Rob's parents. Both parents used a couple of the same curse words that Rob had used and used them in normal conversation (they did not seem to be angry at all).

Go through each step of the Decision-Making Model of Child Guidance to choose a course of action for dealing with Rob's cursing in your classroom.

✓ **SUPPLEMENTAL CASE STUDY: WAIT, WAIT, WAIT!**   Use the following case study to help the student teacher reflect on his practices.

Mr. Nellis's student teacher took the class to the library. Mr. Nellis observed during library period because he was the cooperating teacher and the student teacher was in charge for the day. He noticed that the student teacher seemed frustrated when several of the children, while waiting in line to check out library books, started giggling and wiggling. Then the action escalated with two children getting very loud, in a cheerful sort of way. The group had been in line for 5 minutes before the librarian was even ready to begin checking them out.

The student teacher recorded the names of children that he considered "disruptive," intending to transfer the names to the board when they returned to the classroom. Mr. Nellis, however, quietly intervened because he did not approve of this method of discipline. This is what he did instead when they met after school to reflect on the day.

- He asked the student teacher to reconsider and to look back and figure out what went wrong in the library.
- They talked about whether it was necessary or appropriate to make the children stand in line so long.
- He asked the student to recall what he had observed as the children stood in line (wiggling, pushing, and a little shoving).
- Mr. Nellis asked the student teacher to think about a different system to get the books checked out in a way that did not require such a long wait.

From your perspective, how has Mr. Nellis avoided being judgmental? How did his questions help his student teacher to reflect and to examine his own practices?

REFERENCES

Ainsworth, M. D. S., Blehar, M., Waters, E., & Wall, S. (1978). *Patterns of attachment.* Hillsdale, NJ: Erlbaum.

Baumrind, D. (1996). Parenting: The discipline controversy revisited. *Family Relations, 45,* 405–414.

Bracken, B. (2000). Clinical observation of preschool assessment behavior. In B. Bracken (Ed.), *The psychoeducational assessment of preschool children* (pp. 45–56). Boston: Allyn & Bacon.

Bredekamp, S. (Ed.) (1987). *Developmentally appropriate practice in early childhood programs serving children from birth through age 8* (Exp. ed.). Washington, DC: NAEYC.

Bredekamp, S. (1997). Position statement on developmentally appropriate practice in early childhood education. *Young Children*, 52, 34–41.

Clay, M. (1990). Research currents: What is and what might be in evaluation. *Language Arts*, 67, 288–298.

Clay, M. (1993). *An observation survey of early literacy achievement*. Portsmouth, NH: Heinemann.

Cohen, D., & Stern, V. (1983). *Observing and recording the behavior of young children*. New York: Teachers College Press.

Cohen, D., Stern, V., & Balaban, N. (1996). *Observing and recording the behavior of young children*. New York: Teachers College Press.

Fabes, R., & Eisenberg, N. (1992). Young children's coping with interpersonal anger. *Child Development*, 63, 116–128.

Genishi, C. (1992). Framing the ways. In C. Genishi (Ed.), *Ways of assessing children and curriculum*, pp. 1–24. New York: Teachers College Press.

Harper, L. V., & Huie, K. S. (1985). The effects of prior group experience, age, and familiarity on the quality and organization of preschoolers' social relationships. *Child Development*, 56, 704–717.

Hemmeter, M., Maxwell, K., Ault, M., & Schuster, J. (2001). *Assessment of practices in early elementary classrooms* (APEEC). New York: Teachers College Press.

Hill, B., & Ruptic, C. (1994). *Practical aspects of authentic assessment*. Norwood, MA: Christopher-Gordon Publishers, Inc.

Howes, C., & Matheson, C. C. (1992). Sequences in the development of competent play with peers: Social and social pretend play. *Developmental Psychology*, 28, 961–974.

Izard, C. E. (1982). *Measuring emotions in infants and children*. New York: Cambridge University Press.

Kamii, C. (Ed.) (1990). *Achievement testing in the early grades: The games grown-ups play*. Washington, DC: NAEYC.

Katz, L. (1997). A developmental approach to assessment of young children, ERIC *Digest*, ERIC-EECE, April. www.ericeece.org/pubs/digests/1997

Kohn, A. (1996). *Beyond discipline*. Alexandria, VA: ASCD (Association for Supervision and Curriculum Development).

Kontos, S., & Wilcox-Herzog, A. (1997). Research in review: Teacher's interactions with children: Why are they so important? *Young Children*, 52(1), 4–12.

Malatesta, C. Z., Culver, C., Tesman, J. R., & Shepard, B. (1989). The development of emotion expression during the first two years of life. *Monographs of the Society for Research in Child Development*, 54(102, Serial No. 219).

Marion, M. (2003). *Guidance of young children* (6th ed.). Upper Saddle River, NJ: Merrill/Prentice Hall.

Meisels, S. J. (1993). Remaking classroom assessment with the work sampling system. *Young Children*, 45(5), 34–40.

Meisels, S. J. (1995). Performance assessment in early childhood education: The work sampling system. ERIC *Digest*, ERIC Number: ED382407, 3 pages.

Parten, M. (1932). Social participation among preschool children. *Journal of Abnormal and Social Psychology*, 27, 243–269.

Pelander, J. (1997). My transition from conventional to more developmentally appropriate practices in the primary grades. *Young Children*, 52(7), 19–25.

Piaget, J. (1951). *Play, dreams, and imitation in childhood*. New York: Norton.

Shaffer, D. (1996). *Developmental psychology* (4th ed.). Pacific Grove, CA: Brooks/Cole Publishing Company.

Snow, R. E. (1989). Toward assessment of cognitive and conative structures in learning. *Educational Researcher*, 18(9), 8–14.

WEB SITES RELATED TO THIS CHAPTER

✓ ASCD/Association for Supervision and Curriculum Development

A professional organization for teachers. www.ascd.org

One of the best Web sites for information on assessment. Do a search or visit links to get the information you need. Films, online courses, books, workshops.

✓ ERIC Clearinghouse

This organization is a clearinghouse for information on early childhood as well as other areas in education.

www.ericeece.org

Search for information on assessment in early childhood. A particularly good link would be the ERIC DIGESTS, shortened versions of selected articles published in journals. The DIGESTS are indexed by year. You can read the DIGESTS on the computer or can order a hard copy directly from ERIC. Click on "Publications" and then "Digests."

✓ NAEYC/The National Association for the Education of Young Children

This professional organization is a good source of information on a large number of professional issues, including assessment or discipline.

www.naeyc.org

Go to NAEYC Resources and then to the Position Statement; See the list of statements including "Standardized Testing of Young Children."

✓ Rethinking Schools

www.rethinkingschools.org

This is a publication and contains many different types of articles. One of the topics about which they write is assessment in schools.

CHAPTER 2

The Ethics and Process of Observing

"Above all, we shall not harm children."
   (NAEYC, Code of Ethics)

Chapter objectives

1. *Comprehend and explain* why an ethical approach to observation is essential.
2. *Explain* several ways to protect children's privacy in the observation process. *Adopt an attitude* that shows willingness to protect children's privacy.
3. *Explain* several policies that ensure confidentiality of observations.
4. *Identify* specific times when divulging information from observations is required of teachers.
5. *List, describe, and explain* two major categories of methods of observing.
6. *Describe* the participant and the nonparticipant observer role.
7. *List* several different instruments that are used in observing. *Explain* why each is useful.

HANNAH'S TEACHER

Hannah is 28 months old, a toddler who has been in Mr. Thompson's class for 5 months. Hannah seems to enjoy her time at the center and being with other children. Today, Mr. Thompson was startled when Hannah screamed and smacked Rachael, because the teacher had never seen Hannah hit anyone. "You know," Mr. Thompson said to his aide, "I did hear Hannah yell at Rachael yesterday, and, today, the hitting. I wonder what is going on here. I'd better check things out."

Hannah's teacher, like all early childhood teachers, does **naturalistic observation,** by observing toddlers in the natural environment without controlling the setting. Mr. Thompson will involve himself in the **process** of observing—watching, recording, and analyzing events that occur naturally (Wright, 1960). Ethical early childhood educators plan their observations well and observe systematically. Most important, this teacher's work with children, their parents, and fellow teachers is grounded in ethics.

THE ETHICS OF OBSERVATION

The National Association for the Education of Young Children (NAEYC) developed the Code of Ethical Conduct (NAEYC, 1989, 1997) to guide early childhood teachers in ethical decision making. The following principle is the guiding force in the Code:

> *Above all, we shall not harm children. We shall not participate in practices that are disrespectful. . . . This principle has precedence over all others in this Code.* (Principle 1.1)

In terms of observation, this "first of all do no harm" principle urges teachers to demonstrate respect for children by using ethical observation practices. Ignoring the ethics of observing harms children and damages relationships between parents and teachers and between staff members. An ethical approach to observing and reporting is the most important element in observing.

Here are two examples of teachers who lack a clear sense of ethics in observing and reporting.

Example: A kindergarten teacher has excellent observation skills and uses them to gather good information about children. She also talks openly about her observations, that is, she violates the confidentiality rule. She acts unethically by not protecting the privacy of children and families.

Example: A preschool teacher met Aaron's parents in a fast food restaurant. When they asked how Aaron was doing, the teacher replied, "Aaron is doing fine, just fine!" The parents left feeling good about this casual report. The teacher, however, knew that Aaron constantly interrupts group time. She plans to talk with his parents about this at an upcoming conference.

How has this teacher acted in what appears to be a somewhat unethical way? She has not been honest with Aaron's parents, giving them an inaccurate picture. She has also set herself up for an unpleasant interaction when she does give them information about his disruptions.

A Different Approach.   Teachers need to be prepared for such casual contacts. A teacher is wise not to get into a protracted conversation in a public place. However, a teacher should deal ethically with parents under all circumstances, including unplanned encounters. She could have approached the casual contact more honestly and ethically:

Example: (Dad asks), "How's my boy doing?" Teacher replies, "He loves to count and he loves playdough, which you already know, and he is so kind to the animals. One thing that we do is to teach children some skills for working well in groups. We're working on helping Aaron listen during group times."

The teacher was surprised when the father laughed and replied, "Oh, you've noticed that Aaron has a lot to say! He hardly ever stops talking at dinner. We can use your help." Her honesty has opened the door to a working relationship with Aaron's parents.

This section focuses on some specific and practical strategies for showing respect for young children in the process of observation.

Protect Children's Privacy

Healthy family and classroom systems show respect by having good boundaries (Marion, 2003; Minuchin, 1974). Teachers show respect in the process of observation by developing good boundaries that protect the privacy of families and children and that acknowledge the confidentiality of observation records. Here are several practical suggestions for protecting children's privacy and maintaining confidentiality when you are doing observations (Figure 2.1).

Observing Ethically to Protect Children's Privacy

- **Know who is and is not allowed to read observations.**

- **Safeguard observation notes and final reports** by
  Keeping notes private as you write them.
  Restricting access to your notes after completing an observation session.

- **Treat any observation report as a confidential document** by
  Talking about notes only when you are formally analyzing your notes.
  Never initiating a conversation about observations with unauthorized persons.
  Politely but firmly refusing to respond to questions about your observations.

- **Refrain from labeling children** after gathering information about them.

Figure 2.1

Some Persons Are Allowed to Read Observation Notes or the Finished Report.

- A student doing an observation assignment
- The instructor of a class in which observation is required
- Students working together on an observation, who may read notes of both observers
- A teacher doing an observation
- The principal or director
- Other teachers *directly involved* with a child
- Parents, who may read observation notes placed in a child's permanent file

All persons allowed to read or discuss observations have a professional and ethical responsibility to maintain confidentiality.

Some People Are Not Permitted to Read Observation Notes or the Finished Report (Almy & Genishi, 1979).

- Other students
- Professors not teaching the observation class
- Other teachers not directly working with the child, unless parents have given clear and explicit written permission
- Friends, acquaintances, or family members of an observer

Safeguard Observation Notes.   Information that you acquire about a family or a child is confidential. Any notes that you write or dictate about a child are confidential. Any final record from a child's previous schools or grades is confidential. Thus, the only people who are allowed to read or discuss observation notes or a final report are those authorized to read or discuss the observation. Treat observation notes the way that you would want your physician or psychologist to treat any notes about you (Cohen, Stern, & Balaban, 1996).

Consider the Following Ideas for Maintaining Confidentiality.   First, your notes are for your eyes only when you are observing. Act professionally when taking notes by keeping your notes private and politely refusing requests from others to read your notes as you write them.

Second, restrict access to your notes upon completing an observation session. Never leave notes lying around. Students can easily restrict access to their notes by keeping observations separate from all other class material and by storing observation notebooks or folders in a safe place. Teachers can take precautions by simply storing notes in a secured place, a locked desk drawer or filing cabinet, for example. Anyone taking notes with a computer should secure the computer file with a password known only to that person and never give the password to anyone. Never send observation notes as an attachment. The "bottom line" is that unauthorized persons never have access to your notes about any child.

Talk About Notes Only in the Context of Formal Analysis.   Professionals take observation notes to help understand child development or to plan curriculum or to help make guidance and discipline decisions. Talking about your notes only in these professional contexts goes a long way in maintaining confidentiality.

Example: (infant room) A teacher in the infant room could discuss notes about a baby's eating problems with an aide in order to solve the problem.

Example: (toddler room) A teacher of toddlers might discuss notes about a child who bites other toddlers with an aide or the center director in order to help the toddler.

Example: (primary grade) A first-grade teacher might discuss a series of curriculum checklists with a child's parents during a parent-teacher conference. The teacher may only discuss that parent's child and not other children in the class. The same teacher could discuss the checklist results for any or all of the children with a coteacher or principal in planning curriculum. If the child were evaluated for special education services (CEC, 1999), then the teacher would be expected to share some of this information with professionals who evaluate the child.

A teacher may talk about observation notes with another professional when the teacher needs help in solving a problem.

Use These Ideas for "Saying No" to Talking About Your Notes.

📖 Never initiate a conversation about observations with unauthorized persons. This will be difficult because children do and say extremely funny things at times. You will be tempted to talk about how "cute" or funny a child was or even about a child who was mean to someone else. Resist the urge. Maintain confidentiality.

When you are talking with people about what they are doing at work or school, it is permissible to talk, in generalities, about your work. It is not permissible to give specific information about children or families. For example, you can say something like, "I really do like watching language development in action. Today, we wrote poetry and the children seemed to like doing that." Another example: "Those babies in my class are really on the move! Everybody crawling or walking all over the place!"

📖 Politely but steadfastly, decline to respond to questions about observations. Suppose that you made the comment about the infants in your class really getting around. The person with whom you are talking says, "Hmm, what about that Smith baby? I hear that his parents don't take very good care of him. Is that true, and how is he doing?"

If an unauthorized person asks such a question, it is your responsibility to maintain confidentiality about what you know. You could respond in a friendly tone to an intrusive question with a statement like this: "My intention isn't to offend you. I have to tell you that any information that I have about children is confidential, and I am not allowed to discuss my observations or specific children." Should the person persist, you can say, still politely and firmly, "I am sure that you'll understand my professional obligation to protect this child's privacy by not talking about my observations." Then, immediately, change the subject or go on to some other activity. Ignore further requests.

Refrain from Labeling Children After Collecting Information.

Show respect and protect privacy by taking great care in interpreting information from observing. Refrain from jumping to conclusions about a child prematurely. Hesitate to label a child or her behavior. Say things in a helpful and thoughtful way.

Example: (infant room) Do not say, "Sammy is such a fussy baby." The word *fussy* is a somewhat negative label. Instead, say something more helpful: "Sammy seems to be very uncomfortable because of teething. He has been crying more than he normally does but responds well to soothing techniques."

Example: (preschool room) Do not say, "Nellie is selfish, as demonstrated in several observations in which she has grabbed things from others." The word *selfish* is a label and seems grossly unfair. Instead, say something like this: "We have continued to work with Nellie on perspective taking. She is slowly but steadily making progress in this area."

Example: (primary grades) Do not say, "David is not very good in math." The phrase *not very good* is a vague and an unhelpful label that could find its way into a permanent file and then do permanent damage. Instead, say something like this: "David seemed very

Refrain from labeling children after observing them.

happy today after we worked together on that math concept that has been giving him trouble. I think that he's beginning to 'get it'!"

Develop and Communicate Policies about Confidentiality of Observations

Principle 2.8., NAEYC Code of Ethical Conduct (1989, 1997), states:

> *We shall develop written policies for the protection of confidentiality and the disclosure of children's records. These policy documents shall be made available to all program personnel and families.*

The Council for Exceptional Children (CEC) also includes a statement about confidentiality in its Code of Ethics and Standards of Practice (1997).

Checklist: Policies About Confidentiality of Observations	
Item	*Reflection: Comments and Action Plan*
❑ Written policy statement about confidentiality of observations exists.	(Use this space to document when you completed this element or to create an action plan for getting this element done).
❑ Statement is in operations manual of the school.	
❑ Confidentiality policy statement available as handouts and on any existing Web pages for the school.	
❑ Copy given to **every** person, with no exceptions, who works in the school.	
❑ Teachers	
❑ Director/principal	
❑ Parents	
❑ Every volunteer	
❑ All college students who do any field experience at the school	
❑ Cooks	
❑ Custodians	
❑ Van or bus drivers	
❑ Others	
❑ We go over the privacy statement during orientation sessions.	
❑ Confidentiality statement reviewed on a regular basis.	
❑ Staff has formally discussed the statement.	
❑ We have informed parents about the statement.	

Figure 2.2

Communicate the professional and ethical responsibility to maintain confidentiality of observation records to every staff member. Write a policy statement about privacy protection for your school and insert the statement into the operations manual of the school. Figure 2.2 is a checklist that might help you communicate a policy about confidentiality of observations.

Avoid Triangulation

Principle 2.10, NAEYC Code of Ethical Conduct (1989, 1997), states:

> *In cases where family members are in conflict, we shall work openly, sharing our observa-*
> *tions of the child, to help all parties involved make informed decisions. We shall refrain*
> *from becoming an advocate for one party.*

This principle advises early childhood teachers to avoid what family scientists call *triangulation*. Person 1 tries to pull person 2 into an issue that person 1 has with person 3. Person 2 is in danger of being pulled into the problem and a triangle of relationships. Triangulation creates an "us against him or her" situation, which is unpleasant, unproductive, and unprofessional.

Example: Brenda's parents are divorced. Brenda spends part of each week with her mother and part with her father. Brenda is in your preschool class. Her father begins to ask you questions—attempts to triangulate you—about whether the child seems to have eaten breakfast before coming to school on days that she has stayed at her mother's house.

The NAEYC advises that we avoid entering such triangular relationships—that we avoid using information from observations to take sides with one parent against another. In the example, you could say, in a friendly yet firm voice, something like, "Brenda eats her morning snack eagerly every day, whether she has stayed with her mother or with you. It might be good for you to ask Brenda's mother about breakfasts if you are concerned." Get support by consulting with a center director or principal when questions about such issues come up.

Know When You Are Required to Divulge Confidential Information

On one hand, teachers are required to keep information confidential. On the other hand, they are required to take action to keep a child safe and to make sure that she receives an appropriate education (CEC, 1997; NAEYC, 1989, 1997; Turnbull & Turnbull, 1997). This might seem like a major conflict, but it is not. As professionals, we are required to divulge confidential information under certain conditions.

Child Abuse and Neglect.   Teachers who observe physical or behavioral indicators of child abuse or neglect (Tower, 1999) are required to report their suspicions of abuse to the agency charged with investigating cases of abuse and neglect. Teachers are **mandated reporters**: that is, they are mandated, or required by law, to report suspected cases of abuse and neglect (NAEYC, 1989, 1997).[1] Teachers do not have to

---

[1]All states have a "child abuse law." In Wisconsin, for example, the child abuse law is in Chapter 48, the Children's Code section of the Statutes. The specific number of the law is 48.981. The question of mandated reporters is usually covered in each state's law, as it is in Wisconsin's 48.981.

make a decision about whether abuse has occurred, but they have a legal obligation to make a good-faith report of their suspicions. States usually have the legal authority to penalize a mandated reporter who does not report suspected child abuse or neglect. The agency receiving a teacher's report makes the decision about whether abuse has occurred and has the power to intervene in the child's interest.

Special Education.   All children, ages birth to 21, are entitled to an appropriate education. The Individuals with Disabilities Education Act of 1997 (IDEA) (CEC, 1999) describes the requirements for educating children with special needs. It outlines the responsibilities that a school has in evaluating or reevaluating a student for special education. Any group that evaluates a child for special education writes a plan for that child's education or services needed by the family (CEC, 1999; Turnbull & Turnbull, 1997). Writing these plans presents a wonderful opportunity for professionals and parents to form partnerships that will ultimately benefit a child.

IFSP.   The written plan for very young children (birth through age 2 up to the day that the child is 3 years old) is called the Individualized Family Service Plan (IFSP). An IFSP focuses on the early intervention needs of the infant or toddler as well as on enhancing a family's ability to meet their child's special needs. Legal requirements mandate that an IFSP contain specific elements. The first meeting to develop the IFSP must take place within 45 days after the family's or child's first referral for early intervention services. There must then be at least one meeting every year to review the IFSP. Legal requirements mandate that the following people attend the meetings (Turnbull & Turnbull, 1997):

- The child's parent(s)
- Other family members as requested by parents, when it is feasible to include the others
- Person(s) directly involved in evaluating or assessing the child or family
- Persons who will provide services to the child or family (a caregiver or teacher, for example)

IEP.   The written plan for children ages 3 through 21 is called an Individualized Education Program (IEP). An IEP focuses on the instructional needs of the student. Legal requirements mandate that the IEP contain specific elements. One example is the set of annual goals and short-term instructional objectives in each area requiring specially designed instruction. Another is the projected date for the beginning and the anticipated duration of the services offered to the child. See Turnbull and Turnbull (1997) for other requirements. Legal requirements mandate that local education agencies write an IEP for children who need special education or special services, whether the child is in public or private school. As with the IFSP, an IEP specifies who must attend the meeting:

- One or both of the student's parents
- The student's teacher(s)
- The student, when it is appropriate that she attend

   📖 Representative of the school, someone qualified to supervise or provide special
education
   📖 Other individuals requested by the school or by the parent(s)

Teachers, then, are an important part of ensuring that children who have any
exceptional needs get the help and education to which they are entitled even if they
are not officially classified as disabled. Infant/toddler or preschool teachers, or general
education teachers in primary and elementary grades, can contribute knowledge
about children gained through observing. Teachers have an ethical as well as a legal
responsibility to help children get the services that they need (CEC, 1999).

A teacher might observe, for example, that a child has a developmental delay, might
need some related service but not special education, or has some other condition such
as ADD (Attention Deficit Disorder) for which services are available. This teacher has a
legal obligation to share the observations or knowledge. The Council for Exceptional
Children's Code of Ethics (CEC, 1997) notes in its instructional responsibilities section
that teachers are required to release information about children at specific times.

The bottom line: Teachers are not only ethically responsible but also legally required,
under certain conditions, to relay their observations to specific persons or agencies.

THE PROCESS OF OBSERVING

Observation Is an Active Process

All observation is active. First, even an observer who sits in a booth or on the side-
lines in a classroom observes actively. The observer must concentrate on the action
observed, must pay attention to the objectives of the observation, and must focus on
the mechanics of observing.

Second, an observer is active because she or he brings opinions and values to an
observation. Teachers who observe with empathy and sensitivity acknowledge that
their personal history and biases can easily affect how they observe and interpret what
they see (NAEYC, 1989, 1997). Teachers who do observations well also try to understand a child's background and try to avoid making unfair judgments about a child.

Example: (preschool classroom) Mrs. Vargas, the preschool teacher, has observed that
Oliver seems to curse a lot. This teacher grew up in a home where cursing was both forbid-
den and punished. She brings her background to her observation but she also understands
that Oliver's parents use swear words, allow Oliver to curse, and even laugh at him when he
does. This teacher understands that her upbringing colors her view of Oliver's behavior and
language. She tries to remember Oliver's background and tries not to project her feelings
onto him because she knows that doing so will destroy her observation.

Third, the observation process is active because skilled observers act like scientists (Figure 2.3).

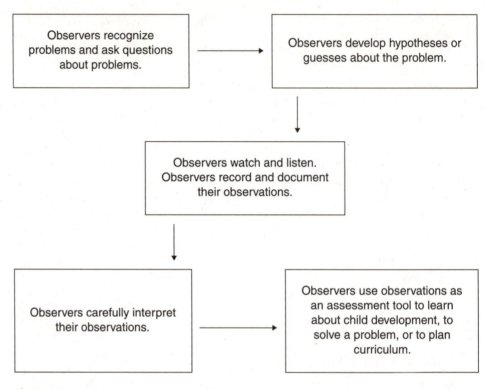

Figure 2.3
Early Childhood Professionals Are Active When They Observe Because They Act Like Scientists

Observers Recognize Problems and Ask Questions About the Problems.   For example, Hannah's teacher (chapter opener case study) asks, "What is going on with Hannah? She hit Rachael today and screamed at her yesterday."

Observers Develop Hypotheses or Guesses About the Problem.   Hannah's teacher developed a hypothesis when he said, "Hannah has never hit anyone else, only Rachael. It looks like something is happening just between those two children."

Observers Watch and Listen.   They take in information. They observe. Hannah's teacher observed Rachael and Hannah playing together or near each other, and he observed for several days and in several areas of the room and playground.

Observers Record and Document Their Observations.   They use a variety of methods to get the information that they need. Hannah's teacher made a series of brief notes called anecdotal records, described in chapter 3.

Observers Interpret Their Observations.   They arrive at a conclusion about their original question and guess about the situation at hand, if they think that they have gathered enough of the right information. Hannah's teacher, for example, observed that Rachael was bullying Hannah, which made Hannah quite angry.

Observers Use Observations as an Assessment Tool.   The teacher can use these tools to learn about child development, to solve a problem, or to plan curriculum. Hannah's teacher, for example, used his information to develop a guidance plan for both Rachael and Hannah (Marion, 2003).

Useful Observation Is Systematic

General Impressions Versus Systematic Observation.   Some people like to base guidance or curriculum decisions on their feelings or impressions and do not like to collect information systematically. Such impressions, however, tend to be unusable for assessing children's development or progress in curriculum. They are not able to back up impressions with solid observational data.

Example: A third-grade teacher said to another teacher, "Two of the children in my class are extremely bright. I think that they are both among the smartest children I've ever taught." This third-grade teacher has never recorded any data about either child's abilities and has made her judgment solely on her general impressions. Her impressions would not be useful at all to the specialist who runs the gifted and talented program at the school.

Observations in early childhood classrooms are most useful and helpful when a teacher collects and records information systematically (Bergen, 1997; Weisz, Chaiyasit, Weiss, Eastman, & Jackson, 1995). Teachers who observe systematically are more likely to notice a variety of behaviors and less likely to have set ideas about a child's behavior.

Example: Hannah's teacher is a good example of this. He observed carefully and systematically and did focus on the toddler's (Hannah's) anger and aggression (hitting). Additionally, his careful observations showed him that Rachael was just as aggressive (pinching Hannah and taking things) but in a quieter way. He also observed that Hannah was kind to the classroom animal and was beginning to use words to express anger. He observed that Rachael did not know how to ask for things that she wanted, including trying to make social contact with another toddler.

Honig and Thompson (1993) studied how toddlers (23 to 33 months) tried to make social contact with other toddlers. The researchers found that most toddler bids for social peer interactions were unsuccessful and that teachers only attempted to assist in 15% of the cases. Therefore, it was good that Hannah's teacher systematically observed toddlers Hannah and Rachael, and that he discovered that Rachael was quite unsuccessful in making social bids to Hannah.

Observing Systematically Requires an Observation Plan.   Observers develop observation plans by making some practical decisions. Decisions center on the purpose of the observation, the methods they will use, the role that an observer should take, the specific instruments they will use to record observations, and how often, how long, and when to observe.

📖 Decide on the purpose of the observation. The first and most important part of developing a systematic observation plan is to figure out the precise purpose for observing. Do you, for example, want to document an infant's level of motor development? Do you want to get a picture of a toddler's language development? Do you want to know how a preschooler expresses anger? Do you want to figure out which type of play your kindergarten children typically engage in? Do you want to document your first or second grader's progress in math or reading? This decision affects other decisions about the plan. It is like taking a trip: knowing your exact destination helps you decide how to get there. Knowing your purpose in observing helps you decide how best to do the observation.

Example: (infant room) The teacher wanted to observe each infant's large motor development.

Example: (preschool) This teacher focused on emotional development and specifically on anger management.

📖 Decide on operational definitions (Bergen, 1997). Specify clearly what you will be looking for. Precise definitions keep observers from drifting away from the original purpose of the observation.

Example: (infant room) The teacher was especially interested in documenting how each infant moved from one place to the next—crawling, scooting, holding onto something for support while walking, walking unassisted.

Example: (preschool) Anger management is still too broad a topic. The teacher narrowed it by focusing on specific words children used for the emotion of anger. She also wanted to know which children used words instead of striking back at another child to express anger.

📖 Decide on an observation strategy. Choose a method that will help you carry out the purpose of the observation. The two major categories of observation techniques are the *narrative* and *nonnarrative* (Wright, 1960). Each of these categories contains different specific techniques. Figures 2.4 and 2.5 highlight some of the main features of each category and the techniques associated with it. Chapters 3, 4, and 5 give an in-depth look at each.

The teacher in the infant room decided to use a checklist (nonnarrative method) to assess gross motor development. The preschool teacher used anecdotal records (narrative method) to assess the children's style of anger management.

Narrative Methods of Observation

- Tell a story about something that has happened (narrates the action)
- Focus on long and continuous segments; observer records original data
- Observer gives enough detail so that readers have a clear picture of what happened

Selected Narrative Techniques

Running Records (chapter 4 gives a full description and examples)
- Longer account of an incident (from 20 minutes to 1 hour)
- Original data recorded with much detail
- Recorded as behavior occurs and maintains original sequence
- Context or information about the setting also recorded
- Used frequently in college classes to learn about child development
- Useful and realistic for teachers if shorter time segments employed

Anecdotal Records (chapter 3 gives a full description and examples)
- Brief account of an incident
- Original data recorded but far less detail recorded
- Can be written as event occurs or after the event
- A flexible technique; teachers can observe almost anything with this technique
- Occasional incidents recorded, that is, observer does not record continuously
- Very useful for early childhood teachers

Figure 2.4

📖 Decide on the observer's role. Observers can take a *participant* or a *nonparticipant role* (Bergen, 1997). These roles depend on whether the observer interacts with the children observed.

Nonparticipant observers have no direct involvement with children observed; a nonparticipant observer sits quietly, watches, and records notes, but does not interact with children. Observers sit in observation booths separate from the classroom, or in the room in an out-of-the-way location, or on the playground. Children occasionally initiate contact with nonparticipant observers by asking, "What are you doing?" Observers respond politely to such questions by saying something like, "I'm writing things down about how children play," and then getting back to the observation.

It is somewhat difficult for classroom or student teachers to observe as nonparticipants because teachers have many things to do while children are present. A teacher who wants to observe as without interacting with his or her children, that is, as a nonparticipant, may do so if there are other adults in the classroom.

There is great learning waiting for teachers who allow themselves to "be still and simply watch" what is happening in their own rooms. A calm, deliberate approach to observing, an approach in which a teacher essentially becomes "wallpaper," that is, uninvolved with the class for a short time, allows her to learn things

---

Nonnarrative Methods of Observation
(see chapter 5 for details and examples)
- Samples or rates behavior; does not tell a story (does not narrate action)
- Observer usually checks things off or indicates a rating
- Focuses on short segments of behavior
- Easy to use and to learn to use

Selected Nonnarrative Techniques

Checklists
- Samples some aspect of development or behavior; does not tell whole story
- Lists behavior or some aspect of development; observer checks presence of behavior
- Gives little or no detail; does not require observer to describe setting; does not say anything about cause of behavior
- Easy to use
- More powerful when combined with anecdotal or running records

Rating Scales
- Samples some aspect of development or behavior; goes on to rate child in area observed
- Based on having done some observation before attempting a rating
- Requires very little training to learn to use
- Can be problematic; calls for rating, but does not require observer to support rating with data

---

Figure 2.5

about the classroom itself or about children. This is difficult to do if a teacher feels compelled to interact with children constantly or if she frenetically presents one activity after another.

Participant observers must observe while they also interact with the children observed. Hannah's teacher took this role, which is probably the most realistic observation role for a teacher. He did a few simple things to organize for observing—carried a pen, placed blank observation forms in different sections of the classroom, and had a simple and effective storage system for observation notes. He also realized that it was a lot easier for him to record observations when he was not working with a small group or dealing with parents.

📖 Decide how to record. Making a record of one's observations adds power to the observation and is an essential part of the systematic observation process. An observer chooses some sort of observational instrument to record what she sees or hears. The choice of instrument depends on the purpose of the observation, the instruments available, and the observer's preferences. Our goal in observing is to get the information needed as simply as possible, and there are a number of observational instruments from which to choose:

Paper and Pen.   This has been the method of choice for decades in child development classes. Classroom teachers find that it is a simple, inexpensive, reliable observation tool.

Photographs.   Pictures are indeed worth a thousand words. Some teachers try, for example, to get photos of children's block structures, of children playing with other children, or of art activities. A teacher might combine pictures with written observations to make a record of the activity. Digital cameras make it much easier to use photographs productively in the observing process. Teachers can easily place digital photographs in observation reports.

Child-Produced Products (Gullo, 1997).   A child produces materials including writing samples, drawings, other artwork such as mobiles, and block or sand structures as she plays and works in an early childhood classroom. Teachers use objects produced by children to assess development and learning. A primary-grade teacher, for example, might collect writing samples from each child over the course of the year to document the change in children's writing.

Children produce many products that cannot be saved for very long—things like block structures, sand structures, or writing or drawing done in sand or on a chalkboard. A teacher who wants to use such products to document an observation and for assessing a child's development and progress would have to preserve the items with a teacher-produced drawing, photograph, or written description.

Videotapes.   This type of technological instrument is useful because information can be viewed and analyzed at the teacher's convenience (Bergen, 1997). High-quality videotaping systems are expensive, however, to purchase, to install, and to maintain. Teachers must be trained to use taping devices. Children have to become accustomed to the presence of taping equipment in the room.

Audiotapes.   High-quality audiotaping systems are useful for collecting different types of information, such as language samples (Bergen, 1997). The teacher must still describe the context or setting from which the sample is drawn.

Computers.   Laptop computers continue to become easier to use. They are a sophisticated and excellent technological aid for a busy, computer-literate student or teacher (i.e., a person who likes and knows how to use computers). Many students in child development or early childhood classes now record observation notes directly into a laptop. Teachers, as participant observers, can set up secure files for the type of observations that they have chosen to do and then record during the day or at the end of the day. Laptops have replaced note cards and filing folders for some teachers and students.

Combination of instruments.   From time to time, you will find it to your advantage to combine different observation tools. For example, combine written running records (done with paper and pencil or computer) and photos of children working at the water table. Consider combining videotapes of infants or toddlers with a checklist (done with paper and pencil or computer) of gross motor skills. Pair child-produced writing samples with anecdotal records or a rating scale. Combining different instruments gives additional power to an observation.

📖 Decide how often, how long, and when to observe. Our goal as observers is to get a good description of a child's development or progress in curriculum areas, whatever role we take and whatever method we use. We need to observe and record children's behavior in a variety of contexts so that we get a good, clear, and accurate picture (Almy & Genishi, 1979; Bergen, 1997). What we see in one observation or even in a whole series of observations might not accurately represent a particular child's development or progress and can lead us to make inaccurate and, often, unfair conclusions.

Example: A parent volunteer in James's first-grade class listened as a small group read segments of a story aloud. The parent noted that James had difficulty with this reading activity and prematurely concluded that James has trouble with oral reading. The teacher wisely advised the parent to observe further when James was alone and using a tape recorder. The parent observed that James read aloud into the tape recorder with great skill when he was alone. She got a different picture of his ability. She saw that James might be somewhat shy in front of other children while reading, but he can indeed read aloud.

Activities to Help You Construct Knowledge and Skills in Observing

ACTIVITY 1

Get a copy of the child abuse and neglect statutes (laws) for your state. You will find the law in a public library, in your college or university library, at a local department of human services, or on the Internet. Look through the law: find and photocopy the part listing teachers as *mandated reporters*. Place the photocopy of that subsection in your observation notebook.

ACTIVITY 2

Examine the policy or operations manual of a school or school district. Find the policy statement on maintaining confidentiality of children's records. Name the things about the statement that are done well. Make a statement about how you would change the policy statement to make it even better.

ACTIVITY 3

Work with other class members and choose one or two aspects of maintaining confidentiality that you want to emphasize. Make a cheerful, friendly poster focusing on your choice for a school used by observers. Ask the center director or principal to review the class's poster and then request permission to put up the poster if it is approved.

REFERENCES

Almy, M., & Genishi, C. (1979). *Ways of studying children* (Rev. ed.) New York: Teachers College Press.

Bergen, D. (1997). Using observational techniques for evaluating young children's learning. In B. Spodek & O. Saracho (Eds.), *Issues in early childhood educational assessment and evaluation* (pp. 108–128). New York: Teachers College Press.

Cohen, D., Stern, V., & Balaban, N. (1996). *Observing and recording the behavior of young children*. New York: Teachers College Press.

Council for Exceptional Children (1997). *CEC code of ethics and standards of practice*. Retrieved March 5, 2003, from http://www.cec.sped.org/ps/code.

Council for Exceptional Children (1999). A primer on IDEA 1997 and its regulations. *CEC Today—Online!* 5(7), 9 pages.

Gullo, D. F. (1997). Assessing student learning through the analysis of pupil products. In B. Spodek & O. Saracho (Eds.), *Issues in early childhood educational assessment and evaluation* (pp. 129–148). New York: Teachers College Press.

Honig, A., & Thompson, A. (1993, December). *Toddler strategies for social engagement with peers*. Paper presented at the eighth Biennial National Training Institute of the National Center for Clinical Infant Programs, Washington, DC.

Marion, M. (2003). *Guidance of young children* (6th ed.). Upper Saddle River, NJ: Merrill/Prentice Hall.

Minuchin, S. (1974). *Families and family therapy*. Cambridge, MA: Harvard University Press.

NAEYC (adopted 1989; amended 1997). *Position statement: code of ethical conduct*. Washington, DC: NAEYC.

Tower, C. C. (1999). *Understanding child abuse and neglect* (4th ed.). Boston: Allyn & Bacon.

Turnbull, A. P., & Turnbull, H. R., III (1997). *Families, professionals, and exceptionality* (3rd ed.). Upper Saddle River, NJ: Merrill/Prentice Hall.

Weisz, J. R., Chaiyasit, W., Weiss, B., Eastman, K. L., & Jackson, E. W. (1995). Multimethod study of problem behavior among Thai and American children in school: Teacher reports versus direct observations. *Child Development, 66,* 402–415.

Wright, H. F. (1960). Observational child study. In P. H. Mussen (Ed.), *Handbook of research methods in child development* (pp. 71–139). New York: Wiley.

WEB SITES RELATED TO THIS CHAPTER

✓ NAEYC/National Association for the Education of Young Children:

http://www.naeyc.org

Contains many good links. Go to the NAEYC Resources link and then to Position Statements, Look for the "Code of Ethical Conduct," a position statement.

✓ CEC/The Council for Exceptional Children

http://www.cec.sped.org

This home page has a number of links.

http://www.cec.sped.org/ps/code

CEC's Code of Ethics and Standards of Practice. Contains several documents. Click on "CEC Code of Ethics for Educators of Persons with Exceptionalities."

http://www.cec.sped.org/bk/cectoday

CEC's online journal, CEC *Today—Online*! This is the archive from which you can select any of several CEC journal articles.

✓ Institute for the Study of Developmental Disabilities

2853 East Tenth Street, Bloomington, Indiana, 812-855-6508. The Institute focuses on providing a seamless system of inclusionary services for individuals across the lifespan.

www.isdd.indiana.edu

Go to the link dealing with services during early childhood. This group produces excellent, practical publications for teachers.

PART II

Methods of Observing and Documenting Progress and Development in Early Childhood

Part One described the power, ethics, and process of observing. This part of the book will give you the practical help that you need to observe well. You will study several major methods for observing, with specific, detailed, and usable information about each strategy, along with a sound rationale.

Chapter 3 Anecdotal Records: A Short Narrative Method of Observation.   Anecdotal records are a favorite method of observing with early childhood teachers, and it is easy to see why. It is an extremely efficient strategy, and it is relatively easy to learn to write good and useful anecdotal records. As a busy teacher, you will appreciate having a brief record of significant incidents in your classroom. Anecdotal records are brief records. You will look at an interesting incident and record its essential details with enough detail to give you a "snapshot" of the action. You will quickly learn the value of using anecdotal records to watch almost any aspect of a child's development or progress.

Chapter 4 Running Records: A Longer Narrative Method of Observation. Anecdotal records are like short stories, whereas running records are longer versions of stories or events. You will occasionally need to record an event in more detail than you could with anecdotal records and will then find running records a good choice. This chapter explains that running records give many options about what to observe and require that the observer watch from the periphery. You will discover that running records are quite useful in doing authentic assessments of children's development or progress. You will learn the skill of writing about a child or an activity without giving your opinion while you record information. You will also learn how to reflect on the data that you have collected.

Chapter 5 Checklists and Rating Scales: Nonnarrative Methods for Observing Development and Progress. These two methods are "shortcut" strategies because they bypass the detail that you would record in either anecdotal or running records. You will not be narrating a story with a checklist or a rating scale, making these nonnarrative strategies. You will learn that both checklists and rating scales are useful and popular strategies to use when you need to gather specific types of information quickly. You will also learn about different types of checklists and rating scales and about how to develop each. Because checklists and rating scales do not give much detail, this chapter describes practical ways to increase their power.

Chapter 6 Documenting and Reporting Development and Progress: Children's Products, Observation Reports, and Portfolios. Chapters 3, 4, and 5 explained the major methods for observing children's development and progress. This chapter focuses on helping you understand the twin processes of documenting and then reporting what you observe. Documentation provides proof of what *is*. Reporting a child's development and progress, like observing and documenting it, is not trivial. This chapter will show you several different ways to document and report children's development and progress: with children's products and work samples, with documentary displays, and with observation reports. This chapter also describes portfolios as a way of documenting and reporting. You will learn practical strategies for using children's portfolios in your classroom.

CHAPTER 3

Anecdotal Records
A Short Narrative Method of Observation

Anecdote: a short narrative of an interesting incident

Chapter Objectives

1. *Summarize* advantages and disadvantages of the anecdotal record method of observing.
2. *List* and *explain* guidelines for writing anecdotal records.
3. *Explain* why it is important to have a focus for anecdotal records.

ANECDOTAL RECORDS

Mrs. Vargas and her assistant teacher, Mrs. Lyndon, were preparing the room for the next day. They used this time to reflect on issues of the day and to evaluate the effectiveness of activities and curriculum for the day. Mrs. Vargas uses informal assessment extensively and talking with assistants or student and intern teachers is one of her favorite methods. She believes that, as a team, the adults in the classroom can work together to help children and to develop appropriate curriculum and activities.

Mrs. Vargas: "How do you feel about your talk with Nellie today?"
Mrs. Lyndon: "It went well. I thought that she should give the boat back to Ralph and told her so. She had just taken it and had not even asked. Then she was surprised that Ralph got mad."
Mrs. Vargas: "I agree that she should have given it back and she did what you asked right away. I saw her take something without asking last week, too. The strange thing, though, is that Nellie also seems generous at times."
Mrs. Lyndon: "I know. Today, she broke an apple slice in half so that Kim could have another piece. She's a puzzle; sometimes she seems so *selfish*, just taking what she wants. What do you think that we ought to do?"
Mrs. Vargas: "I'd feel better if we got a little more information about her sharing and about her not asking for things. How about trying some observation? I think that that would be a good starting place."

These teachers face a challenge common to all early childhood teachers, whether they work with infants, toddlers, preschoolers, or kindergarten or primary-grade children. They need information about a child so that they understand her needs and abilities. They will be better prepared to help Nellie only when they have enough of the right information. They plan to get the necessary information through observation, not by guessing. They have decided to observe Nellie by using one of the major methods of observing young children—*anecdotal records*.

Anecdotal Records—Description

An **anecdotal record** (Figure 3.1) is an *open, narrative, brief* form of observation that early childhood teachers tend to like to use. This type of observation is easy to learn to do and is one of the most efficient observational methods available to early childhood teachers. A teacher looks at or observes an interesting incident in his classroom and writes it down or records it. He then has a record of the incident or anecdote: an anecdotal record. An anecdotal record is like one snapshot of a child's development or activity in a classroom.

An anecdotal record, then, results from a teacher's direct observation. To get an anecdotal record, a teacher carefully and purposefully observes a specific event and then records data about that incident. Knowing how to write an anecdotal record is a professional skill that has to be learned and then practiced.

An Anecdotal Record Is an Open Form of Observation.   The observer is free to watch a variety of behaviors or interactions or almost any aspect of a young child's development. Mrs. Vargas and many other teachers at her school favor this method of observation, although she does use other observational methods. She has used the anecdotal record method many times and for several different aspects of her children's development and interaction. Here are just a few examples.

Example: Mrs. Vargas observed how Pete's ability to initiate contact with other children developed over the course of several months. She taught one of her assistants how to observe the types of activities that Ralph engaged in during the play/work periods. She decided to use anecdotal records to define the circumstances under which Kim cursed. She developed anecdotal records of when Moshe participated in large-group time without interrupting.

An Anecdotal Record Is a Narrative Form of Observation.   An anecdote is a story. When a teacher writes anecdotes about some aspect of a child's development, she essentially writes a very short story. She describes or narrates an incident or a series of incidents.

The teacher records the information and preserves the data about when a child, for instance, curses or shares or interrupts a group time. She records the incident in enough detail so that rereading the story will bring back the incident to her mind. As with any story the teacher, at some future time, can pick up the anecdotal record, read it, picture the incident in her mind, and think about or analyze it.[1]

An Anecdotal Record Is a Brief Record of an Incident.   Anecdotal records do give some detail, but they do not describe prolonged actions as a running record usually does. Teachers who use the anecdotal record method avoid describing details that might be interesting but are essentially unnecessary in such a brief story.

Mrs. Vargas decided to make brief notes about when and where Kim cursed. Did he, for example, curse during large group, small group, when playing during play or work periods, outdoors, only with certain children, when he was frustrated or angry? Each observation and its recording took only about 1 to 1½ minutes. She preserved the essential information that would help her recall incidents of cursing. She wanted to record and keep original data but just enough data to give her a good picture of when Kim cursed.

Use Anecdotal Records for Preplanned or Spontaneous Observations

One thing that makes anecdotal records so appealing is that teachers can use this method either for preplanned observations or for spontaneous moments.

---

[1]**Event sampling (with narration)** is an observational method that is similar to anecdotal records because of the narration or storytelling aspect. In event sampling, an observer chooses an event, a *category* of behavior such as prosocial behavior, and lists examples of behaviors in that category—sharing, helping, cooperating, showing compassion. The observer records instances of the specific behaviors, describing the behavior or event in enough detail to give an accurate picture of the event. The observer also interprets the action when it seems appropriate to do so.

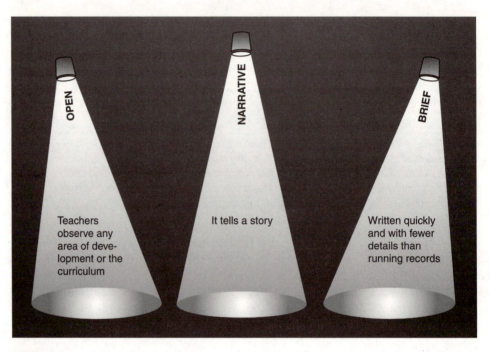

Figure 3.1
Spotlight on Anecdotal Records: An Anecdotal Record is . . .

Preplanned Anecdotal Records.   At times, a teacher plans to observe something specific.

Example: (infants) A teacher used anecdotal records to document examples of the infants recognizing themselves in a mirror.

Example: (toddlers) A student teacher wrote anecdotal records about how each toddler fed him- or herself at meal time.

Example: (kindergarten) The teacher observed his class in the computer lab as they worked with a computer teacher and a student teacher. He recorded anecdotes about each child's ability to follow directions.

Example: (second grade) Teachers in a bilingual second grade (Fournier, Lansdowne, Pastenes, Steen, & Hudelson, 1992) used brief observations to record some of the children's problems during reading. They also noted what the child did after coming to a trouble word (e.g., looked at illustrations, went back and read over, skipped the word, substituted a word, sounded out).

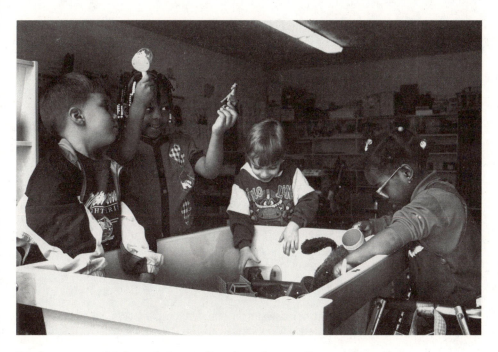

Teachers use anecdotal records to record preplanned or spontaneous observations.

Spontaneous Anecdotal Records.   At other times, teachers have opportunities to observe those spontaneous moments that they have not set out to record, but that can tell them a great deal about a child or the curriculum.

Example: (infants/toddlers) The teacher was delighted to witness Josie's first steps and hurried to make a note, an anecdotal record, of the event. She even recorded the exact hour and minute as well as the date so that Josie's mother and father would have this information. Josie's parents framed that observation.

Example: (first grade) Teacher watched the assistant with a small group of children. The assistant gave each child one cracker. Then he broke his cracker into three parts and asked Todd, "Who has more cracker, me or you?" Todd replied, "We both have the same. All you did was to break yours in three pieces." The head teacher quickly grabbed an anecdotal record form and recorded Todd's response, which was the first indication that Todd understood conservation.

Guidelines for Writing Anecdotal Records (Bergen, 1997)

Figure 3.4, at the end of this section, is a checklist listing all of the guidelines described here. Consider using the checklist to analyze your own anecdotal records.

Guideline 1: Develop a Plan for Collecting the Anecdotes.   Teachers spend a lot of time planning, and teachers who make the most of anecdotal records carve out a small amount of planning time to decide how they will collect anecdotes about children. They plan:

- What they will look for or observe
- How often they will collect anecdotes
- When they will observe, that is, the time of day
- Where they will observe

Decide what to look for or observe. Stating or specifying a range of behavior to observe is an important part of doing anecdotal records well. Observing a range of behavior enables a teacher to produce an even-handed description of a child's behavior. Observing a range of behaviors, therefore, can help teachers avoid the problem of bias in anecdotal records. Bergen (1997) noted that a plan that included the teacher's intention to record a range of social skills and not just negative or hurtful behaviors, for example, should precede a set of observations of social skills. Here is what the teachers developed for a sampling plan of Nellie's behavior:

Example: Mrs. Vargas's and her assistant's observation plan. "We will do anecdotal records of Nellie. We are interested in two things.

"1. We want to record examples of when Nellie shares things with other children.

"2. We also want to observe and record examples of when Nellie takes things from other children and whether she asks for things first."

This type of statement is not elaborate and will be relatively short in most cases. The main idea is for teachers to think through clearly the exact nature of the type of observations that would be most useful to them in helping a specific child. This requires that an early childhood professional has already casually observed a child's behavior and has formulated some preliminary questions about that child. Mrs. Vargas and her assistant have done that when they began to notice that Nellie was occasionally generous with others, but also seemed to grab things from them.

Decide how often to collect anecdotes (Almy & Genishi, 1979). Mrs. Vargas, for example, decided to try to collect at least three anecdotes about Nellie each week. Other teachers might need a different timetable for collecting observations. Mr. Nellis, the teacher of the multiage K–2 classroom in the same school, collected vignettes or anecdotes about Todd's understanding of conservation after setting up a situation to check his understanding.

Decide when and where to observe. Teachers often, but not always, decide to observe at specific times or within a specified period. Mrs. Vargas decided to observe Nellie during the time when children chose from a variety of activities in the room. The two teachers reasoned that they had noticed that Nellie seemed to either share or grab things most often then.

Teachers also often decide on the place for the observation. Mrs. Vargas and Mrs. Lyndon decided to concentrate on observing Nellie during the indoor work/play period and decided to observe her in any of the several areas of the preschool classroom. Their decision hinged on prior, but undocumented, observations of Nellie's sharing or having grabbed things in different parts of the classroom. Their colleague, Mr. Nellis, decided to observe Todd during playtime outside where he set up the conservation experiment.

Guideline 2: Record the Anecdote as Soon as Possible After It Happens.   *Helps with recalling the incident*. Busy teachers, like the teacher who recorded evidence of Todd's understanding conservation, have many things to do and to remember, and they might forget to record the incident at all if they do not do it almost immediately. They would then have an incomplete record of the events that they wanted to observe. Recording an anecdote long after the incident occurred forces a teacher to rely on memory to recall the incident, and this might well result in inaccurate recall of essential details.

Example: Mrs. Lyndon could not remember exactly with whom Nellie had been playing in the sandpit a couple of days prior to the initial conversation about Nellie's habit of grabbing. "I also recall watching Nellie share things but can't remember exactly when or with whom."

Effective observers are well prepared. How do teachers with so many things going on in a classroom record anecdotes right away or almost immediately after an incident occurs? They do it by being prepared for observation. Many teachers keep note cards and pencils or pens in two or three different places in the room. They do not have to spend time to go and get items needed for observation and are therefore much more likely to record an incident and record it immediately.

Write very brief notes and add detail later. Any observational method that a teacher chooses must be realistic. There are times when teachers simply cannot stop what they are doing to write a complete anecdotal record. At these times, they compose a very brief note using telegraphic speech. Then they expand the note shortly after the incident. This compact version gives them just enough information to jog their memory of the event that took place a short time before. Mrs. Vargas encouraged her assistant to use this skill and observed that the assistant teacher did write an extremely short anecdotal record the next day.

Example: Mrs. Lyndon was preparing the snack when she noticed that Nellie handed one of her blocks to another child in the block area; Nellie had shared. The assistant teacher could not take much time from the task at hand, so she quickly jotted down the following note: "Nellie/Ralph/blocks. N shared block with R."

Such a concise record would not be sufficient, however, to help the teacher accurately remember the incident a month or even a week or a few days later. There simply would not be enough information. So, teachers who want to preserve the scene in enough detail write a more detailed anecdotal record as soon as possible.

Example: When the snack was prepared and set out, Mrs. Lyndon wrote, "Nellie and Ralph were playing in the block area. They had each built a patio. Ralph needed one small block to complete his patio but had exhausted his supply. Nellie picked up one of the small blocks she had in a pile and handed it to R, saying, "Here's a block, Ralph. I have lots of blocks."

At other times, teachers do not even have time to write a brief, telegraphic note. They remember the incident and record it as soon as possible. Mrs. Vargas, for example, could not stop to write a note when the children and teachers went on a walk. So, just as soon as they returned to the playground, she jotted down her note and placed the note card in the child's file.

Guideline 3: Describe the Context in Which the Incident Occurs.   An observer usually watches only a small portion of a child's total activity or development. The observer, then, gets only a snapshot of behavior or development, not the complete movie. A teacher who accurately describes the context in which the incident takes place puts a frame around the incident, an important step in effective observations. Without a good description of the context, or *frame*, we are likely to see a child's behavior as separate from the context or setting. The teacher can mistakenly ignore cues from the context that partially explain the child's behavior.

Frame the incident well by describing the context in which the action takes place:

- Describe the setting
- Note date and time of day
- List names of children and adults involved in the incident

Describe the setting. Record important information about the setting where the incident took place—block corner, computer center in a first- or second-grade classroom, dramatic play center, or library—or was the class on a field trip? Recording the setting on anecdotal records of Nellie sharing or grabbing things will eventually pinpoint places where Nellie's behavior tends to occur.

Note date and the time of day. This information will become important when a teacher collects a number of anecdotes about the same type of behavior for a child because the teacher has better information about the timing of problems and about any change over time.

List names of others involved in the incident. Children's behavior does not happen in a vacuum. Therefore, it is important to document who else was involved in an incident. List names and ages of other children with whom the observed child was involved. Note whether there were other children in the area but with whom the child was not playing. Record the names of any adults present.

Adopt a simple format for recording contextual information. Teachers are much more likely to do observations if the observation system is uncomplicated. A practical idea, then, is to use a simple form like the one in Figure 3.2 for quickly recording contextual information. Another practical idea is to duplicate the form and leave copies in different parts of the classroom. Teachers who use a form like this view it as a real time-saver that reminds them to record this essential information without spending a lot of time doing it. See Figure 3.2.

List the name of each child involved in an incident when writing anecdotal records.

Anecdotal Record

Goal for this observation:
Setting:
Date/day:
Time of day:
Basic activity:
Focus child:
Others involved:

The Anecdote:

Reflection/Comment/Interpretation:

Figure 3.2
Suggested Format for Recording Anecdotal Records. Part One Is for Context; Part Two for the Anecdote; Part Three for Reflecting/Commenting

Guideline 4: Write Useful Notes About the Activity. Record Enough Detail So That You Have a Good Snapshot of the Episode.   Place notes about the activity in a separate section on the form. Figure 3.2 shows where to write notes about the anecdote.

Observers have to concentrate, write quickly, and record enough detail to get a rich description of an incident. Observers create a much better, more useful, and more sharply focused snapshot of the activity because sufficient detail tells more about what was going on.

Example: (anecdotal record with good detail) Nellie and Justine had each been playing peacefully together for several minutes with the marble machine, each girl taking turns dropping in her marbles. When N finished dumping her marbles into the device, she looked over and eyed J's marbles. Without a word, N then leaned over and closed both hands over a bunch of J's marbles. N scooped them up and put them in front of her.

J's eyes opened wide, giving her a look of surprise. Then J cried out indignantly, "Stop it, Nellie! They're *my* marbles, and you're supposed to use your words for asking." N finally glanced up at J but said nothing. N went right back to dropping J's marbles into the contraption. J cried. Mrs. V looked at and walked over to them. She calmly asked the girls what had happened. N exasperatedly said, "I wanted the marbles. I needed them!"

Guideline 5: Use a Person's Exact Words When Writing Dialogue.   Writing a word-for-word record gives the reader a much better sense of the conversation. Use quotation marks around a speaker's exact words. Do not use quotation marks when paraphrasing (rewording or restating) the speaker's words. When it is not possible to record a child or teacher's precise words, then record essential phrases.

Example: (direct quote) Justine said to the teacher, "Nellie took my marbles." Then, quietly, firmly but with great emphasis, "I WANT THEM BACK!" (Exact words are in quotation marks.) This statement gives a clear idea of Justine's desire to get her marbles returned.

Example: (paraphrasing) The following statement—Justine told the teacher that she wanted the marbles back—paraphrases or summarizes the speaker's words and does not contain the exact words. Therefore, the paraphrasing does not need to have quotation marks.

Example: (writing essential phrases) The assistant teacher recorded essential phrases when Mrs. Vargas talked with Nellie about taking things. The assistant teacher was not able to get the exact wording but did capture the essence of the statement by writing – "To Nellie, 'Classroom rule . . . not to grab . . . ask first.'"

Guideline 6: Include Information About How Others Respond to the Main Speaker's Words or Actions.   Describe how other children or adults respond with words, actions, or a combination of the two. Most observers describe reactions of those directly involved in the activity. It would also be wise to describe the responses of people in the back-ground. Such information gives a better portrayal of the incident.

Example: Yesterday, at arrival time, Nellie's dad was talking to Ms. V while N placed her coat and boots in her cubby. Danielle was also stowing things, including her backpack, in her cubby, next to N's cubby. N took the backpack from Danielle's cubby and put her arms through the straps when N's dad turned his attention to his daughter. He looked irritated and said, "Nellie, put the backpack away. It's not yours." He then asked Mrs. Vargas about how to handle something like this.

Guideline 7: Write the Anecdotal Record in the Proper Sequence.   (Using first-grader Todd's conservation example.) Describe the setting first—teacher and small group of children at snack table. Then describe what you see and hear in correct sequential order: Teacher gave each child a cracker, gave himself one, broke his cracker into three pieces, asked question of Todd. Finally, write about how the incident ended: Todd answered the question.

Guideline 8: Aim for Complete and Accurate Data. Be as Objective as Possible When Recording Data.   *Complete data.* In order to help children or to learn about their level of development, teachers need observations that give enough of the right type of information. Therefore, when doing an observation, including when doing short anecdotal records, take care to observe carefully and then to record the data as completely as possible. Concise reports are admirable, but it is possible to write a report that is too concise, too brief. Avoid this problem by getting enough facts to give a clear idea of the event. Getting enough facts also contributes to the accuracy of an observation. Having enough data will also enable you eventually to begin to interpret the child's behavior or development more accurately.

Objectivity. Be objective, which means to avoid making interpretations when describing an action. This is a difficult thing to do. It is easy to slip in to interpreting, for example, saying something like "John is really an aggressive child." The word *aggressive* is an interpretation of John's actual behavior, but the teacher has not described the behavior.

One way to deal with this problem is to review an observation, check for interpretations, and then eliminate them. Consider having another person check for interpretations in your observations, particularly when you are first learning to do observations.

One realistic technique for keeping interpretations out of the activity section of an observation is to record data and only data. Write about what a child did or said. Write about what you saw, heard, and smelled. In this way, you will be writing only the facts, the data. You will achieve a much greater degree of objectivity.

Accuracy. Be as accurate as possible when recording facts from an observation. Make sure that the data are factually correct. For instance, did Nellie take a shovel that Ralph was the first to play with that day? Alternatively, did Nellie take the shovel back after Ralph took it from her? Accuracy in this case is crucial when you get to the reflecting and commenting (interpretation) stage.

Consider observing with another person while learning observation skills. You can then check both observations for accuracy in recording facts. The assistant teacher asked Mrs. Vargas to do an anecdotal record of the same episode along with her and then to check how accurately Mrs. Lyndon recorded the event. Here are their two observations of the same event.

In the past, Moshe has had trouble participating at group time on occasion, but at other times seems to have participated joyfully. The teachers needed specific information on when he participates without interrupting and when he interrupts. Their goal was to observe Moshe's participation in the large-group activity.

Example: (Mrs. Vargas's anecdotal record) Gerry's mother volunteered to read a story to the children. Pete, Kim, and Moshe sat next to each other on the outer ring of the group. Moshe leaned back on his hands, which he had positioned behind him. He listened to the story and did not turn to or talk to anyone. Pete and Kim assumed the same pose, and both boys also listened quietly for the first part of the story. Then Pete's left hand started moving, slowly and crablike, toward Moshe. Pete's hand then seemed to slide sideways. Pete fell slightly to the left and fell into Moshe. Moshe moved aside and continued to listen to the story. Pete glanced at Moshe, narrowing his eyes, smiling, and then poked Moshe on the shoulder. Moshe called over to the teacher, "Teacher!" Gerry's mother stopped reading and looked at Moshe.

Example: (Mrs. Lyndon's anecdotal record) Moshe sat with all the other children in the class and listened to the story that Gerry's mother was reading. Pete and Kim were sitting on either side of Moshe. All three boys listened closely for a few minutes when Moshe rudely said, "Teacher!" Everybody stopped and looked at Moshe. (Please note: It is *not* acceptable to use a judgmental label such as *rudely*.)

Difference between the two observations. Mrs. Vargas, an experienced observer, has given more comprehensive data than has the assistant teacher, who is just learning to observe. A reader looking at the head teacher's observation would know that Moshe seemed to want to listen to the story but was disturbed by Pete. The reader would not get that same information from the assistant teacher's report because there were no data about either Pete's facial expressions or his touching and pushing Moshe. Mrs. Vargas's observation, therefore, was more accurate than was Mrs. Lyndon's.

The assistant teacher's observation was judgmental. In addition, she interpreted when she said that Moshe "*rudely* said." It was her opinion of how Moshe talked in the group and should not have been included in the observation. Such an opinion in the body of the report decreases the objectivity of the report.

Guideline 9: Interpret Observations Carefully If It Is Appropriate to Interpret.   The assistant teacher interpreted Moshe's behavior inaccurately when she wrote, "Moshe *rudely* said . . . ," because she had recorded so little information about the incident. She presented a biased interpretation with no data to support what she wrote.

Observers bring their own selves to an observation, and this makes it almost impossible to be completely neutral or objective. Nevertheless, there are some reasonable strategies for keeping interpretations to a minimum.

Record only data (what you see, hear, smell, feel) in the body of the anecdotal record. Do not make interpretations in the body of the record. In the 1960s-era detective show *Dragnet*, when Sergeant Friday, the main character, interviewed witnesses to crimes, they frequently insisted on giving their interpretation of the crime, with too much information. Sergeant Friday, in his dull, monotone voice, would drone, "Just the facts, ma'am." Perhaps we should also take Sergeant Friday's famous advice and stick to recording facts—and be sure we have enough of them before we give our opinion about what they mean.

Separate comments/interpretation from fact. If it is necessary to make a brief interpretation, then separate the interpretation from the facts by enclosing your interpretation in brackets or parentheses.

Example: (Mrs. Vargas's observation) Nellie and Ralph had been working together in the sand pit, and they had made a tunnel together. Ralph had been working with the one shovel and Nellie had been carting the sand to another area of the pit. It was Nellie's turn to dig, but Ralph said, "No, Nellie. I have the shovel." Nellie said, "It's my turn!" Ralph ignored her. Nellie, her face turning a bright red (interpretation: she seemed to be angry!) said, "It's *my* turn. Give me the shovel." (Interpretation: some people would see Nellie as aggressive if they had not examined the whole situation carefully. Others would view Nellie's behavior as *active resistance*, a healthy form of anger management [Fabes & Eisenberg, 1992]. They would say that Nellie has asserted her right to her turn.)

Create a separate reflection/comment (interpretation) section for the anecdotal record. Please see Figure 3.2.

Decide on whether and when to write comments (interpretations) for observations. Do not feel compelled to explain immediately why you think that a child did or said something, or how a child felt. It is not always necessary to write interpretations, especially when you are just beginning to gather data or information. In fact, it is often best *not* to interpret. If you decide that it is not necessary to make an inference or an interpretation, then make a notation in the interpretation section, "N/I." This means *no interpretation*.

Example: The first-grade teacher who observed Todd's understanding of conservation simply noted, "N/I. Look for other examples or set up a few conservation experiments for Todd to check his understanding."

Look for patterns before interpreting. Gather several anecdotes and look for patterns in the record. When you do this, an interpretation often becomes evident, even without

---

Goal for this observation: observe Nellie's generosity, learning to ask for things instead of grabbing, and conditions surrounding grabbing behavior
Setting: area with puzzles and other small manipulative equipment
Date/day: Tuesday, September 14
Time of day: 9:17 a.m.
Basic activity: four children working with a variety of small manipulatives
Focus child: Nellie
Others involved: Kim mainly; Ralph and Justine in same area but only onlookers

The Anecdote: Nellie sat facing Kim, each child working with the small lock-together blocks. They each had a pile of blocks. Nellie worked quietly for three minutes and then looked up and around at the pile of blocks in front of Kim. She said, "Can I have one of your blocks?" Kim replied, "I need all of the blocks for my boat." Nellie then reached over and took one of Kim's blocks anyway. "Hey! That's my block, Nellie. I want it back," shouted Kim. "I NEED it," replied Nellie and then went on to place Kim's block on her own structure.

Reflection/Comments/Interpretation: (This is the first interpretation or reflection that we've made about this part of Nellie's behavior.)

    Nellie has taken things from children several times in the time that we have been observing (anecdotes 1, 4, 6, and 8, with #8 today's observation). We have requested that she ask first if she wants something and she did so for the first time yesterday. Today she also asked—progress! Therefore, she now seems to know *how* to ask others for what she wants. However, she still does not seem to understand that the other child has a right to continue to play with a toy that he or she has chosen. When Kim refused her request, Nellie took the blocks anyway. We think that Nellie is just not getting it because she is still somewhat egocentric and seems not able to take another person's perspective, which is not unusual for a child Nellie's age. We plan to continue working on perspective taking with Nellie.

Figure 3.3
Reflecting on an Observation: Making Appropriate Comments

you coming up with it (Figure 3.3). Figure 3.4 is a checklist of the guidelines for writing anecdotal records.

ADVANTAGES AND DISADVANTAGES OF USING ANECDOTAL RECORDS

No method of observation, including anecdotal records, is perfect, but each has its merits. Teachers have used each method successfully, and each method has some distinct advantages as well as disadvantages.

Advantages of Anecdotal Records

There are some very good reasons for using anecdotal records to observe young children.

Checklist: Guidelines for Writing Anecdotal Records

Use these criteria for analyzing an anecdotal record. Check the appropriate box next to each numbered statement. Write comments that will help in your analysis.

	Met	Not met	Comment
1. Develop an observation plan	_____	_____	_____
2. Record the anecdote as soon as possible after it happens	_____	_____	_____
3. Describe the context in which the incident occurs	_____	_____	_____
4. Write useful notes about the activity. Notes are in separate section of form	_____	_____	_____
5. Exact words recorded in writing dialogue in quote marks. Paraphrased remarks not in quote marks	_____	_____	_____
6. Information about how others responded to speaker's words or actions	_____	_____	_____
7. Written in proper order: Describe setting, then action, then how incident ended	_____	_____	_____
8. Complete enough in data recorded to get clear idea of event. Written objectively	_____	_____	_____
9. Interpreted carefully (interpretations in body of anecdote in brackets; most interpretation done in separate section)	_____	_____	_____

Figure 3.4

Anecdotal Records Help Early Childhood Professionals to:

- Understand child development
- Make wise decisions about guidance and discipline
- Assess a child's needs, interests, and abilities
- Plan and evaluate curriculum
- Document change or the lack of change
- Document suspicions of child abuse or neglect
- Observe both unusual and typical behavior

Anecdotal Records Are Uncomplicated.   Anecdotal records are an understandable, dependable narrative method. They are particularly well suited for busy teachers, and preprinting forms and leaving them in various parts of the classroom further simplifies the process. Teachers are much more likely to observe behavior if the process for observing is simple and reliable.

Anecdotal Records Are Easy to Learn to Use.   The guidelines for writing anecdotal records provide the means for you to learn to write good and useful observations. Practicing recording a number of anecdotes will show you that you can indeed record enough of the right type of information about what you observed.

Disadvantages of Anecdotal Records

There are a few major potential problems or disadvantages you might encounter when using anecdotal records.

An Observer Can Slip into Making Biased or Prejudiced Judgments.   Mrs. Lyndon, for example, made a hasty judgment about how *selfish* Nellie seemed to be by taking things from other children. The head teacher realized that her assistant was making a judgment with very little evidence. If the assistant teacher had started her observations with this in mind, she might well have chosen to observe mainly what she viewed as *selfish* behavior. She might not have even looked for examples of when Nellie was generous, such as when she shared a block.

Anecdotal Records Are Open to Invalid or Insupportable Interpretations.   The danger is that an observer can make groundless or unconvincing statements. That is why it is a good idea to record only facts and to avoid interpreting when recording facts or data.

If Mrs. Lyndon had only observed Nellie taking things, then the assistant teacher could easily have interpreted Nellie's behavior as selfish. As it turned out, after collecting many anecdotal records, the teachers concluded that Nellie is at the very beginning stage in learning to take another person's perspective (e.g., seeing that Kim had the right to play with the marbles, too).

They also realize that Nellie still has a way to go in perspective taking (Dixon & Soto, 1990), and they decided to continue to help her with this skill. Teachers can easily make mistaken negative value judgments about children if they interpret observations, including anecdotal records, carelessly.

USING ANECDOTAL RECORDS EFFECTIVELY

Organize the Anecdotes Well

Decide on the Best Way to Store Observations.   Consider using a simple filing box or cabinet for larger sheets of paper with a separate filing folder for each child in the class. Alternatively, consider using index cards for observations and make a section in a filing box for each child in the class. Keep the method simple and make it easy to get to the storage unit.

Decide When to File Observations.   Some teachers file notes as soon as they write the notes or they set a time each day or week for filing observations. Either method works well and becomes a pleasant classroom routine when done consistently.

Note the Goal for Writing the Anecdote (Almy & Genishi, 1979).   Write a brief note on the observation form about the goal for a specific anecdote (Figure 3.2). Mrs. Vargas noted that her goal was to observe Nellie when she takes things from other children. A simple notation about the goal will make it easier for teachers to use each child's file later. When Nellie's teachers were ready to analyze the observations about Nellie, Mrs. Vargas asked her assistant to go over Nellie's file and take out the anecdotes related to sharing or grabbing behavior. Their task was easier because they had clearly written the goal for every anecdote at the top of each card.

Have a Clear Plan for Analyzing and Using Information from Anecdotes

Review Observations Regularly.   Mrs. Vargas holds regular planning meetings with her assistant teacher. A part of their planning involves their observations of children. She scheduled time twice each month for going over observations of children for the most recent 2-week period. Their purpose for reviewing the observations was to consider the information that they had gathered about each child observed. They made interpretations when it seemed appropriate and decided when they needed more information before they could justifiably interpret.

Analyze the Observations.   Then they decided how the information could help them plan for that child. Nellie's teachers, for example, decided that they needed to continue to help her understand that other children had a right to keep on playing with toys, that is, that other children had a different perspective than did Nellie. The teachers collaborated on how they might both tell Nellie about using words to ask for things instead of just grabbing. Additionally, they decided to talk with Nellie's father because he had requested information on how to deal with this behavior.

Activities to Help You Construct Knowledge and Skills in Observing

ACTIVITY 1

Analyze the following anecdotal record of three second-grade children by using Figure 3.4, Guidelines for Writing Anecdotal Records. (Mr. Nellis recorded this incident about 3 minutes after he finished talking with each child involved.)

Class: K–2 classroom, Mr. Nellis, lead teacher
Setting: *"NASA" dramatic play center*   Focus of observation: *Jasmine's*
Date/time of day: *9/9, 9:45–9:47 a.m.*   *reactions to background anger*
Focus child: *Jasmine,* 6-6 (6 years, 6 months old)
Others involved: *Patrick (6-10) and Tim (6-9)*

Body of anecdote: Patrick, Tim, and Jasmine had been working on a project about space and had constructed their version of the control room. They had been working in the control room for several minutes. Patrick and Tim were going through their take-off checklist and Jasmine was now off to the side while she put on her blast-off suit. Patrick and Tim started to argue about taking turns at the controls. Jasmine turned her head toward them slightly as if listening. Jasmine stopped getting dressed and looked directly at Patrick and Tim, blinking her eyes rapidly. Jasmine looked back and forth, at whomever was talking.

"It's my turn at the controls," said Tim. "I'm not done yet," replied Patrick, his voice getting louder with each word. Tim: "But, I want my turn. Mr. Nellis told me that it was my turn next!" Tim tried to take the control panel from Patrick who held on tight and pushed Tim away. Patrick cursed at Tim. Jasmine seemed to be holding her breath and then she started to cry (interpretation: seemed to be alarmed). Then Jasmine picked up her space helmet and hurled it at the wall while she declared loudly, "I don't care WHO uses the control panel. I just know that I can't live here any more!" Then Jasmine rushed out of the project center. (Adapted from a similar case study written by Terri Swim, Indiana University-Purdue University Fort Wayre, for the 1999 New Orleans NAEYC conference presentation of Marian Marion and Terri Swim.)
Interpretation: Jasmine has lived in two different foster homes. Her first set of foster parents argued a lot in front of her, that is, she heard a lot of *background anger.* She frequently responds to other children's arguing in somewhat the same way as she did today, except that her reaction today was even stronger. Usually, she just gets very quiet and watches the argument. Today, Jasmine seemed quite agitated by Patrick and Tim's argument.

ACTIVITY 2

Write at least three anecdotal records. You may choose one child and record three observations about that child. Alternatively, you may choose to record one observation about three different children. Analyze your observations by using Figure 3.4, the guidelines for writing anecdotal records.

ACTIVITY 3

Here are three anecdotal record observations of the same incident in a preschool. Each is written with a different amount of detail. Why does the first example's amount and quality of detail make it the most helpful and descriptive account of the marble incident? What do you know about Nellie after reading the first example that you would not have known if you had read only the second or third examples?

FIRST EXAMPLE.   Nellie and Justine had each been playing peacefully together for several minutes with the marble machine, each girl taking turns dropping in her marbles. When N finished dumping her marbles into the device, she looked over and eyed J's marbles. Without a word, N then leaned over and closed both hands over a bunch of J's marbles. N scooped them up and put them in front of her.

J's eyes opened wide, giving her a look of surprise. Then J cried out, "Stop it, Nellie! They're *my* marbles and you're supposed to use your words for asking." N finally glanced up at J but said nothing. N went right back to dropping J's marbles into the contraption. J cried. Mrs. V looked at and walked over to them. She calmly asked the girls what had happened. N exasperatedly said, "I wanted the marbles. I needed them!"

SECOND EXAMPLE.   Nellie and Justine played with a marble machine. Nellie took Justine's marbles. Justine cried, but Nellie said nothing. The teacher talked to the girls to find out what happened.

THIRD EXAMPLE.   Nellie and Justine had been playing with the same marble machine. Nellie ran out of marbles and took some of Justine's marbles. Justine was surprised and told Nellie to give the marbles back. Nellie did not give the marbles back, and then Justine cried. The teacher talked to each girl to find out what had happened.

REFERENCES

Almy, M., & Genishi, C. (1979). *Ways of studying children* (Rev. ed.). New York: Teachers College Press.

Bergen, D. (1997). Using observational techniques for evaluating young children's learning. In B. Spodek & O. Saracho (Eds.), *Issues in early childhood educational assessment and evaluation* (pp. 108–128). New York: Teachers College Press.

Dixon, J. A., & Soto, C. F. (1990). The development of perspective-taking: Understanding differences in information and weighting. *Child Development, 61,* 1502–1513.

Fabes, R., & Eisenberg, N. (1992). Young children's coping with interpersonal anger. *Child Development, 63,* 116–128.

Fournier, J., Lansdowne, B., Pastenes, Z., Steen, P., & Hudelson, S. (1992). Learning with, about, and from children. In C. Genishi (Ed.), *Ways of assessing children and curriculum* (pp. 126–162). New York: Teachers College Press.

WEB SITES RELATED TO THIS CHAPTER

✓ High/Scope Educational Research Foundation (known widely as High/Scope)

This organization has published an assessment system that uses anecdotal records as a primary observation tool.

www.Highscope.org
Go to the Assessment link and look for the High/Scope Child Observation Record for Ages 2½ to 6 (COR).

CHAPTER 4

Running Records
A Longer Narrative Method of Observation

Running: fluid, continuous

Chapter objectives

1. *Summarize* advantages and disadvantages of the running record method of observing.
2. *Explain* why it is important to have a focus for a running record.
3. *List and explain* at least three different things on which to focus for running records.
4. *List* parts of the running record. *Explain* why it is so important to describe the context of an observation.
5. *Write and analyze* running record observations.

RUNNING RECORDS

Doing a running record well is a professional skill, and becoming a skillful observer is the first step in doing authentic assessments of children. Skillful observation also enables teachers to evaluate and plan activities and curriculum. Good observation helps students learn about child development. It also helps teachers focus on a child's development, which is the basis of developmentally appropriate practice (Bredekamp & Copple, 1997).

The running record is a tried and true method. A bit more complex than an anecdotal record, the running record is a traditional and time-honored way of learning about child development. For several decades now, instructors of child development and early childhood courses have used the running record when they want students to see child development in action (Bergen, 1997).

RUNNING RECORD: DESCRIPTION

A written **running record** observation is a narrative, open, longer form of observation. It is similar to an anecdotal record in several ways, but it is also different from the anecdotal record method (chapter 3).

A Running Record Is a Narrative Form of Observation

Like the anecdotal record, a running record tells a *story*. The anecdotal record is a very short story, whereas the running record is a longer story because an observer watches a child, a group, or an activity for a much longer period. An observer records as much as possible about a chosen focus and preserves that data. He records enough detail so that the story, when he reads it later, will make sense.

A Running Record Is an Open Form of Observation

It is open because an observer can choose to observe a wide range of child development, interactions, or activities. An observer can watch a single child, the whole group, a specific activity, or a specific aspect of personality development and can even observe a teacher's behavior and interactions (Cohen, Stern, & Balaban, 1996).

A Running Record Is a Longer Form of Observation Than an Anecdotal Record

Observers using the running record method gather much more information about an incident and, therefore, spend more time doing the observation. If, for example, the observer's focus for the day is on how a child initiates play with other children (a social skill), then he observes a single child for an extended period. He records what he sees or hears and then analyzes his record with the focus clearly in mind.

Observers Do Not Participate in Activities When Doing Running Records

A running record, like an anecdotal record, results from an observer's direct observation. Unlike an anecdotal record, however, the observer is a *nonparticipant* and does *not* participate in the classroom while doing a running record.

Instead, an observer doing a running record watches from the periphery, observing but not interacting with the children he is observing. The observer places himself in a place where he can observe as unobtrusively as possible—a special observation booth, a quiet corner of a classroom, or a spot on the playground.

Early childhood teachers tend to shy away from using running records because of the amount of time involved. As busy teachers, they worry about using a method that would take them away from their classes for so long. An early childhood professional does place the needs of his class first.

However, a modified form of the traditional running record could easily be one part of an authentic assessment plan for busy teachers. Teachers can observe for shorter periods, say 20 to 30 minutes, when they need good data for decision making and when anecdotal records would simply not be appropriate. Teachers might also consider using one running record to complement anecdotal records or even other types of observations.

Use a running record to observe an activity, an individual child, or a group of children.

FORMAT OF A RUNNING RECORD

Suggested Form

The format for a running record is simple and straightforward. The goal is to record information about the context of an episode, and then to do an intensive recording of what the observer sees and hears. Finally, an observer reflects on the data collected and comments on data *only* when it is appropriate to comment. Figure 4.1 shows a suggested format for a running record observation.

Parts of the Running Record Report: Explanation

A running record report has three parts: context and background comments, intensive observation, and the reflection/comment sections. Figures 4.1, 4.3, and 4.4 illustrate these parts.

Context and Background Comments.   Get a clear idea of the context. As with anecdotal records, it is essential to understand the context of any observation. Record information about the setting, people, your impression of the mood of the group of children, and the child's activity. Then, you will have this context as a backdrop to the main body and the reflection part of the observation.

- *Name the activity or situation.* Snack? Science? Outdoors? Field trip?
- *Describe the setting.* Be brief and clear. Record enough detail to help you remember what was happening. Note the time and record it.

Context/Background Comments	Intensive Observation	Reflection/ Comments

Figure 4.1
Format for a Running Record Observation

📖 *List names of children and adults* involved in the activity.

📖 *Comment on the "mood" of the group* if it seems appropriate. For example, "It was nap-time, but the group seemed restless and agitated by the noisy fire truck that had just passed by the school."

📖 *Make sketches whenever they would be helpful.* Experienced observers know that "a sketch is worth a hundred words." Do a quick room sketch or a drawing of the specific area that you are observing. Figure 4.4, for example, described four children, Aiko, Kenny, Sam, and Molly, as they found and explored a large block of ice on the patio of their school. There is a sketch of where each child, plus the teacher, stood when they first saw the ice.

Intensive Observation.   The second part of a running record observation is the intensive observation. An observer writes an accurate, detailed description of an incident in this section, describing children's actions and speech, as well as how they seem to feel.

📖 *Write accurate notes.* Your notes about a child, an activity, a teacher, or an incident should be accurate, that is, there should be enough detail so that you or any other reader can picture things as they really happened.

📖 *Record good detail, enough information* so that you will have a good description of this incident whenever you read the observation.

📖 *Write objective notes.* Avoid giving your opinion in this section. Here, write data. Some examples: What did the child do? What did he say? What did others say in response to him? Describe facial expressions. Describe body movements that seem significant. (Follow Sergeant Friday's advice and give "Just the facts, ma'am," or "Just the facts, sir.")

📖 *Use good descriptive words.* An *objective* observation is not necessarily a bare bones description of an incident or a child. Use good descriptive words that give a clear picture of the action or of the child. Use good descriptive words to characterize the tone of interactions. Consider the following examples.

Example: Andy went to the bathroom. He washed his hands. Then he went to the table and sat down between two children. He told the teacher that he had washed his hands.

Example: Andy *raced* to the table from the bathroom and *plopped* himself into the chair between George and Sandra. "I washed my hands, Mr. Nellis, see?" Smiling *broadly,* eyes wide open, he first showed the palms of his hands and then *flipped* them over for the teacher. He sniffed one of his hands and said, "I can even smell the soap."

The first example gives the dry facts. The second example describes the same incident but is a richer picture of the tone of Andy's actions. A reader gets a picture of the speed with which he got to the table (raced) and how he seated himself (plopped). We know that he smiled and did so broadly. He went beyond just telling the teacher. Andy showed his hands and smelled the soap.

📖 *Tie descriptive words or phrases to behavior.* Use powerful and descriptive words and phrases, but tie these words to behavior for greatest effectiveness. The next example says only that a child seemed very happy and excited but does not tie the impression to any specific behavior. A reader would not know what it was that led the observer to conclude that this child seemed happy or excited.

Example: Janna seemed *very happy and excited* when she arrived at school today.

The next example describes specific behavior that led the student observer to view 6-year-old Janna as "very happy and excited."

Example: Janna burst into the room today, pulling her mother along with her. "Come on, Mom! Mr. Nellis . . . LOOK!" Bouncing in place and flashing a big smile and a photograph at the teacher, she said, her words tumbling out faster than I have ever heard her talk, "LOOK, here's my puppy! Her name is Maxine. She's a beagle. She came from the Humane Society. Isn't she bee-u-ti-ful? She has a chew toy and a bed and a crate and a bowl and a leash! She sleeps in MY room." Janna used her "pointer finger" on her right hand to tap her chest as she said "MY room."

Reflection or Comment.   Gaining skill in reflecting on and then interpreting data takes effort and time. It is like most aspects of development and occurs over time. Give yourself the time that it takes to develop initial skill in reflection on your observations. Be extremely cautious about interpreting. Three things will help you.

📖 *Reflect, but avoid guessing about the cause of the behavior.* The reflection/comment column is the place to reflect on the incident, thinking carefully about what happened. This is not the place to make wild guesses about why a child acted a certain way. Behavior is complex enough that there are many possible causes of any behavior. For example, you see a child standing next to the chain link fence, grasping it with both hands, and staring out at the trees beyond the fenced area. There really is no way that anybody can say with accuracy why this child is at the fence and staring out. Think about all the possible explanations. Therefore, it is best *not* to jump in and start guessing. Our guesses are not relevant or important until we have a large enough mass of information on which to reflect.

It is better much of the time just to gather data, read it over, and let the data sit there for a time. The observer who recorded Figure 4.4, Ice on the Patio, left the comment column blank at first. She concentrated on recording what children did and said and what adults did and said. She then read her notes for accuracy, and then reflected on the episode. She made a conscious decision not to interpret every action. Instead, she focused on what her long observation told her about how each child approached the activity and how the children were constructing knowledge about the concept of melting.

Comment only when it would contribute to your understanding of this child's behavior or development, of the group's dynamics, or of the curriculum's effectiveness. Do not interpret every little detail. Making comments on every single aspect of the observation yields a jumbled mass of detail that is simply not relevant. Please see the reflection/comment sections of the running record observation form in Figures 4.3 and 4.4.

📖 Use *descriptive phrasing. Avoid using interpretive phrasing.* Your words and phrases should describe observable behavior, behavior that another observer could easily verify. Another observer could never verify interpretive phrasing because such phrasing makes judgments about a child's behavior but gives little or no observable data to justify such judgments.

Example: (interpretive phrasing) "Aubrey was eager to go to the aquarium." This statement makes an uncalled-for assumption about how Aubrey was feeling. There is no way to confirm this interpretive phrase.

Example: (descriptive phrasing) "During large-group time, Aubrey talked about his two books on aquariums and described the aquarium in his mom's office. When the teacher announced that it was time to line up for the bus to the aquarium, Aubrey took a deep breath, let it out, clenched his fists, and shook them. At the same time, he closed his eyes and smiled. Then he chanted, 'Let's go! Let's go!'"

This statement gives just the facts and avoids interpretive phrases. Another observer could easily verify the observation because of the descriptive phrases. When an observer gets enough descriptive phrases, enough good data, then the child's underlying feelings shine through and we do not have to make wild guesses. Recording, reading, and then reflecting on observable data is a humbling experience for any observer who is breaking a habit of jumping to early and often erroneous conclusions.

📖 *State comments tentatively, if you decide to make comments.* Be cautious and careful when making comments. An observer who has reflected on information thoughtfully might decide that it is appropriate to make a comment about the data. Even at this point, no observer can be sure that her interpretation of an event is accurate. We can never be sure that we are interpreting accurately because our conclusions are a *best guess* based on our perspective.

Suppose that you recorded all the descriptive data about Aubrey's behavior before the group went to the aquarium. It certainly looks as though he might be eager to get to the aquarium. It is also possible that this is not the case. Aubrey might be truly bored with school today and might just want to escape the boredom. He might not be all that enthralled with the aquarium. If you do think that he is eager to go, state your comments cautiously.

Example: (comment) "Aubrey *seemed* eager to get to the aquarium."

Example: (observation) "Alice sat back in her chair and folded her arms across her chest. She lowered her chin to her chest. She narrowed her eyes and glanced at the teacher who was restating a direction, 'It is time to put the tape recorder away now. It's time to have a snack.'" (Comment) "Alice's body posture and facial expressions *were consistent with* those of a person who is angry. Alice *might well have been* angry."

Avoid interpretive phrasing	Instead, use descriptive phrasing
"Jessie is so *selfish*."	"Jessie took the marker from Kee and the hat from Marc."
"Saul was really *aggressive* today."	"Saul grabbed back the book that Shari had taken from him, saying, 'Give it BACK!'"
"Roberto was *shy* when the rescue dog was here."	"Roberto sat quietly and looked at the rescue dog as the trainer explained the dog's job. Roberto did not ask, as did the others, if he could pet the dog. Roberto just sat and listened."
"Those two boys acted *so silly* today."	"Ben and Adam looked in the mirror and then contorted their faces, giggling at first and then laughing loudly each time they made a new face. They laughed more loudly each time until Adam rolled on the floor, laughing. Ben joined him and laughed."
"Libby *did not want* to go home with her father."	"Libby was going to her dad's house for the weekend. When her father arrived, Libby looked at him and then quickly averted her eyes. She whined when the teacher told her to get her things. She sat in front of her locker and did not move when Dad called to her to get her coat on."
"Shondra *loves* to paint."	"Shondra headed straight for the easel this morning, painting for almost 15 minutes, using four colors. Holding one brush in each hand, she swirled, dabbed, and swiped the brushes across the paper, humming as she painted."
"Caleb is *afraid* of storms."	"Caleb stood still when he heard the thunder and saw the lightning. He covered his ears."
"Carrie was *angry* with Pete today!"	"Pete took one of Carrie's colored pencils without asking. She looked directly at him, narrowing her eyes, and said, "You have to ask first!"
"Sean was *stressed* during that test."	"Sean chewed on his lip throughout the test and kept rubbing one fist against his face."
"Janet was *tired* yesterday."	"Janet yawned several times during the work period. She fell asleep during a story."

Figure 4.2
Avoid Interpretive Phrasing and Use Descriptive Phrasing.

Example: (observation) "Ella picked up a piece of carrot and put it in her mouth. She immediately spit the carrot out and across the table. 'Yuck, aggh!' she said as she wrinkled her nose, stuck out her tongue, and shook her head." (Reflection) "I immediately concluded that Ella must not like carrots, but then I heard her say something else." (More observation/data) "Ella pointed to the carrot and to the insect crawling away from it, 'A bug, a bug! A bug on my carrot!'" (Comment) "*My guess is that* crunching into a carrot with an insect on it startled Ella. I still don't know if she likes carrots, but am reasonably sure that she does not like insects on her food."

ESTABLISH A FOCUS FOR RUNNING RECORDS

Reasons for Having a Focus

Although the running record is an open method, it is not a "free-for-all." The most effective and coherent running records have on a clear focus. It is confusing and difficult to go into a classroom, into an observation booth, or onto the playground and begin to observe. There is usually so much activity that an inexperienced observer can easily feel overwhelmed.

It is important, then, to establish a clear focus for the observation, that is, to limit the range of what to observe. A clear focus allows an observer to pay more attention to a specific aspect of the classroom and far less attention to other ongoing activities. A clear focus enables an observer to have some control over the observation by helping to center attention.

A clear focus is like a zoom lens on a camera. An observer zooms in on a specific area, activity, or behavior. The zoom lens of a clear focus effectively blocks out other activities and stimuli competing for attention as an observer watches a classroom filled with children.

Example: Mrs. Vargas, the preschool teacher, and her assistant, Mrs. Lyndon, arranged the morning schedule so that the assistant teacher was in charge for a short time. Mrs. Vargas wanted to spend 20 minutes observing, focusing on how one child approached different activities during the morning work period. The head teacher faded into the background and zoomed in on her intended focus. Although she was well aware of the entire classroom, she maintained her focus. She did not shift her focus to any other child.

Selecting the Focus

Observers can focus on any of several things: one child, one activity, the overall group, a single aspect of development, or the teacher.

Focus on One Child.   Choose one child who seems especially interesting to you. Watch that child very closely for about 15 minutes. Some students who are just learning how to observe tend to choose a quiet child or one playing alone. It is good practice to describe what the child looks like first and then observe what the child does.

Context/Background Comments	Intensive Observation	Reflection/Comment
8:02 a.m. Background comments/context: Kenny is a slim but solidly built 4-year-old. He is one of the tallest children in his class. His dark brown hair is very short all over. He has bright dark brown eyes. I would say that Kenny appears to be a healthy, strong, sturdy child. Yet, he moves gracefully. He seems to be alert all the time and he smiles easily. Today, he wore clean shorts, a tee shirt, sneakers, and socks. His dad told him to leave his cap in his cubby. This incident took place indoors, at the water table, just after arrival time. It was August and was hot. About half the class was there and children chose an activity after saying good-bye to parents. (8:04, end of background comments.)	8:04 Kenny's dad had just left after bringing Kenny (K) to school. K kept his cap on. Dad had told K, "A gentleman does not wear his hat inside, K. Put your cap in your cubby." K complied with this limit and then waved good-bye to his dad. He then made a beeline to the water table, which contained several boats. Ritchie (R) and Sam (S) were there. S was already playing in the water with a boat and R, also wearing an apron, was watching S play. K quickly put on an apron and stationed himself on one side of the table. "I'm gonna play with this boat" he announced to the other children. "It's a ferryboat. Toot, toot . . . it has to go pick up the people on the island." After that announcement, Kenny said nothing as he slowly steered his ferryboat through the water, from one end of the water table to the other end. He turned from the table, went to a nearby shelf to get some small plastic figures of people, and then returned to the water table. "Time to get into the ferry! Time to go to the mainland. Toot, toot." He ferried the passengers to the other end of the water table. "Everybody out, please. Watch your step. Careful there, Sir." K picked up each figure and placed it carefully on the ledge of the water table. The teacher (T) had heard this whole episode and now smiled. "Did you visit your Grandma this weekend, Kenny?" (K's grandmother lives on a nearby island and K and his family visit her often, riding a ferry to and from the island.) "Yep, we did. We rode on the ferry. The captain saluted at me and I saluted back! My Grandma gave me a cookie that was still warm. The chocolate chips were all gooey!" He looked away from the T and bobbed the boat in the water. "Toot . . . toot.	Did not argue with Dad. Complied with the limit. Kenny seemed to be eager to get to the water table, to play. Unlike Ritchie, K did not hesitate to play. He jumped right in and then became absorbed in his play. K seems to understand the role of ferryboat captain. K's play is based on a real experience, an experience that seems to have been a pleasant one for him.

Figure 4.3
Kenny the Ferryboat Pilot. An Excerpt From a 15-Minute Running Record Observation (Focus: One Child)

We have to make another trip now. Bye." K looked over at S and said in a deep voice, "Wind's blowin' up. Do you have any passengers over there for my ferry? We're leaving soon for the island. All aboard!"

K piloted the ferry across the water table a few more times and seemed to be absorbed in this play. Ritchie, a child with Down's syndrome, had moved closer and closer to K. K looked surprised (and angry?) when R reached for K's ferryboat. "No, Ritchie! I'm playing with the ferryboat now. I had it first. You have to wait until I'm done." K looked at R who had backed away quickly and who looked as though he might cry.

K did not just go right back to playing but stopped and talked to R. "I'm sorry, R. Here's a good boat for you to play with. It's just like mine." R perked up when K picked up the other boat, gently took R's hand, and placed the boat in R's hand. K; "Let's make boat sounds together, toot . . . toot. Put your boat right next to mine, R. That's good. Now, make the boat sound, toot . . . toot!" R never did make the sound but steered his boat along with K's boat, R looking at K frequently. Whenever K said, "Toot-toot!" R smiled. 8:11 End of excerpt.

K imitated the captain's voice. His memory seems to be well enough developed so that he remembers the exact words as well as the sound of the captain's voice.

K's expression of his frustration was positive and nonaggressive.

K showed empathy. K even put the boat in R's hand. K did not get frustrated with R when R could or simply did not make the boat sounds. K just played with R in the way that R seemed able to play.

8:11 (K and R continued to play ferryboat captain for several more minutes and then K left the watertable for the dramatic play area where he put on a ferryboat captain's jacket. He then sat at the steering wheel and piloted the ferry to the mainland.)

Figure 4.3

Figure 4.3 is an example of an intensive observation focusing on one child. It is an excerpt from a 15-minute observation focusing on 4-year-old Kenny. You will notice several indicators of Kenny's personal style as he chooses an activity, interacts with teachers, asserts himself nonaggressively, and shows compassion for another child.

Focus on One Activity, Interest Center, or Play Material.   Figure 4.4 is an excerpt of an intensive observation from a 15-minute observation in the same classroom. The observer focused on one activity, a small group of the 4-year-olds as they investigated a large cube-shaped block of ice on the concrete patio on the playground. The teacher had placed the ice block there because of the children's interest in how some regular ice cubes had partially melted when the group had made a gelatin dessert. The children had noted that ice melted in warm liquid. The teacher decided to focus on having them predict what would happen to the large block of ice just sitting on the patio on a hot day and not immersed in liquid.

Appendix B in this text lists specific questions on which you can focus as you observe a play material or an activity.

Focus on the Overall Group.   Consider switching focus from one child to the whole group. Watch the entire group closely for about 15 minutes at large group, snack, or lunch, during transitions, or even during naptime.

Focus on One Aspect of Development.   Observe one specific aspect of development. For example, observe stages of play or observe how children initiate contact with other children. There are hundreds of possibilities when focusing on one aspect of development, and this textbook focuses on many of these.

Focus on the Teacher.   Watch the teacher closely for about 15 minutes. How does the teacher talk to the children, set limits, restate limits? What does the teacher do to help children get started with an activity? How does the teacher guide an angry or an aggressive child? How does the teacher lead small or large groups?

Figure 4.5 is a suggested list of things to observe with a running record.

ADVANTAGES AND DISADVANTAGES OF OBSERVING WITH RUNNING RECORDS

Disadvantages of Running Records

The first disadvantage of running records is that an observer can easily make an *invalid interpretation,* an erroneous and insupportable conclusion.

Example: Mrs. Lyndon had watched as Ralph mixed dry soil and water with his hands in the sensory table. When she observed the joy that Ralph got from making mud, she made a careless judgment by concluding too quickly, "Ralph likes *sloppy* activities."

Context/Background Comments	Intensive Observation	Reflection/Comment

9:49 a.m. This took place on a hot, hot day in late August at the university lab school in the group of 4-year-olds. The children, each dressed appropriately for the hot weather, had just come outside to the playground. They seemed to survey the yard eagerly. In spite of the heat, each child raced to a specific area. Four of the children spotted an ice block on the patio and dashed over to it.
 	
Teacher
 	
Molly
Aiko
Kenny
Sam
 	
Patio ↑
	9:51 a.m. Molly (M), Aiko (A), Kenny (K), and Sam (S) ran to the edge of the patio where they had spotted a very large cube of ice. The teacher (T) walked over there, too. K squealed, "Look! Ice! A BIG ice cube! Look . . . you can almost see through it." He ran his hand, first over the block of ice, and then over his face, smiling as he did this. "That feels good," K said. S stood back about a foot from the ice and just looked at the cube, his mouth gaping open. He watched as K, A, and M all felt the ice, smoothing their hands over its slick surface, each making little sounds of contentment— "Ooh, m-m-m." "Sam, feel the ice. It's smooth," called A. "It's cold," chimed in K. The teacher (T) stood back a little, watching as the children explored the ice. S moved closer to the other children and put out his hand cautiously. K encouraged him, "Feel it right here, S," as he pointed to one of the flat surfaces.
	
	    S placed his right hand on the ice and a look of surprise lighted up his face. K: "See. It is cold." S did not say anything, but he grinned as he looked at his now wet right hand and touched it lightly to his face. He seemed to lose his caution and placed his hand back on the ice block, now moving it in quick, tight little circles. When he removed his hand, it was dripping water. S's eyes followed the drops as they landed on the dry patio. S: "Look, it's water. Teacher, it's water." He opened his eyes wide and opened his mouth.
	
	    T: "That's a good observation, Sam. You do have some water dripping from your hand. You rubbed the ice and then you had water dripping from your hand. What do you think happened?" S looked at T as T spoke. S seemed to be listening intently to T
		The children's words and facial expressions seemed to indicate that they were *surprised*!
		
		Sam did not seem to be afraid but did hesitate to touch the ice.
		
		S seemed to trust the other children and later really seemed to enjoy this activity.
		
		S's face had a look that made me think that he was surprised and confused.

Figure 4.4

Ice on the Patio. An Excerpt From a 15-Minute Practice Running Record (Focus: One Activity)

because he focused on T's face and scrunched up his face in concentration. "I put my hand on the ice and when I took it off, I had water on my hand. The ice turned to water on my hand."

The other children continued to rub the ice, dripping water onto the patio. They were listening to the interchange between S and T. A, "Look, I'm dripping water, too," as she shook her hand vigorously, spraying water in an arc. T: "What's happening to that ice when you touch it?" S suddenly lost his look of confusion. He looked like a person who has just said A-HA, I have it!, when he blurted out, "That ice melted." "Yeah, it MELTED," agreed K. A and M continued to smooth the ice and watch the water drip from their hands to the patio.

By this time, the block of ice had started to turn to liquid, water observable at the base of the block as the melted ice turned the light gray patio a much darker color. A: "Look, there's water under the ice now," as she pointed to the base of the ice block. "H-m-m," said T. "None of us even touched the ice on the base of the block. What do you think is happening?"
9:58 a.m. End of excerpt

9:58 (The teacher and children continued this exchange of ideas for several more minutes. Other children joined the group and A and M left. Questions about frozen water changing to liquid flew around the group. The teacher made connections to the gelatin activity from the previous day.)

T led a discussion of how ice turns into water—from some sort of heat source—for example, warm hands or from heat from the sun.

Figure 4.4   (*continued*)

Focus on One Child or One Aspect of Development

• Record a child's language and action in dramatic play.
• Identify the type or classification of play in which a child engages: unoccupied, solitary, onlooker, parallel, associative, cooperative.
• Identify the activities that a child seems to prefer.
• Gather information on a child's competence in both gross and fine motor skills.
• Record a verbatim (word-for-word) observation of a child's speech. Record dialogues between the child and others, teachers or children.
• Gather information on a child's ability to represent her experiences with words, drawings, and dramatic play.
• Focus on how a child reacts to anger-arousing events or to things arousing fear.
• How does this child react to someone being aggressive toward him? How and when does this child show aggression toward others?
• Record how the child relates to other children. Observe whether he chooses to work and play with others. Note responses of other children to him (reject, accept, ignore him?). Observe his body movements and postures or facial expression during work and play.
• Observe social skills: How does she enter groups, deal with conflict, assert her rights, ask for things from children or adults, demonstrate respectful behavior?
• Observe how a child responds to positively stated limits.
• Observe how this child responds to transitions.

Focus on One Activity, Area of the Classroom, or Material

• Observe a group of second or third graders as they work together on a project.
• Observe very young children encountering a completely new activity or material.
• Record words and behaviors of children on a field trip.
• Focus on how children work with blocks.
• Observe children's use of small manipulative types of toys, such as snap-together blocks.
• Observe how young children work with puzzles with fewer pieces; observe how primary-school children deal with more complex puzzles.
• Observe how preschool, kindergarten, or primary-grade children working with math manipulatives.
• Observe how children approach work with a computer.
• Record the reactions of children to a messy material, either indoors or outdoors.
• Record words and behaviors during snack or lunch.
• Record information about children's behavior during naptime.

Figure 4.5
Suggested Behaviors and Situations to Observe with a Running Record[1]

[1]This list is an extensive list of situations and behaviors that you can observe with a running record. The list is, however, not a complete list. You will undoubtedly think of other things that can be observed best with a running record.

• Observe children's behavior when a visitor comes to the classroom, especially one who demonstrates some skill.
• Record information about behavior during oral reading.
• Observe during standardized testing. Record children's behavior during testing.
• Observe children as they participate in a teacher-initiated discussion about a question or concept identified by the children, such as in Figure 4.4.
• Observe children's reactions to and behaviors during a teacher initiated and dominated activity such as preparing for a "program" for parents.

Focus on the Group

• Record reactions of the group to cleanup and transitions.
• Observe the group and identify types (classifications) of play (unoccupied, solitary, onlooker, parallel, associative, cooperative).
• Describe how a group of children functions during group inquiry or instruction.
• How would you characterize a particular group's style after observing them for several hours straight or for three or four running records on different days? Is this group generally calm, frenzied, cooperative, friendly?
• Record the group's style of reacting to unexpected events, such as a fire drill.
• Observe the group's reactions to positive limit-setting.

Focus on the Teacher

• Observe how a preschool, kindergarten, or primary-grade teacher states limits.
• Record a teacher's reactions to children who comply with reasonable, well-stated limits; to children who test reasonable and well-stated limits.
• Observe how a teacher deals with an openly defiant child.
• Record examples of guidance and discipline strategies, both positive and negative. Avoid commenting at first; just record the data.
• Observe a teacher's interactions and language with both boys and girls. Just get the data. Reflect and, if appropriate, comment on how equitably and fairly this teacher seems to treat each gender.
• Observe how this teacher models responsible anger management.
• Observe how a teacher models prosocial behavior, that is, cooperation, helpfulness, and compassion.
• Make a record of how a teacher treats classroom animals and what he models for children with his behavior.
• Observe a teacher to record how well she has provided a climate for discovery. Record information on how she introduces ideas, materials, or activities that will help children construct knowledge about their world.

Figure 4.5 (*continued*)

Mrs. Vargas urged her assistant teacher to look through her observation notes carefully for other examples of Ralph having participated in activities that many people would consider messy.

Another disadvantage is that *an observer might not be able to write quickly enough* to record every one of a child's behaviors. Even a diligent observer might not notice certain behaviors when he is busy recording what he has just watched.

Finally, *observer fatigue* can strike even the most dedicated observer. All observations require close attention to the task at hand. Running records, however, require an observer to be attentive, alert, and focused for quite a long time. Observers sitting in one position get tired; their hands often hurt from quick writing, or their wrists hurt when using a laptop for a long time. Observers can actually become exhausted when doing a running record. Fatigue might make an observer less focused or attentive, thereby rendering the observation less useful.

Advantages of Running Records

There are distinct advantages to using running records to observe children (Bergen, 1997).

Generous Amount of Time. Running records give teachers enough time to record important data. An observer needs a minimum of about 15 minutes for a "mini-running record" but most often takes from 30 minutes to about 1 or $1\frac{1}{2}$ hours. Anywhere in that range does seem like enough time to record an incident in enough detail.

Sharp Focus. Students or teachers using a running record get to focus their attention on one child or curriculum area or activity for a significant amount of time.

Variety of Behaviors Because of Longer Observation Period. The generous observation period (20 minutes to over an hour) gives an observer a better chance to see a variety of behaviors in the same child. Recall Figure 4.3 (Kenny the Ferryboat Pilot). The observer watched Kenny choose his activity, comply with a limit, interact with his teacher, interact with other children at the water table, reenact a real ferryboat ride, and assert himself nonaggressively. Finally, the observer was able to see Kenny demonstrate compassion for another child.

An anecdotal record, in its compressed period, simply would not have allowed an observer to see the larger number of behaviors. Consequently, when done well, running records yield good and abundant information about children. This makes the running record an advantageous method.

More Details Possible. A careful and thorough observer usually records many details about the child's behavior during a running record. The large number of details, if carefully interpreted, can give the observer insights about the child that might have gone unnoticed up until then.

Example: Mrs. Lyndon followed Mrs. Vargas's suggestion to look through all of her observations of Ralph. She detected a pattern centering on Ralph's apparent delight in playing with water. She had observed that he had walked with head tipped up and rain hitting his face. He had let water run slowly over his hands at the sink and he dictated a story about his swimming lesson. Yes, he did seem to enjoy making mud, but the enjoyment could just as easily have come from playing with the water with which he made the mud.

Activities to Help You Construct Knowledge and Skills in Observing

ACTIVITY 1

Label each of these statements as descriptive or interpretive. If a statement is interpretive, please explain what led you to this conclusion.

- "Darnell said, 'No, I don't want to play baseball.'"
- "Sam does not like orange juice."
- "Amanda hurt Andy's feelings at snack time."
- "Choua (pronounced 'chewa') was sad when the gerbil died."
- "Young-He handed two apple slices to Sam."

ACTIVITY 2

This activity is an opportunity to write a running record observation. If you are not currently working with young children, then consider observing in a public place such as a food court in a shopping center. Alternatively, consider watching a video about children and do a running record of one of the children in the video.

Write one 15-minute practice running record observation. Focus on the child. Record the context for the observation first. Then do the intensive observation. Finally, reflect on the information and judge how well you avoided interpretive phrasing. Circle examples of interpretive phrasing. Think back to the incident, about how you can change any interpretive phrasing to descriptive phrasing. Finally, decide whether you want or need to interpret or whether you might need more information.

ACTIVITY 3

Write a 15- or 20-minute running record observation. Focus on the teacher in a preschool, kindergarten, or primary-grade class. Specifically, focus on how this teacher states or restates limits. Record the context for the observation first. Then do the intensive observation. Again, reflect on the information and judge how well you avoided interpretive phrasing. Change any interpretive phrasing to descriptive if you can recall the episode clearly enough. Finally, reflect on your information about this teacher and limit-setting, commenting when appropriate.

REFERENCES

Bergen, D. (1997). Using observational techniques for evaluating young children's learning. In B. Spodek & O. Saracho (Eds.), *Issues in early childhood educational assessment and evaluation* (pp. 108–128). New York: Teachers College Press.

Bredekamp, S., & Copple, C. (Eds.) (1997). *Developmentally appropriate practice in early childhood programs*. Washington, DC: National Association for the Education of Young Children (NAEYC).

Cohen, D., Stern, V., & Balaban, N. (1996). *Observing and recording the behavior of young children*. New York: Teachers College Press.

WEB SITES RELATED TO THIS CHAPTER

✓ NAEYC/The National Association for the Education of Young Children

National organization for early childhood professionals and parents.

www.naeyc.org

Go to "NAEYC Resources" link, then to "Position Statements." Look for "Guidelines for Appropriate Curriculum Content and Assessment in Programs Serving Children Ages 3 Through 8." Click on "View the Full Position Statement." This document describes appropriate assessment, which includes running records.

CHAPTER 5

Checklists and Rating Scales
Nonnarrative Methods for Observing Development and Progress

Checklist: an inventory
Rating: a relative estimate or evaluation

Chapter objectives

1. *Explain* what checklists and rating scales are in observing young children.
2. *List and describe* different ways in which checklists can be used, and summarize guidelines for developing checklists.
3. *List and describe* three different types of rating scales.
4. *Summarize* the differences between narrative and nonnarrative forms of observation. *Explain* why checklists and rating scales are nonnarrative forms.
5. *Explain* the advantages and disadvantages of checklists and rating scales.
6. *List and explain* at least three ways of increasing the power of checklists and rating scales.

At the beginning of the school year, Mrs. Vargas and her assistant, Mrs. Lyndon, were having a planning meeting and were looking at photographs of the 4-year-olds in the class. The two teachers had made a home visit for each child that summer and so had met each family and were acquainted with each child.

Mrs. Lyndon pointed to Moshe's photo: "Moshe was so eager, when I visited, to show me his picture books. He likes books and even has a library card. I found out that Ralph's mother is a painter and his dad is a musician. Ralph knows a lot about color mixing and the names of exotic colors. He's well beyond just naming colors. I took a picture of him at his own easel."

"I know what you mean," said Mrs. Vargas. "Pete's parents own the nursery in town, and Pete is already helping his dad and older brothers plant perennials. Pete can identify many perennials at the nursery. He wrote this list for me and even defined 'perennial.'" The teacher showed the yellow sheet with Pete's list of plants, complete with invented spelling.

"I like knowing something about each child, and I've already written some notes and want to place Pete's list and Ralph's photo in their portfolios," said the assistant.

"I agree," the lead teacher said. "That's a great start. I'd also like to use a few checklists to get more information quickly about each child so that we can plan." Mrs. Vargas scanned the photos. "We don't have a lot of time, and finding out who knows the names of basic shapes or who can hop, skip, or jump, or can produce labels for emotions really doesn't require a lot of anecdotal or running records. Checklists would do the job nicely. We'll be meeting with the rest of the early childhood faculty about our assessment plans. I know that we plan on using a ready-made checklist for looking at each child's motor development."

These two teachers had begun their year by facing the challenge of gathering information about children's needs, interests, and abilities. They knew that they would be much better prepared to make wise curriculum and guidance decisions when they had done an appropriate assessment. Again, they obtained the essential facts through observation. This time they needed less detailed information, so they used methods of observation that yield less detail than do anecdotal or running records.

Mrs. Vargas and Mrs. Lyndon had decided to observe the children in their class by using two nonnarrative observational techniques—*checklists* and *rating scales*. Almy and Genishi (1979) called the two "shortcut methods" because they bypass details. They do not narrate a story; they merely check or rate development and progress. Therefore, they are called **nonnarrative methods.**

CHECKLISTS

Description

In observing young children, a **checklist** is a list of characteristics or behaviors. A teacher observes a group of children and notes whether each child does or does not show that characteristic or behavior. The teacher records a check if a child shows the behavior or leaves a blank space if a child does not yet show the behavior. A checklist is an efficient way to determine the presence or absence of a behavior. Checklists are an efficient way to acquire certain types of information.

Hand Washing Checklist

	Ralph	Kim	Moshe	Nellie	Justine	Roxanne
Proper hand washing		×	×	×		×
Washes hands before preparing food	×		×	×	×	
Washes hands before eating		×	×	×	×	×
Washes hands after using tissue			×	×	×	
Washes hands after using toilet	×	×	×	×	×	×
Washes hands after painting, etc.	×	×	×			
Washes hands at other times	×		×	×		

Figure 5.1

Example: Out of concern for the health and safety of the children in their class, Mrs. Vargas and Mrs. Lyndon wanted the children to learn and use some basic health practices. Consequently, one of the first things that they taught was how to wash hands properly and when the children needed to wash their hands. Then they used a simple checklist (Figure 5.1) to determine whether the children were following the hand-washing procedures.

In this example, the teachers have used the checklist method of observation to keep track of children's progress toward a set goal (Almy & Genishi, 1979). You will

The children's teacher is keeping track of a set goal, hand washing, *by using a checklist.*

quickly observe that a checklist yields less information than they would gather with a running record or even with anecdotal records, which were discussed in chapter 3. A checklist, then, is an observation method that samples behavior.

We do not know, for example, when Kim first used the proper hand-washing technique. We only know that he used it. We do not know whether a teacher had to remind Ralph to wash his hands before he helped prepare a snack. We know nothing, when we read this checklist, about the discipline encounter when Ralph actually defied the rule about washing hands after using the toilet.

Teachers usually design checklists to gather a minimum amount of detail because they need so little detail about some things. Therefore, the only thing that we know by reading the checklist in Figure 5.1 is that each child did or did not show the behavior.

Different Ways to Use Checklists

Teachers who learn how to construct good checklists tend to like using them because there are so many ways to employ this efficient observation tool. Early childhood teachers have used checklists to do the following.

Observe Children's Development (Krechevsky, 1998).   Teachers can observe specific aspects of each domain or area of development using checklists and can observe every age group. Using motor development as an example, teachers of infants, toddlers, preschool, kindergarten, and primary-age children can develop checklists to gather information about different aspects of a child's gross and fine motor development.

Teachers can also use existing or ready-made[1] checklists to observe children's development.

Example: Mr. Nellis and his colleagues plan to use the Peer Interaction Checklist from Project Spectrum (Krechevsky, 1998) to observe each child in their classes. They are not going to use it this year, but have voted to use it in the second phase (1 year from now) of adopting some of Project Spectrum's assessment strategies.

Assess, Document, and Reflect on Children's Progress (Fournier, Lansdowne, Pastenes, Steen, & Hudelson, 1992).   Fournier and colleagues (1992) believed in using types of assessments congruent with their beliefs about appropriate ways of teaching in their bilingual second-grade classroom. Therefore, the teachers relied on a variety of informal classroom-based observations of children and documentation of their work.

The teachers identified goals for reading and writing and reflected those goals in objectives and kinds of literacy behaviors they were helping their children develop.

[1]Chapter 8 describes different categories of observation and assessment tools. Ready-made or existing instruments is one category.

Reflecting this belief, the teachers developed checklists and then used them at the end of each quarter to reflect on and to document student progress.

In the checklist, for example, for *writing quality*, the teachers checked off such things as self-selects topic, uses revision strategies, and experiments with style. When assessing a child's *mechanics of writing*, the teachers checked off such things as handwriting, uses periods, uses questions marks, and uses quotation marks. They did the checklist three times and marked either no evidence, developing, or controls. The checklist had a space for comments.

Observe One Child on a Single Checklist.   Use checklists to observe one child on a single checklist. One way to use checklists is to set up a single checklist for each child. The checklist described in the paragraph just before this was used for individual children. Primary-grade teachers (Fournier et al., 1992; Mobley & Teets, 1992) constructed checklists on math and writing skills. In these cases, the teachers documented an individual child's progress in specific curriculum areas by checking off skills as a child demonstrated a skill.

Checklists set up like this enable teachers to get a good idea of an individual child's progress in one curriculum area from one checklist. Teachers in these second-grade classrooms then looked at a specific child's checklists in math, writing, or reading skills when reflecting on that child's overall progress.

Observe the Entire Group or Several Children on a Single Checklist.   Many teachers use a single-page checklist that concentrates on a specific task to observe all or several of the children on that task. Mrs. Vargas used this type of checklist to assess the children's progress in hand washing (Figure 5.1). Then, to ascertain how a specific child is progressing overall, a teacher would look at the different group checklists.

Another helpful type of group checklist is a *participation checklist*. Teachers find this type of checklist helpful because it tells them a lot about children's interest in the variety of learning centers or areas in a center or classroom, thus helping teachers to plan the curriculum. Figure 5.2 is an example of a participation checklist that teachers Vargas and Lyndon developed for their preschool classroom for a single day. They used a similar form for other days, changing names of areas of the room or activities when appropriate.

Teach Children How to Document Their Progress.   Children can also record their own participation. Each of Patsy Foote's kindergarten children filled in a participation checklist on a daily basis (Foote et al., 1992). Their checklists designated each area of the room or each activity with drawings. Preschool children could also keep their own records if the checklist was simple.

Use checklists to teach children how to document their progress. Mobley and Teets (1992) told how the children in a second-grade classroom kept a mathematics skills checklist in the front of their state-mandated test booklets. Each child checked off each skill as he or she mastered it. The authors emphasized that they did not

	Participation Checklist						Date: *October 20*		
NAME	Dram. play	Reading	Easel	Chalk drawing	Blocks	Computer	Counting game	Music	Writing center
Ralph		×		×	×				×
Nellie		×	×			×	×	×	
Pete		×		×	×	×			
Kim		×			×	×			
Moshe		×		×			×		×
Justine			×	×				×	×
Gerry		×		×		×			×
Danielle	×	×					×		×
Kao		×				×	×		×

Summary comments based on this observation: Only two children have played in the dramatic play area in the past 2 weeks. The reading and writing centers usually are heavily used. No girl used blocks today, which is unusual.

Figure 5.2

teach skills in isolation. Katz (1997) noted that one of the major purposes of assessment is "to assist a child with assessing his or her own progress."

Guidelines for Developing Checklists

This section describes five guidelines for developing checklists (Almy & Genishi, 1979).

Guideline 1: Clearly Define Behaviors Before Beginning to Observe.   This entails being sure about what you are looking for. For example, do you want to know whether everybody knows the fire escape route? If a teacher names a shape, do you want to know whether a child can then point to or pick out the shape? If a teacher points to a shape, do you want to know whether a child can name that shape? Do you want to know whether a child can match two identical shapes? Do you want to know whether a second-grade child can identify antonyms?

Defining behaviors for a checklist is often quite simple, such as when a teacher wants to know if children can name the primary colors. At other times, a teacher has a more difficult job because he will have to do a task analysis first.

Example: Suppose that a teacher wants to know whether a child is popular, ignored, or rejected. The teacher would have to look at each of these and say specifically what each meant.

Guideline 2: Prepare the Checklist Ahead of Time, Before Doing the Observation.   Plan a checklist alone or work with another teacher, as Mrs. Vargas and Mrs. Lyndon have

Can pick out facial expression of an emotion as the teacher names the emotion.

	Yes	No
Happy	_X_	____
Sad	____	_X_
Angry	_X_	____

Figure 5.3
Section of Checklist on Emotional Development, Used Here as an Example

done. Consider involving children in constructing checklists when it seems appropriate. For example, involve children in defining behaviors, have them write their names in the names column, have them decide on colors or symbols to use, or ask children to help decide where to place a checklist. Mrs. Vargas introduced the idea of daily classroom tasks at large-group time. She and the children developed a checklist for daily tasks with children offering several suggestions for the chart.

Guideline 3: Try to Achieve an Appropriate Degree of Specificity in Listing Behaviors.
Avoid merely listing large categories of behaviors. Divide some categories into smaller units. For example, when Mrs. Vargas and Mrs. Lyndon were constructing a checklist on emotional development, they wrote:

Can pick out facial expression of an emotion as the teacher names the emotion.
Yes_____ No_____.

The problem here is that a child might be able to do this for one emotion but not for another (Figure 5.3). Moshe, for example, could pick out facial expressions for *angry* and *happy*, but not for *sad*. Therefore, the teachers divided this large category into smaller units by specifying each emotion.

They could then be far more accurate in checking Moshe's abilities in this area of development.

Guideline 4: Organize the Checklist Logically.   How you do this depends on the domain of development, behavior, or curriculum area for which you are designing the checklist. It is easier to read and work with an orderly and logically arranged checklist. Many teachers arrange checklists according to the level of difficulty of the items. Mrs. Vargas did this when she arranged the part of the math checklist dealing with one-to-one correspondence (Figure 5.4).

Mobley and Teets (1992) developed a second-grade mathematics skills checklist and arranged it logically. Figure 5.5 shows how they arranged the addition facts section in order of difficulty of the items.

Can do one-to-one correspondence for	Yes	No
• Two objects	____	____
• Three objects	____	____
• Four objects	____	____
• Five objects	____	____
• More than 10 objects	____	____

Figure 5.4
Section of a Checklist, Used Here as an Example

Guideline 5: Make Sure That the Checklist Does What It Is Intended to Do.   Ask yourself, before and after you have developed the checklist: "What do I want this checklist to tell me?" For example, do you want to know that a behavior merely occurred? If so, then you need only list spaces for checking Yes or No. Do you also want to know when a child first showed the behavior? If yes, then add a column for recording the date. Mobley and Teets (1992) did this with the math skills checklist, a small section of which is shown in Figure 5.6.

Advantages of Using Checklists

Efficiency.   Checklists have two major advantages. First, they are efficient, extremely easy, and quick to use. Checklists are ideal for observing a behavior that requires only a check to determine its presence or absence.

Flexibility.   Second, checklists have a great deal of flexibility. For example, teachers can choose when they check off behaviors—during the school day or at the end of the day. Flexibility is also evident in that there are so many ways that a teacher can use checklists, as explained in a previous section. Such flexibility makes it possible for teachers to plan realistic, effective, and efficient ways to observe with checklists.

	Yes	No
Match word names to numbers	____	____
Count/write by twos through 98	____	____
Read/write numbers through 999	____	____
Count/write by threes through 99	____	____

Figure 5.5
Section of a Checklist Showing Additional Facts Section Arranged in Order of Difficulty, Used Here as an Example

	Yes	No	Date mastered
Match word names to numbers	___	___	_____
Count/write by twos through 98	___	___	_____
Read/write numbers through 999	___	___	_____
Count/write by threes through 99	___	___	_____

Figure 5.6
Section of a Math Skills Checklist, Used Here as an Example

Disadvantages of Using Checklists

Lacks Information About Quality.   Checklists also have two major disadvantages. One problem is that a checklist provides very little or no information about the quality of the behavior or the *how* of the behavior. A checklist tells an observer whether a child can run, but does not indicate *how* that child ran: quickly? Gracefully? Awkwardly?

Example: Mrs. Lyndon, in using the participation checklist (Figure 5.2), observed that Justine had painted at the easel and then checked off *easel* next to Justine's name. The teacher was somewhat frustrated because all she could record was that Justine painted at the easel—she would need an anecdotal record to capture the joy that Justine seemed to derive from this activity.

No Information on Frequency.   Second, a checklist gives no information on how frequently or the degree to which a child shows a behavior. Again, Figure 5.2, the participation checklist, shows that Justine participated in easel painting. How frequently, for example, did Justine paint at the easel? How long did she stay at the easel? Did she merely flutter by the easel and dab at the paper, or did she slip on an apron, roll up her sleeves, and immerse herself in easel painting for quite a long time?

RATING SCALES

Description

Rating scales, like checklists, are a "shortcut" method in observing young children, because a teacher summarizes observations and makes a judgment about a child's regular performance. The two methods described in this chapter are called shortcuts because none call for recording original data. Rating scales, in fact, are very useful when a teacher needs less information and does not need original data. Rating scales are a popular method of observing because they help a teacher quickly organize information in an orderly way (Almy & Genishi, 1979).

Child's name: *Ralph* Date: *November 10* Circle one: Indoors/outside (playground)

Circle one phrase from this list describing child's participation in cleanup.
- Blocks efforts to clean up
- Does not stop playing unless teacher (T) makes a firm request
- Does not participate
- Cleans up only with supervision from T
- Cleans up without supervision from T

Figure 5.7
Example of a Forced Choice Rating Scale

A *rating scale* is a listing of characteristics or activities. An example is a listing of how a child participates in cleanup time in a classroom or on a playground. An observer marks the observation sheet to show how she rated that child or group of children. Ratings can be descriptive or numerical (quantitative). A teacher who uses a rating scale shows how much of something she observed, but she cannot show the quality of the child's performance.

Types of Rating Scales

The three types of rating scales—*forced choice, numerical, and graphic*—described in this section require a teacher to make a summary judgment. Each type is illustrated with the same behavior: whether a child participates at cleanup time.

Forced Choice Rating Scales.   Figure 5.7 shows a *forced choice rating scale.* An observer makes a judgment about a specific behavior or aspect of development. In this case, Mrs. Vargas has asked Mrs. Lyndon to use a forced choice rating scale to make a judgment about each child's participation in cleanup either inside the classroom or outside on the playground. She read the set of descriptions of how a child could participate in the cleanup routine. Then, she was *forced* to choose the one phrase that most accurately described, in her opinion, how a specific child participated and to indicate that choice by checking the space in front of the phrase. Figure 5.7 is her rating of how Ralph participated in cleanup outside.

Numerical Rating Scales.   Figure 5.8 shows a *numerical rating scale,* a list of descriptive phrases or categories. In this case, it is the same list as on the forced choice rating scale. Here, an observer assigns a numeral to each behavior on the list. Mrs. Lyndon could have used a numerical rating scale to judge how each child functioned at cleanup time, either inside the classroom or on the playground. She would have thought about each child's participation and then circled the numeral next to the statement that most accurately depicted her view. She could have made her choice

Child's name: *Ralph* Date: *November 11* Circle one: indoors/outside (playground)

Circle the number of the phrase describing child's participation in cleanup.
1. Blocks efforts to clean up
2. Does not stop playing unless teacher (T) makes firm request
3. Does not participate
4. Cleans up only with T supervision
5. Cleans up without T supervision

Figure 5.8
Example of a Numerical Rating Scale

right after observing or even later. A teacher can use this type of rating scale for each child only once or even several times. Mrs. Lyndon, for instance, could observe the children at cleanup on several different days. She could then calculate each child's average score. Figure 5.8 is her rating of Ralph's participation in cleanup using a numerical rating scale.

Graphic Rating Scales.   Figure 5.9 shows a ***graphic rating scale,*** which is a straight line in format. Most ***graphic rating scales*** require an observer to make a judgment about some behavior and then to record the judgment on a scale from high to low. In this case, the observer is asked to give a rating from "always" (high) to "never" (low) after recalling how specific children have participated in either indoor or

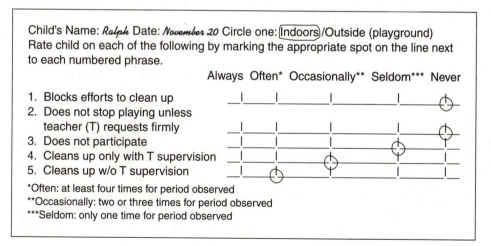

Child's Name: *Ralph* Date: *November 20* Circle one: Indoors/Outside (playground)
Rate child on each of the following by marking the appropriate spot on the line next to each numbered phrase.

	Always	Often*	Occasionally**	Seldom***	Never
1. Blocks efforts to clean up					⊕
2. Does not stop playing unless teacher (T) requests firmly					⊕
3. Does not participate				⊕	
4. Cleans up only with T supervision			⊕		
5. Cleans up w/o T supervision		⊕			

*Often: at least four times for period observed
**Occasionally: two or three times for period observed
***Seldom: only one time for period observed

Figure 5.9
Example of a "Graphic Rating Scale"

outdoor cleanup. The marks along the line are cues, and the function of the cues is to help an observer decide where to record a judgment about how a child participates. Figure 5.9 is Mrs. Lyndon's rating of Ralph's participation in indoor cleanup over a 2-week period.

Advantages and Disadvantages of Using Rating Scales

The principal advantage of rating scales is that they are **easy to use** and do not require much training to learn to use. Observers tend to like using rating scales because an observer gets to make a judgment and does not record raw data.

Nevertheless, there are three significant disadvantages to using rating scales. First, personal bias is always a potential problem when there are no data supporting an observer's judgment. A rating scale is the least objective observational tool because it lacks such data. Second, many raters tend to rate most children at the midpoint on a scale, essentially rendering this method useless in many cases. Third, developers might use unclear terms in a rating scale. For example, what do terms such as *frequently* or *unfriendly* or *extremely* mean? The problem here is that different raters might have different definitions of terms like these, and ratings that they make of the same group would not be valid or reliable.

SUGGESTIONS FOR INCREASING THE POWER OF CHECKLISTS AND RATING SCALES

Checklists and rating scales are useful **shortcut methods of observation** that give helpful information quickly and efficiently. The very efficiency of the methods is also a drawback that teachers can avoid or overcome. It is possible to increase the power of a checklist or a rating scale by a number of methods, all of which are easy. Here are three ideas for making the most of checklists and rating scales.

Combine Checklists and Rating Scales with Anecdotal or Running Records[2]

Consider the outcome of combining anecdotal or running records with checklists or rating scales. The result? A teacher would have the evidence or data collected over time from the narrative observations (anecdotal or running records) linked to information from a checklist and or a rating scale. There is power in this combination, power missing from checklists or rating scales alone (COR, 1992). The COR, or Child Observation Record, developed by the High/Scope Education Group requires that ratings from rating scales be backed up by evidence from anecdotal records. This combination is much more powerful and useful than a checklist or a rating scale alone.

---

[2]**Anecdotal records** are explained in chapter 3, **running records** in chapter 4.

Add Space to Checklist and Rating Scale Forms for Comments, Date, Summary

Checklists and rating scales do not give information about the quality of a child's behavior. Nor do they say anything about when a teacher first saw the behavior. Mobley and Teets (1992) solved this problem by expanding their checklists to include columns labeled Date of Mastery and Notes. Similarly, Beatty (1998) constructed the Child Skills Checklist to include two columns labeled Evidence and Date. Teachers using these checklists would be able to make brief notes about what they observed and would be able to note the date on which they first saw the behavior. We do not always need such information, but comments and dates are valuable at certain times.

Teachers can use a summary section to begin to analyze their observations, or at least to make relevant notes. In the participation checklist (Figure 5.2), for example, Mrs. Lyndon made brief notes about the fact that only two children had played in the dramatic play center (set up as a housekeeping corner) in the past 2 weeks.

Develop a Checklist or Rating Scale Plan

Have a plan for when to check things off or to make ratings, for organizing and storing forms, and for analyzing and using information from checklists and rating

These teachers schedule time to analyze observations.

Checklist: Timeline for Assessment
Early Childhood Classes: Oaklawn School

Sept. 1–14 ___Social Attributes Checklist (existing, ready-made)
___Williams' Motor Development Checklist (existing, ready-made)
___Explain concept of portfolios to children and parents
___Portfolio items as appropriate: writing samples from all children
Sept. 15–30 ___Portfolio items as appropriate: art samples for each child
___Anecdotal or running records for 1/3 of the class
Oct. 1–15 ___Math skills checklist (all children)
___Portfolio items as appropriate
___Anecdotal or running records for 1/3 of the class
Oct. 16–31 ___Social Attributes Checklist (second time for this checklist)
___Anecdotal or running records for 1/3 of the class
___Begin Project Spectrum Motor Development Assessment
Obstacle Course
___Portfolio items as appropriate; writing samples
___Review portfolios for one-half of the class
Nov. 1–15 ___Portfolio items as appropriate
___Review portfolios for other half of the class
___Rating scale: cleanup
___Math Skills Checklist
Nov. 15–
Dec. 10 ___Portfolio items as appropriate: writing samples
___District administers standardized test for motor skills to all early
childhood classes
___Emotional development checklist
Dec. 27–
Jan. 8 Holidays (work on observation reports and portfolios)
___Consolidate observational data for each child: write observation report
___When school starts up again: Portfolio Review & Reflection
___Work with each child to review portfolio's contents
___Organize for parent conferences
___Write helpful comments for parents as appropriate
Jan. 12–14 ___Parent conferences
___Portfolios contain midyear observation report and analysis of
children's work samples

    This is the timeline for observation and assessment for the early childhood
classes in Mr. Nellis's school for the first semester. Mr. Nellis has made a checklist to
help track assessment activities. He has also made a notation of each item in his
day planner.

Figure 5.10

scales. Think about when to check things or to do ratings. Some teachers do this during the day; others decide that the end of the day is a better time. Still others will see the benefit of doing it either way, depending on the specific checklist or rating scale.

Checklists or rating scales for individual children are best stored in a child's folder or portfolio. Group checklists might best be stored in category folders. A simple but well-organized filing system encourages almost all teachers to pay attention to the checklists or rating scales and is a good use of a professional's time.

Mrs. Vargas schedules time twice each month for going over observations of children for the most recent 2-week period. She and her assistant consider the information that they have gathered from all types of observations and then interpret it when it seems appropriate. They use information from anecdotal and running records plus checklists or rating scales for assessing children's needs, abilities, and interests and then for planning curriculum and for making guidance and curriculum decisions.

For example, their participation checklist showing that the children had used the housekeeping corner so rarely (Figure 5.2) spurred the teachers to reflect on and then make significant changes in the dramatic play area. They also use the information from many types of observations to help them prepare for conferences and other activities with parents.

Place Observations and Assessments on a Timeline

Identify a target date on which your observations and assessments must be done—midyear conferences? IEP or IFSP meeting? End-of-year conference? Curriculum and instruction committee meeting? Whatever the date or event, let it motivate you to gather observations and do other assessments in an organized, systematic way. Consciously blend and combine all of your methods toward that target date for which you must have the information (Figure 5.10).

Break down your gathering task into smaller, manageable chunks. Place tasks on your calendar and let observation and assessment become a part of your daily teaching. This will help you avoid the common but preventable frenzied atmosphere of frantic data gathering at the beginning and end of the year.

Activities to Help You Construct Knowledge and Skills in Observing

ACTIVITY 1

Use each of the rating scales given in the chapter—forced choice numerical, and graphic—to rate one child's participation in cleanup in a classroom. Observe the child both inside the classroom and then on the playground.

ACTIVITY 2

This is a follow-up to Activity 1. Observe the same child who you observed in Activity 1. Add to your knowledge about this child by doing *one* of the following:

- Two 15-minute running records
- Five anecdotal records
- One 15-minute running record and two anecdotal records of that child at cleanup in a classroom

ACTIVITY 3

Reflect on the difference between your findings from Activities 1 and 2. If you were to have a conference with the child's parent to report your findings, would you feel more confident using the results of Activity 1 or those of Activity 2? Why?

ACTIVITY 4

Working alone or preferably with another student, develop a group checklist for cleanup time in the same classroom. Follow the guidelines for developing checklists presented in the chapter.

REFERENCES

Almy, M., & Genishi, C. (1979). *Ways of studying children* (Rev. ed.). New York: Teachers College Press.

Beatty, J. J. (1998). *Observing development of the young child.* Upper Saddle River, NJ: Merrill/Prentice Hall.

Child Observation Record (COR), (1992). Ypsilanti, MI: High/Scope Educational Foundation.

Fournier, J., Lansdowne, B., Pastenes, Z., Steen, P., & Hudelson, S. (1992). Learning with, about, and from children. In C. Genishi (Ed.), *Ways of assessing children and curriculum.* (pp. 126–162). New York: Teachers College Press.

Katz, L. (1997, April). A developmental approach to assessment of young children. ERIC Digest, ERIC-EECE, www.ericeece.org/pubs/digests/1997.

Krechevsky, M. (1998). *Project Spectrum: Preschool Assessment Handbook.* New York: Teachers College Press.

McClellan, D., & Katz, L. (2001). Assessing young children's social competence. ERIC/EECE Publications-Digests, March, E00-PS-01-2, ericeece.org/pubs/digests/2001/mccle/01

Mobley, J., & Teets, S. (1992). Informal assessment in second grade: A Foxfire story. In C. Genishi (Ed.), *Ways of assessing children and curriculum* (pp. 163–190). New York: Teachers College Press.

WEB SITES RELATED TO THIS CHAPTER

✓ Project Spectrum

Project Spectrum is a research project of Project Zero. Project Spectrum uses both check-lists and rating scales, as well as other methods, in their assessment tools. See the Peer Inter-action Checklist (Table 42, Krechevsky, 1998) and the Visual Arts Scoring Criteria (Table 47, Krechevsky, 1998).

www.harvard.edu

This is the main Web page for Harvard and another way to get to Project Zero and then Project Spectrum. Purchase Krechevsky's book at the Project Zero Web site. The checklists are printed in the book.

CHAPTER 6

Documenting and Reporting Development and Progress
Children's Products, Observation Reports, and Portfolios

Document: to give factual or substantial support for statements made
Report: to give an account of; to make a written record or summary of

Chapter objectives

1. *Explain* the role of documentation and reporting in assessing and evaluating young children's development and progress.
2. *List* and *explain* three different ways to document and report development and progress.
3. *List* and *describe* the functions of an observation report. *State in your own words* why an observational report is an important part of the assessment process in early childhood education.
4. *Explain* what a portfolio (in early childhood) is and *summarize* its role in the assessment process.
5. *Summarize* the benefits to teachers and to children of using portfolios.
6. *Name* and *describe* the two major categories of materials placed in children's portfolios.
7. *Summarize* the differences between a current year and a permanent portfolio.

DOCUMENTING AND REPORTING DEVELOPMENT AND PROGRESS

Chapters 3, 4, and 5 in this text explained several different methods for observing children's development and progress. The teachers in this chapter all use the twin process of documenting and then reporting what they observe. The teachers also use portfolios to pull together the different types of documentation into one central place for each child in their class.

Documentation

Documentation is an old and respected practice in early childhood education (Carbonara, 1961; Cohen & Stern, 1983; Cohen, Stern, & Balaban, 1996; Cross & Dixon, 1997; Helm & Katz, 2001; Katz, 1995; Katz & Chard, 1996). Documentation provides "proof" of what exists and is an essential and logical companion to the process of observation.

Example: K–2 teacher Mr. Nellis noticed at the beginning of the school year that David seemed to hesitate when writing. The teacher decided that he should *document* information about David's writing with brief teacher's observations and some concrete examples of David's writing. To do this, he collected writing samples and wrote a set of anecdotal records about David's writing.

Documenting development and progress is not trivial. It is indispensable in the science as well as in the art of teaching and is important for a number of reasons (Helm, 2003; Helm, Beneke, & Steinheimer, 1998; Katz & Chard, 1997; Krechevsky & Stork, 2000). Documentation gives strong evidence of taking a child's work seriously and allows us to see the evidence.

Teachers use documentation of children's work to plan and then to evaluate curriculum and activities. Documenting children's progress is also an important part of adapting curriculum and instruction for children with special needs in inclusive classrooms (Cross & Dixon, 1997; Dixon, Davis, & Schmidt, 1994). Krechevsky and Stork (2000) led a research project concerned with documenting the learning that takes place within *groups* of children.

Reporting

Teachers who carefully observe and document also **report** a child's development and progress, also an old and venerated practice in early childhood. Reporting development and progress, like observing and documenting it, is not a trivial thing; reporting is a professional responsibility and a major part of a teacher's job.

A teacher reports a child's development and progress to parents through casual contacts, formal conferences, and formal reports (Figure 6.1). A teacher reports children's progress to other teachers so that they can develop guidance plans, curriculum, or activities together. A teacher reports children's development and progress to administrators and might be called on to report a child's progress to other teachers or specialists: a special education group doing an assessment of a child for special services, for example.

DIFFERENT WAYS TO DOCUMENT AND REPORT DEVELOPMENT AND PROGRESS

Document and Report with Children's Products and Work Samples

Over time, members of the early childhood profession have agreed that it is a good idea to document children's development and progress with children's products and samples of their work (Almy & Genishi, 1979; Helm, Beneke, & Steinheimer, 1998; Katz & Chard, 1996). In the past decade, teachers have renewed their commitment to using samples of children's work to assess and evaluate children's progress in a more developmentally appropriate way.

Documenting with children's products can be an exciting part of teaching because a teacher can pick from a wide array of samples of children's work. Just a few examples are samples of children's work at different stages of completion, photographs showing work in progress, comments by a teacher working with children, or transcriptions of children's comments. Roskos and Neuman (1994), for example, gathered and interpreted samples of children's literacy behaviors, such as writing samples. The preprimary schools of Reggio Emilia, Italy, as another example, focus extensively on using photographs and children's work samples to document children's experiences, memories, ideas, and thoughts (Edwards, Gandini & Forman, 1998; 100 Languages of Children display; Katz & Chard, 1997).

Documentary displays help children clarify and strengthen their experiences.

Document and Report with Documentary Displays

Schools in Reggio Emilia have rekindled interest in creating displays of the documentation of children's work (Katz, 1995; Katz & Chard, 1996, 1997). Creating such displays tells children that teachers value their work. Preparing and displaying children's work encourages teachers and children alike to revisit the experience, which clarifies and strengthens understandings in the experience. Such displays also make it easy to convey solid evidence to parents about the mission and curriculum of the school.

Document and Report with Observation Reports

It is as important for a teacher to document development with a written summary of observations as it is to collect samples of children's work. The two types of documentation work together to give a good clear picture of a child's level of development and progress. A teacher puts any observations (anecdotal records, running records, checklists, and rating scales) together and summarizes them to arrive at that picture of development (Almy & Genishi, 1979; Cohen, Stern, & Balaban, 1996; Helm, Beneke, & Steinheimer, 1998).

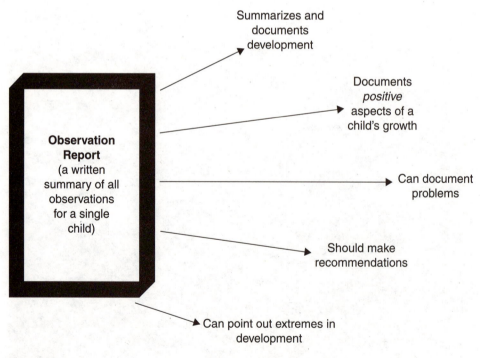

Figure 6.1
Teachers Document Their Observations of Children's Development with an Observation Report

Observation Reports Summarize and Document Development. Child development students have been learning for several decades that an observation report summarizes a child's development in the different domains of development (Carbonara, 1961; Cohen & Stern, 1983). A summary of areas of development gives a teacher a coherent picture of each child's development. Such a summary also makes it easy for a teacher to report this information to a child's parents. Please see Appendix A, in this textbook, for a suggested outline for final observation reports for an individual child.

Observation Reports Also Document Positive Aspects of a Specific Child's Growth. A teacher analyzes and summarizes the accumulated observational data and then makes a judgment about a child's growth in various domains of development. The teacher then reports the judgment in writing. Teachers do not ignore areas in which the child has needed help and teachers do not just say that "everything is wonderful." Instead, they report findings, document positive change, and say it in a nonjudgmental way. Here are some examples:

Example: (toddler classroom) "Jenny has really grown! She used to cry when Mom or Dad left but now waves good-bye and goes to a favorite activity."

Example: (preschool) "John is growing in his ability to approach other children. He has entered many playgroups this past semester and has watched what the other children were doing, and then quietly joined them in play. He has been accepted by the other children."

Example: (primary classroom) "We are encouraged by Patrick's growth this year in how he approaches academic work. At the beginning of the year, Patrick hesitated to begin projects in almost every area of the curriculum. We noticed a big change in his attitude and work habits when he started writing in his journal. He seems to have gained a lot of self-confidence from the daily writing and this has rippled out nicely to other work."

Observation Reports Can Also Document Problems. Growing up is a bumpy process and seems bumpier for some children for a variety of reasons. Remembering that children do encounter problems as they develop and try to learn things in school helps many teachers maintain a helpful perspective on a child's behavior. Teachers are in a good position to notice a variety of potential problems that children might have. A periodic or final observation report should include information about such problems.

Example: (kindergarten classroom) Mr. Nellis wrote this statement for a midyear observation report and used it in a conference with Janna's parents.
    "Janna is having a difficult time with managing her feelings. My observations show that she needs us to help her learn to use words to label angry or sad or disappointed feelings. She now strikes out when angry or tends to yell or do name-calling when she is sad or disappointed or frustrated. We are working on teaching her to use more appropriate words when normal but unpleasant feelings wash over her."

Observation Reports Should Make Recommendations. A child's new teachers or parents not only need to read a summary of development but also need to get well-reasoned recommendations from a teacher (Cohen, Stern, & Balaban, 1996). Teachers and parents can work together to help a child with such recommendations. New teachers can follow up on work begun the year before to continue to help a child.

Example: (same K–2 classroom) This is the recommendation that Mr. Nellis made in May, in his final observation report for Janna.

"Janna has made good progress in managing her feelings this semester, especially her anger. She has begun to label her feelings and that has helped her 'stop and think.' She still needs adult help to find the right words for her feelings. She has also begun to use words to express anger instead of hitting other children, but we still remind her. Janna delights in recognition for her efforts, and we think that she will continue her good emotional progress with adult help and encouragement."

Janna will be in Mr. Nellis's K–2 class again next year. Mr. Nellis writes midyear and final reports because his assistant teachers change and new aides need to read about each child. He also uses midyear and final observation reports to communicate with parents. He realizes that families move and he wants to be ready with an observation report to send to a child's new teacher, if needed.

Observation Reports Should Point Out Exceptionalities or Extremes in Behavior or Development. We are teachers and are not qualified to diagnose major problems, but we can document behaviors indicating that a child is dealing with some specific troubling issue. You might have more confidence talking about extremes in behavior or development if you work with qualified personnel (a school psychologist, social worker, or child development expert) to document and then to write this section of the report.

Extremes in behavior or development might well signal a real problem. For example, pretending to set fires or somehow actually setting fires, cruelty to animals, excessive expression of fear or anxiety, extreme passivity, or extreme aggression (including cruelty to animals) signal that a child needs help. Having the courage to document and then report the behaviors is the first step toward getting the child some help.

Extremes in development can also signal a special talent or giftedness. Thinking in terms of identifying each child's special talent can give a whole new meaning to observation for teachers. Mr. Nellis's colleague Mr. Lee, who taught the third and fourth combined class, had this experience with third-grader Sam. The experience solidified Mr. Lee's already strong beliefs in the value of observing his children carefully and then using the observations to adjust curriculum and activities to meet the interests of specific children.

Example: Sam had transferred to Mr. Lee's third grade in August. From the start, Mr. Lee observed that Sam had good social skills and the other children liked him. However,

Sheldon's teacher will document his new skill of tying his shoes.

Sam showed little enthusiasm for reading or any of the other curriculum areas, although he did complete his work. One day, Mr. Lee was trying, unsuccessfully, to tie a rope securely on a pulley for a science experiment.

"Hey, Mr. Lee. Want some help?"

The teacher looked around to find Sam. "Sure. Do you know about tying knots, Sam?"

"Yep. My dad and I are sailors! He taught me to tie knots." Sam then expertly tied the appropriate knot, grinned at his teacher, and even gave the name of the knot.

Mr. Lee, having discovered a special talent in a child, recorded his observation in an anecdotal record, which he placed in Sam's portfolio. He then decided to use this documentation to adjust the curriculum to try to help Sam enjoy school and academic work. He first asked Sam to teach the other third and fourth graders how to tie knots, one knot at a time. The class then made a display of their knots, complete with labels. Sam and three other children made a short video on knot tying for the library, and they wrote a brief illustrated manual explaining how to tie the knots shown in the video. Sam then chose a library book on modern sailing for a report.

PORTFOLIOS: PULLING IT ALL TOGETHER

In early January, with school on holiday break, Mr. Nellis, the lead K–2 teacher, prepared for upcoming midyear conferences with parents. His school relied on authentic assessment and used *portfolios* as a way to gather in one place all of the observations and documents on each child. Mr. Nellis prepared portfolios with care because he realized how important they were to parents as well as to children. He had found how useful a child's portfolio was in painting a picture of each child's current level of development and in highlighting each child's academic achievements.

What Is a Portfolio?

There was a flurry of writing about portfolios in early childhood in the 1990s, with Genishi (1992), Grace (1992), Gullo (1994, 1997), and Meisels (1993, 1995) as examples. These writers agree that a portfolio is a good and convenient way to collect, store, and document information about a child.

A teacher who uses a portfolio assembles and reviews a collection, or portfolio, of a child's work and of observations about the child. The teacher can use portfolios to document children's progress throughout the year. The teacher uses the information to assess the child's development and progress and to make decisions about curriculum and guidance for that child (Bredekamp, 1987).

Portfolios grew out of a movement that questioned and then rebelled against the use of standardized testing for young children. Portfolios grew out of a need for early childhood professionals to use authentic or performance-based assessment. The early childhood profession views portfolios as a part of authentic assessment because portfolios contain observations and documentation of a child's abilities to function in real, rather than in artificial, testing situations. Portfolios, then, are a part of developmentally appropriate assessment and evaluation of children's development and progress (Helm, 2003).

Benefits of Portfolios

Portfolios, when done well, serve many purposes. They are enormously beneficial for children. Developing children's portfolios also enriches a teacher's professional life. Finally, reading their child's portfolio has real meaning for parents.

Benefits of Portfolios for Children

Portfolios and Children's Self-Esteem.   Children also have a lot to gain when their teachers use portfolios. Carefully developed portfolios encourage children to evaluate themselves (Gelfer & Perkins, 1991; Grubb & Courtney, 1996), which is a part of developing self-esteem. Self-esteem, which develops during early childhood, is the evaluation that a child makes about the "self" (Coopersmith, 1967). This evaluation develops when a child examines and then judges three things about his or her self: competence, control, and worth (Marion, 2003).

A child who has the right to choose or reject items for his portfolio, for example, will likely feel a sense of control. A child whose teacher uses portfolio-based assessment can see and track his progress over time, thus giving him direct evidence of his competence in specific areas.

Children tend to judge themselves worthy when they perceive that others like them and are willing to take the time to help them. When a teacher uses a portfolio, children see that the teacher will indeed take the time to carefully collect important work and will show respect by talking with them about the contents of and the child's ideas on the portfolio.

Tips for Talking with Children About Portfolios.   Help children understand the process of developing their portfolios.

   📖 Explain what a portfolio is. Do this at the beginning of the school year or when a child moves to your class. Figure 8.1, in chapter 8, shows that Mr. Nellis schedules a specific time when school starts to talk about portfolios to both children and parents.
     Present the concept of a portfolio as a way for children to show what they know and can do. Emphasize the child's role in choosing many of the items that go into the portfolio.
   📖 Assist children in the process of portfolio building. Younger children and older children who are new to portfolios will need more help than children who have already used portfolios.
   📖 Talk with children about their portfolios.

Example: Mr. Nellis observed George, one of his kindergarten children, as he built a structure from both large and small unit blocks. Previously, he had written a few anecdotal records about George's block building. Now he wanted to place this information in George's portfolio. The teacher took a picture of the latest building and talked with George about it.
    Here is an example of how Mr. Nellis talked with George about his block building.

   📖 "Yes, this *is* a picture of your building! You used all of the longest blocks for the driveway but yesterday you used the shortest blocks for the driveway. If you make a driveway again, which blocks would you use?"
   📖 "You can put the picture of your building in your portfolio. That would be a good way to show your mom and dad how well you solve problems with blocks."
   📖 "OK . . . , when you build other things this year, we might want to take other pictures and put those pictures in your portfolio, too. Then we could look at all the pictures and see the different ways that you've built things."

Benefits of Portfolios for Teachers

Teachers have a lot to gain by using portfolios—better knowledge about their students, a good base for developmentally appropriate practice, and a good starting point for talking with parents. Portfolios enhance a teacher's professional life.

Documents Development.   Portfolios enable teachers to document children's development. Teachers then use the developmental information to report to parents about their child's development. Teachers also use developmental information in meeting with special education professionals who might be assessing a child for services.

Supports Developmentally Appropriate Practice.   Portfolios support developmentally appropriate practice by supplying information on children's development (Shores & Grace, 1998). This gives teachers a strong child development foundation on which to build age- and individually appropriate programs.

Provides Documentation for Curriculum Planning and Assessment.   Portfolios supply documentation that teachers need to plan curriculum and to assess the curriculum's effectiveness. At the same time, portfolios give a teacher the chance to check the effectiveness of his or her teaching practices (Gelfer & Perkins, 1991; Giffin & Long, 2001; Grubb & Courtney, 1996; NAEYC, 1996).

Aids in Planning Parent Conferences.   Well-developed portfolios enable teachers to plan effective parent conferences (Grace, 1992). For example, Mobley and Teets (1992) collected writing samples for several weeks from the children in a second-grade classroom and placed the samples in each child's portfolio. They documented the children's progress in writing over time, and, at conference time, parents saw this documentation. One child's parents, for example, saw the dramatic change in their son's writing. He had started the year by drawing pictures with only a few words scrawled on crumpled paper and, in the weeks of collecting writing samples, had written a story with five paragraphs.

Portfolios were helpful to the same teachers in demonstrating to parents that a child might need additional work or help. They showed writing samples from one child

Well-developed portfolios help teachers plan effective parent conferences.

that documented how incoherent the child's writing was. The parents then talked with the teacher about a way to work on this problem.

Aids in Explaining the Program.   Teachers can use well-constructed children's portfolios to explain the center or school's program to parents. Gelfer (1994) conducted research with parents of preschool children to discover whether portfolios helped parents understand the program and curriculum of the school. Findings showed that parents whose children had portfolios had a better understanding of the preschool's program than did parents of children who did not have portfolios.

Benefits of Portfolios for Parents

Parents also have a lot to gain with portfolios. They gain a relationship, a partnership, with a teacher. They further their understanding of their child's development by reading the teacher's observation reports. Parents can better understand their child's academic performance by reading authentic assessments in portfolios. Finally, parents will understand the goals of their child's school when teachers use portfolios well.

TYPES OF PORTFOLIOS

Gullo (1994) described types of portfolios that are helpful to teachers. One type is the ***current-year portfolio*** and the other is the ***permanent portfolio.*** Consider building the current-year portfolio in two different stages, as explained in this section (Figure 6.2).

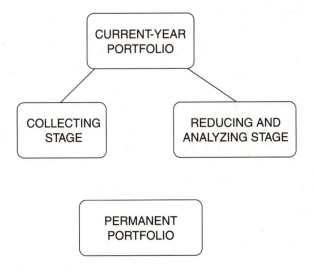

Figure 6.2
Teachers Use a Current-Year Portfolio to Document
Progress and Development for the Current Year—A School
Might Maintain a Permanent Portfolio for Each Child

Current-Year Portfolio

There are actually two stages in developing a child's current-year portfolio; the *collecting stage* and the *reducing and analyzing information stage*.

Collecting Stage.   A portfolio, at this stage, is the collection site for the material that the teacher uses in assessing and evaluating a child's development and progress. Think about a portfolio during the collecting stage simply as the child's file into which you and the child deposit the child's work samples, your anecdotal or running records, rating scales, checklists, audio or videotapes, and other relevant items.

The danger at this stage is to toss every item imaginable into the child's portfolio, quickly making it unmanageable and useless for assessment. Avoid this problem by thinking selectively. You do not have to put every painting, every story, and every writing sample into the file, only those items that illustrate a point about and will help you report on the child's development or achievement.

Avoid getting overwhelmed by all the material that can quickly pile up with portfolios for a whole class. Adopt a disciplined and systematic approach to make the collecting stage as simple as possible. Figure 6.3 describes several principles that will help you organize children's portfolios well.

Use a simple, uncomplicated system to organize materials
  Choose ordinary inexpensive folders or boxes (children can decorate)
  Clearly label each child's folder or box
  Use a straightforward filing system (line up boxes/folders alphabetically by
    child's last name)
Date every work sample and observation
  Write date on each item, in upper right corner (date is then visible when filed)
  Tells reader when item was created
Place items in chronological order in the portfolio
  Older items in front; more recent items behind older ones
  Saves a teacher's valuable time
  Enables teacher to assess development and progress without additional sorting
Place all items from similar categories together, for example
  Easel painting samples from beginning, middle, end of school year
  Photographs of playdough products
  Writing samples (filed chronologically)
File all items promptly
  Avoid letting things pile up
  Consider filing items immediately, or
  File at end of each day
  Children can file a work sample after teacher has dated it

Figure 6.3
Organize Portfolios Well: Develop a Good System

Reducing and Analyzing Information Stage.   If the first stage was the collecting stage, then think about this as the "weeding out" stage. A teacher can more readily carry out the professional responsibility to analyze data or items in the portfolio when there is a reasonable number of items, rather than a mountain of data. Additionally, portfolios are only effective if parents or administrators are willing to read them, something they will not likely be willing to do if they are presented with an unorganized folder.

People will object to and lose patience with a portfolio crammed with paintings, checklists, anecdotal records, and self-portraits of children. It is not a parent's job to put a portfolio in order. Portfolios that are simply a jumbled collection of "stuff" with no analysis are not useful. The goal is for the teacher to go through the portfolio, reduce the amount of data or information, and turn it into a coherent picture of the child's development and accomplishments.

A current-year portfolio that is thoughtfully developed and analyzed helps teachers in planning curriculum. The observation reports in the portfolio contain information that should help teachers assess and report on a child's current level of development and should help them develop good guidance and discipline plans for a child. It will also contain your analysis of the child's work and will contain a well-developed teacher's observation report.

Consider the following suggestions to reduce the amount of information in a child's current-year portfolio (Figure 6.4).

1. *Write a teacher's observation report.*[1]   A teacher can clear out original observation checklists, running records, or rating scales after she writes an observation report based on the original data. Do not wait for the end of the year to write a final report. Avoid the end-of-the-school-year stress by writing at least one periodic report about one-third to about halfway through the year. You will use the midyear observation report with parents. You will find the midyear report extremely useful in helping you reflect on and assess a child's development and progress. Reflection and assessment enables the teacher to plan helpful adjustments in activities, the curriculum, or guidance strategies for children.

Keep periodic observation reports in the current-year portfolio. Consider attaching a few highly selected items, such as a checklist that illustrates one of your points particularly well. For the most part, though, you will not need or want to include original notes. Mr. Nellis wrote a midyear observation report, placed it in the current-year portfolio, and used it for midyear parent conferences. He wrote a final observation report at the end of the school year and placed it in the permanent portfolio.

2. *Designate some child-produced materials for keeping.*   Select work samples that you or a child thinks best illustrate a point you wish to make. When you have finished reducing the amount of material, the portfolio will contain selections of the child's work.

---

[1]Please see the first part of this chapter as well as Appendix A for instructions on writing observation reports.

Write observation reports
    Reason: Clears out original notes from teacher's observations. Makes it easier for teachers to present information from the portfolio.
    How often should I write a report? At least once, and preferably two times, for each half of a school year. Write a final report at the end of the school year.
Designate some child-produced materials for keeping
    Reason: Clears out items that illustrate the same point. Encourages teachers to examine materials and think about what they represent.
Analyze materials chosen for keeping
    Reason: Further encourages teachers to think through reasons for keeping specific materials.

Figure 6.4
Tips for Reducing the Amount of Information in a Child's "Current-Year" Portfolio

Example: Mrs. Vargas, the preschool teacher, had collected 10 easel paintings for one of the children. She looked through the 10 samples and decided to select two, the first and the last. These samples seemed to illustrate significant changes in this child's development.

Example: Andy is a kindergarten child in Mr. Nellis's K–2 classroom. The teacher wrote a set of anecdotal records about Andy's speed in running. He did this because he was surprised that Andy seemed to be so well coordinated and could run much faster than most of the older children. He had observed Andy's speed and coordination after completing a motor development checklist for all kindergarten and first-grade children. He then supplemented his written observations with videotape that further documented Andy's speed and coordination.

    3. *Analyze materials chosen for keeping.* Write a brief analysis of the items that you or a child decided to keep in the portfolio. This analysis will help readers see the logic in the portfolio. The analysis also lets readers know that a teacher has given thoughtful consideration to the job of organizing the child's portfolio.

Permanent Portfolio

A **permanent portfolio** goes with a child to the next class or grade, or even a new school if a child moves. Therefore, choose items carefully from the current-year portfolio to place in the permanent portfolio. The final observation report done by the current-year teacher should give the new teacher a good picture of a child's developmental status and any special talents or problems. It is simpler to do a final observation report if the teacher has written one or two brief reports at other times during the year.

    The selection of children's products or work samples should be quite limited. Because of this, the very few child products chosen for the permanent portfolio should clearly illustrate a specific aspect of that child's academic as well as artistic or athletic accomplishments.

Example: Mr. Nellis had to decide how much of the original data about Andy he needed to keep in the permanent portfolio. He placed his final observation report in the permanent portfolio and only cited his original notes. He discarded the original observation notes after placing the final report in the permanent portfolio. Because he wanted to emphasize Andy's physical prowess as a special talent, Mr. Nellis decided to place the videotape in the permanent file.

CONTENTS OF PORTFOLIOS

The previous section on types of portfolios alluded to contents of portfolios for children. Early childhood portfolios contain

- Child-produced materials
- Material produced by the teacher
- Occasionally, but certainly not always, material from someone other than a teacher or child

Child-Produced Materials

Work Samples.   Samples of a child's own work are the core of every early childhood portfolio.

- *Examples* of the types of child-produced items that teachers have included in children's portfolios are:

Writing samples	Reading logs
Poetry	Audiotapes
Artwork	Dictations or transcriptions of
Mathematics work samples	children's conversations or interviews
Photographs of children's work	Self-portraits
(e.g., block structures, writing	Songs written by a child
or drawing in sand,	Videotapes
math manipulatives)	Checklists

These are only suggestions. Include only those items that seem most relevant for each child. Items included should help a teacher achieve the goals of using a portfolio.

When to Include the Same Items for All Children in Class.   On occasion, it is quite appropriate to place the same type of item in every child's portfolio.

Example: Teachers in Mr. Nellis's school are opposed to a mandated standardized test of motor development. They decide to do their own checklist of motor skills for every child and include the checklist in each child's portfolio because the checklist is a better example of authentic assessment and is easier for parents to understand.

Example: Mr. Nellis decided to include writing samples from all of his second graders so that he could document their change in writing over time. He also included a basic skills checklist in math for second grade for each second-grade child in his K–2 classroom.

Example: Ms. Vargas, the preschool teacher, collected some form of artwork—easel paintings, drawings done in a variety of media, photos of how playdough was used, or collages—from each child to document developmental changes (Gullo, 1994).

At other times, it is appropriate to individualize portfolios. A teacher would often notice, then document and report something about a specific child's development or progress. When this is the case, the teacher collects the necessary information for that child, and often only for that child.

Example: Mr. Nellis soon realized that Jeb, one of the second-grade boys, was quickly acquiring basic math skills. Jeb had completed the checklist of basic skills for second-grade math in an amazingly short time. The teacher conferred with the principal and Mr. Lee, the teacher of grades three and four, to individualize the math program for Jeb. Mr. Nellis wanted to document Jeb's advanced mathematical skills, so he and his colleagues decided to place the basic skills checklist in math for the third grade in Jeb's portfolio.

As much as possible, get samples of children's work from the range of activities that a child has available and from all curriculum areas. Consider including samples from the beginning, middle, and end of the year to show change over time.

Figures 6.5 and 6.6 will help you make decisions about the contents of children's portfolios.

Choose items for portfolios wisely. Focus sharply on the "end" that you have in mind for the portfolios, that is, your purpose or goal in using portfolios. Ask the following questions to help you decide whether to place that painting or writing sample or readings log in a child's portfolio.

- What useful information does this item tell me about this child's development?
- What does this material tell me about this child's academic progress?
- Can this material or information help me plan or evaluate the curriculum? Can it help me decide whether and how to individualize an activity or curriculum for this child? (Gullo, 1997)
- How can this information help me make wise child guidance or discipline decisions?
- Do I already have adequate documentation, or do I need this item as an example, too?
- Does this child want to place this item in his or her portfolio?

Figure 6.5
Choosing Items to Place in a Child's Portfolio

Item	Belongs	Does not belong	Rationale
Handprint on paper (each child had to do one)		✓	Information about child insignificant; does not help teacher plan curriculum.
Series of handprints for Jon, with 5, then 4, then 3, and then 2 and 1 fingers printed (different classroom from first example)	✓		Jon did this on his own at easel. Gives useful information about interest in math (he learned labels "greater than," "fewer than"). Helps teacher plan curriculum for Jon. Jon asked to include it to show his mom.
Anecdotal records of Terri's questions about plants—lots of questions!	✓		Gives information about first grader's interests. Teacher has no other information about this interest. Would help teacher plan curriculum.
Dittoed handout of a pumpkin that each child "colored"		✓	An inappropriate activity and waste of time in first place. Tells nothing useful about child's development or academic progress. Does not help teacher plan curriculum.
Social skills checklist for K–2 class, each child in class	✓		Yields important information about each child's development in social skills. Can help teacher plan for each child (in terms of social skill building). Good information for making guidance decision.
Antonio's variation on the "Bingo" song. He substituted different letters for the "B." Teacher did anecdotal record observation.	✓		Good information about Antonio's understanding of sounds of letters. Also showed development of child's sense of humor when he slapped his thigh and laughed when singing the seemingly silly new names for the dog Bingo. Can help teacher plan curriculum. Is an authentic assessment document.

Figure 6.6
Examples: Items That Belong/Do Not Belong in Portfolios

Teacher-Produced Materials

Children's work samples might be the heart of a portfolio, but it is a teacher's analysis and explanation of the child's work that lends coherence to the collection. The teacher-produced materials include a brief statement of purpose, a table of contents, the teacher's analysis of work samples, the teacher's observations, and the teacher's observational report.

Table of Contents: Jeb's Portfolio (second grade)	**Pages**
Teacher's (Mr. Nellis) observation report	1–2
Curriculum areas	
Math	3–10
Language Arts (including reading)	11–12
Social Studies	13–14
Science	15–17
Jeb's comments on his work	18

Figure 6.7
Table of Contents for a Portfolio

Statement of Purpose.   Use three to four sentences maximum. Write a concise statement of purpose to go in the front of each portfolio. Anyone reading this statement should immediately know why you put the portfolio together. Then, everything else that follows the statement will make sense to that person. They are more likely to understand why, for example, you included a child's paintings from three different parts of the year in the portfolio.

Example (teacher's statement of purpose):   "This is Jeb Smith's portfolio for the second grade. Every item in the portfolio documents some part of Jeb's growth and development or his progress in the curriculum. Brief notations explain individual items. Our school also involves each child in developing his or her portfolio, so Jeb chose many of the items himself and has agreed to all items placed in his folder."

Table of Contents.   Again, make this concise but useful. Limit the table of contents to about one-half page maximum. List the different sections of the portfolio so parents have a good idea of what to expect and so that they know the order of your presentation. Consecutively number every page, including teacher's observation notes, teacher's notes about a curriculum area, and samples of a child's work. Figure 6.7 shows what Mr. Nellis wrote for the table of contents in Jeb's portfolio. Notice the large number of pages devoted to mathematics.

Teacher's Analyses of Child's Work Samples.   Sift through the child-produced material, analyze it, and then report the findings. On occasion, a teacher might write the analysis as a brief set of remarks so that a reader can understand a specific work sample.

Example: Mr. Nellis wrote a brief set of remarks about Jeb's progress in math skills as documented by the second- and third-grade math skills checklists. He attached the remarks to the two checklists. This is what he wrote.

"January 10. Jeb seems to like math and seems to understand concepts in mathematics quickly and easily. Jeb completed the second-grade math basic skills checklist right before the holiday break. He has already started using the third-grade math textbook. He is now well on his way to completing the third-grade basic math skills checklist, which I have attached to this comment."

This type of brief note attached to the child's work sample is much more helpful to parents than if they just look at the two checklists. It shows that the teacher has examined and analyzed the checklists for what they document about Jeb's ability in a specific curriculum area.

At other times, a teacher might write a summary comment about a curriculum area on a separate sheet of paper. Then the teacher includes the curriculum area report in the portfolio and places it in with and in front of any work samples from that curriculum area. Alternatively, the teacher could write a multipage progress in curriculum areas report and place it in front of work samples from the curriculum areas. Mr. Nellis will write curriculum area reports for the final parent conference in May.

Teacher's Observations.   This includes all of the observations that a teacher makes, such as anecdotal and running records, checklists, and rating scales.[2] A teacher writes periodic observation reports at appropriate times during the year (Meisels, 1995). Then, at the end of the year, the teacher writes a final observation report.

Example: Mr. Nellis, when he had first seen how easily Jeb acquired math concepts, decided to do a set of anecdotal records to accompany the checklists that the district mandated. He intended to write at least one anecdotal record per week on Jeb dealing with math, but he actually wrote more.

Example: Mr. Nellis met with Jeb's parents during the January parent-teacher conferences. He combined his anecdotal records of Jeb and math with the basic skills checklists for math into a midyear report. The following statement is his periodic observation report.

"In addition to the math skills checklists, I have observed and recorded information about how Jeb approaches math and the enjoyment he seems to get from it. On his own, he has created a math notebook that he uses to organize all of his math papers. Although he takes pleasure in other curriculum areas, he gravitates toward math. Jeb often takes out his math notebook after he completes some other task. He seems to ponder a concept and then asks me to clarify some point or to let me know that he understands something or to explain it to me.

"He is now occasionally working with others as a mentor but does this quietly, smoothly, and in the most humble way. Jeb is not arrogant about his superior math knowledge. The other children, even the third graders, seem not to be threatened by Jeb's ability, largely because he does *not* make a big deal of it."

[2]Chapters 3, 4, and 5 in this text explain how to use each of these observational methods.

Items Produced by Others

Occasionally, teachers might want to include items produced by someone other than the teacher or child. They might include something generated by a specialist. For example, a teacher might include a screening test from a speech and hearing specialist. Even here, a teacher should include the item only if he or she is willing to tie it in with the rest of the portfolio. The teacher should write an explanation for why the item is in the portfolio.

Make sure that any report that a specialist contributes to a portfolio is free of jargon. The specialist should also avoid making comments that a parent might not understand. Again, the teacher should take the lead in ensuring that all elements of a child's portfolio are understandable, are clearly written, and serve a useful purpose.

PORTFOLIOS ARE USEFUL FOR ALL YOUNG CHILDREN

Portfolios were originally used with older children (Genishi, 1992). However, portfolios are suitable for assessing children throughout the early childhood age range. A teacher can use a portfolio to assemble information about infants, toddlers, and younger preschool children just as a teacher can use a portfolio to collect information by and for older children. Portfolios for younger early childhood children would likely look a little different from those for older children, but the purpose would be the same (Grubb & Courtney, 1996).

Teachers of infants would still deposit their observation notes about an infant or toddler in the child's portfolio. The teacher would still collect and save checklists, rating scales, and anecdotal or running records—whichever method for observing the teacher uses. The teacher would then analyze the data and write a report about a very young child just as a teacher of older early childhood children does. Infant and toddler teachers must report developmental information to parents, and using a portfolio would serve the same purpose for them.

Portfolios for very young children would contain examples of the child's activities, just as portfolios for older children contain their work samples. Teachers observe infants and toddlers playing, and then the teacher documents the play.

Example: Mr. Thompson, the toddler teacher, uses portfolios. He observed Howard at the water table and took a photograph to place in Howard's portfolio. He dated the photo and wrote a note on it: "Howard played in the water today. He seemed to enjoy the feel of the water. He played next to Mia."

The teacher also dated one of Howard's easel paintings and then placed it in his portfolio. The teacher planned to show it to Howard's parents at their conference. The teacher also documented the types of puzzles that Howard had worked with from the beginning of the year to the time of the conference and wrote a summary describing the changes that this signified.

Activities to Help You Construct Knowledge and Skills in Observing

ACTIVITY 1

Several portfolio examples follow. Please state in writing the purpose that each example would serve.

- Photograph of a young toddler gazing at and reaching for a large bubble created by the teacher
- Writing samples from second graders
- Teacher-drawn line sketches of how kindergarten children used math manipulatives
- Series of haiku poems by a third grader (child did these on her own after learning about haiku. All children wrote one poem, but this child was the only one in the class to produce poems on her own)
- Checklist of development of large motor skills for an infant
- Report transcribed from teacher notes of an interview with a 4-year-old who explained the "limitlessness" meaning of "infinity" as ". . . first, you get some. Then you get some more. Then you just keep on getting more."
- List of library books about wolves, some of them reference books, chosen and read by a third-grade girl (teacher urged children to read about something that they *really* wanted to know more about). A tracing that she made of a wolf's picture from one of the books.

ACTIVITY 2

Volunteer to help a teacher create an attractive display of children's works, a *documentary display*. The content will depend on what the teacher wants to document, but here are some ideas. Plan a display of photos of children working with math manipulatives, including captions explaining the photos. Plan a display of playdough creations, either the real thing or photos. Plan a display of children's easel paintings or drawings.

REFERENCES

Almy, M., & Genishi, C. (1979). *Ways of studying children* (Rev. ed.). New York: Teachers College Press.

Bredekamp, S. (Ed.). (1987). *Developmentally appropriate practice in early childhood programs serving children from birth through age 8* (Exp. ed.). Washington, DC: NAEYC.

Carbonara, N. T. (1961). *Techniques for observing normal child behavior*. Pittsburgh, PA: University of Pittsburgh Press.

Cohen, D., & Stern, V. (1983). *Observing and recording the behavior of young children*. New York: Teachers College Press.

Cohen, D., Stern, V., & Balaban, N. (1996). *Observing and recording the behavior of young children*. New York: Teachers College Press.

Coopersmith, S. (1967). *The antecedents of self-esteem*. San Francisco: W. H. Freeman.

Cross, A. F., & Dixon, S. D. (1997). *Adapting curriculum and instruction in inclusive early childhood classrooms*. Bloomington, IN: Institute for the Study of Developmental Disabilities.

Dixon, S. D., Davis, K., & Schmidt, M. K. (1994). *Assessment in action: Ongoing observation in the classroom*. Bloomington, IN: Institute for the Study of Developmental Disabilities.

Edwards, C. P., Gandini, L., & Forman, G. (Eds.). (1998). *The hundred languages of children: The Reggio Emilia Approach Advanced Reflections* (2nd ed.). Norwood, NJ: Ablex.

Gelfer, J. I. (1994). Implementing student portfolios in an early childhood program. *Early Child Development and Care, 97,* 145–154.

Gelfer, J. I., & Perkins, P. G. (1991, April). Developing student portfolios for young children: A grading, marking, and reporting alternative that fosters communication with families. Paper presented at the annual meeting of the National Coalition for Campus Child Care, Inc., Minneapolis, MN.

Genishi, C. (1992). Framing the ways. In C. Genishi (Ed.), *Ways of assessing children and curriculum: Stories of early childhood practice* (pp. 1–24). New York: Teachers College Press.

Giffen, D., & Long, K. (2001, November). Using formative assessment strategies to deepen student learning. Paper presented at the NAEYC National Conference, Anaheim, CA.

Grace, C. (1992). The portfolio and its use: Developmentally appropriate assessment of young children. ERIC D*igest*, ERIC No.: ED351150.

Grubb, D., & Courtney, A. (1996, March). *Developmentally appropriate assessment of young children: The role of portfolio assessments*. Paper presented at the Annual Conference of the Southern Early Childhood Association, Little Rock, AR.

Gullo, D. F. (1994). *Understanding assessment and evaluation in early childhood education*. New York: Teachers College Press.

Gullo, D. F. (1997). Assessing student learning through the analysis of pupil products. In B. Spodek & O. Saracho (Eds.), *Issues in early childhood educational assessment and evaluation* (pp. 129–148). New York: Teachers College Press.

Helm, J. H. (2003). The importance of documentation. In J. H. Helm and S. Beneke (Eds.), *The power of projects* (pp. 97–102). New York: Teachers College Press.

Helm, J., Beneke, S., & Steinheimer, K. (1998). *Windows on learning: Documenting young children's work*. New York: Teachers College Press.

Helm, J., & Katz, L. (2001). *Young investigators: The project approach in the early years*. New York: Teachers College Press.

Katz, L. (1995, October). *Lessons from Reggio Emilia: An American perspective*. Paper presented at the conference on "Nostalgia del futuro: Liberace sperange per una nuova cultura dell'infanzia," Milano, Italy.

Katz, L., & Chard, S. C. (1996). The contribution of documentation to the quality of early childhood education. ERIC D*igest*, ERIC No. ED393608.

Katz, L. & Chard, S.C. (1997). Documentation: The Reggio Emilia approach, *Principal, 76*(5), 16–17.

Krechevsky, M., & Stork, J. (2000). Challenging educational assumptions: Lessons from an Italian-American collaboration. *Cambridge Journal of Education, 30*(1), 57–74.

Marion, M. (2003). *Guidance of young children* (6th ed.). Upper Saddle River, NJ: Merrill/Prentice Hall.

Meisels, S. J. (1993). Remaking classroom assessment with the work sampling system. *Young Children, 45*(5), 34–40.

Meisels, S. J. (1995). Performance assessment in early childhood education: The work sampling system. ERIC D*igest*, ERIC No.: ED382407.

Mobley, J., & Teets, S. (1992). Informal assessment in second grade: A Foxfire story. In C. Genishi, (Ed.), *Ways of assessing children and curriculum: Stories of early childhood practice* (pp. 163–190). New York: Teachers College Press.

NAEYC (1996). *Guidelines for preparation of early childhood professionals*, Washington, DC: NAEYC (National Association for the Education of Young Children).

100 Languages of Children. Documentary display presented at NAEYC's 2000 annual convention, Atlanta, GA.

Roskos, K. A., & Neuman, S. B. (1994). Of scribbles, schemas, and storybooks: Using literacy albums to document young children's literacy growth. *Young Children*, 49(2), 78–85.

Shores, E., & Grace, C. (1998). *The portfolio book: A step-by-step guide for teachers.* Beltsville, MD: Gryphon House.

WEB SITES RELATED TO THIS CHAPTER

✓ ASCD/Association for Supervision and Curriculum Development

http://www.ascd.org
Locate the "search" box. Type in "portfolios." You will get many responses, one of which is an ASCD PD-Online course.

✓ ERIC, a clearinghouse for information on education

http://ericeece.org
This is the main Web site in ERIC for information on early education.

http://www.ericeece.org/reggio.html
This is a section of the ERIC Web site with information and resources about the Reggio Emilia approach to early childhood. This site is excellent, with ERIC Digests, articles, and other resources about documentation in the Reggio approach.

http://ericeece.org/reggio/regvid
This part of the ERIC/Reggio link lists videos on the Reggio approach, including a video on the 100 Languages of Children display.

✓ Project Zero/Harvard

Project Zero is a major research effort at Harvard. One of the research projects within Project Zero is called "Making Learning Visible," specifically about documenting the learning that can occur in groups.

www.harvard.edu
Search on "Project Zero" and go to its main page; then to "Research Projects," to "Making Learning Visible."

PART III
Using Observation

Parts One and Two described the power of observation, explained an ethical approach to observing, and gave detailed descriptions of major observational methods. This section of the book concentrates on using observation for different purposes.

Chapter 7 Observing Behavior: Cracking the Code.   Children's behavior is like a code. You can use observation to try to crack the code, to unravel the meaning of children's behavior that saddens, irritates, or cheers you. In this chapter, you will learn about several good reasons for observing children's behavior. For example, you can observe children's behavior as the first step in dealing with challenging or difficult behavior. You will approach challenging situations with children more confidently if you have observed behavior well.

Chapter 8 Using the Eclectic Approach to Observe Motor and Cognitive Development.   One of an early childhood teacher's main goals is to uncover and then to build on a child's strengths. This chapter will show you how to use an eclectic approach to observation, that is, choosing one or more observation methods most likely to give you the most helpful information about a child's development. This chapter focuses on two areas of child development—gross or large motor development and cognitive development—to illustrate the eclectic approach to gathering information about those domains. You will see how the early childhood teachers at Oaklawn School use several different observational strategies to obtain accurate information about the development abilities of the children in their classes in these two domains. Some of the methods are teacher-made and some ready-made.

Chapter 9 Using the Eclectic Approach to Observe Emotional and Social Development.

Teachers spend a great deal of time trying to figure out how to help children who are sad, angry, or even so happy that the child has difficulty focusing. Teachers are also concerned about children's relationships and their ability to play and get along with others. This chapter, like chapter 8, uses the eclectic approach to observe development in two domains—a child's feelings or emotional development, and a child's relationships, or social development. You will understand how to observe and document children's development in these two domains by using a variety of informal, ready-made, and teacher-made observation instruments.

Chapter 10 Using Observation to Prevent and Solve Problems.

As a reflective teacher, you will use your ability to make active conscious choices and decisions about dilemmas that you encounter. This chapter will urge you to consider adopting an attitude that says, "This is a problem and I am willing to try to solve it." As an ethical and reflective teacher, you will value observation as one of your most valuable skills in preventing or solving problems. This chapter will demonstrate the power of observation in a problem-solving approach. You will see how the early childhood teachers at Oaklawn choose observational strategies that will give them the most helpful information about a problem.

Chapter 11 Using Observation to Become a Reflective Practitioner.

Effective teachers reflect on their own as well as the practices of others, that is, they examine and think about their practices. In this chapter, you will read about how a reflective teacher uses observation and assessment to examine or think about their practices. You will see that the early childhood teachers at Oaklawn School approach reflection systematically and willingly. They, like all reflective teachers, are not afraid to examine their practices. You will see in this chapter how teachers can use specific observational tools to reflect on their practices. You will also have a chance to assess your own ability to reflect on your practices.

CHAPTER 7

Observing Behavior
Cracking the Code

"Children demonstrate their strengths through behavior."
(Marion, 2003, p. 69)

Chapter objectives

1. *Summarize* the role of observation in authoritative caregiving and teaching.
2. *List, explain, and give examples of* several reasons for observing children's behavior.
3. *Identify* behavioral indicators of stress and child abuse and neglect.
4. *Explain* the usefulness of asking specific questions about a child's behavior.

AUTHORITATIVE CAREGIVING AND OBSERVATION (CASE STUDY)

"Withdrawn. That's what I'd call it," concluded the assistant teacher. Ms. Vargas, the lead teacher, later reflected on that conclusion about the behavior of Jordan, Chelsea, and Calvin, three of the 4-year-olds in their class. She agreed that their behavior did seem to show that they are all withdrawn, but their behaviors also indicate that they are withdrawn in very different ways.[1]

Calvin.   Calvin played alone much but not all of the time: he did not appear to be anxious about not playing with others. In fact, he seemed comfortable playing by himself. He usually chose an activity quickly and worked on it industriously. He looked around occasionally while he worked quietly. He was not aggressive toward the other children and did not object if they played near him.

Chelsea.   Chelsea participated, very quietly, in group activities. During individual choice times, Chelsea usually stood at the edge of a playgroup or at the entrance of an area, often biting her lip or clenching her fists as she surveyed the activity. Ms. Vargas had observed that a sad and downcast sweep of her eyes generally replaced her once hopeful facial expression as she turned away from a group. This child's mother also reported that Chelsea was exceptionally nervous whenever she had to meet new people, such as at a summer playgroup, at the playground, or in a ballet class.

Jordan.   Right away, at the beginning of the school year, the teachers had noticed that Jordan responded aggressively to other children, and the aggression most often seemed unprovoked. He barged into playgroups, seeming not to pay attention to what others were doing at the time. He had a very difficult time in either large or small groups because he so frequently blurted out questions or comments. The other children had already begun to stop playing with or talking to Jordan.

Ms. Vargas is committed to helping each of these children. She realizes that there is no single answer about withdrawn behavior. She will observe Calvin, Chelsea, and Jordan and try to get more information about each child. She and other early childhood professionals know that observing children's behavior does not provide easy answers, but it does yield information that teachers can use for making sound decisions about how to support children.

The assistant teacher's conclusion was correct. All three children do seem to be withdrawn, but it is up to the teachers to pinpoint the differences in the withdrawn behavior among these children. Ms. Vargas's willingness to try to *crack the code*, to unravel the meaning of Calvin's, Jordan's, and Chelsea's withdrawn behavior, will make it possible for both teachers to help these children.

[1]Please see Fujiki, Brinton, Morgan, and Hart (1999) for a review of research on withdrawn behavior.

REASONS FOR OBSERVING CHILDREN'S BEHAVIOR

Several factors motivate authoritative early childhood professionals to observe children's behavior:

- 📖 Children communicate with behavior
- 📖 Children demonstrate their strengths through behavior
- 📖 Children's behavior often highlights a special need
- 📖 Children's behavior gives clues about challenging behavior
- 📖 Children's behavior expresses feelings, signs of stress, and signs of child abuse and neglect

Children Communicate with Behavior

A 3-year-old whirls with delight, trying to catch snowflakes. Another child's face turns red with anger as he strikes out at another child. A 5-year-old twirls her hair tightly around her finger as she sits hunched over a workbook page. A boy in the same class lowers his head until it nearly touches his workbook and turns his head from side to side, eyes darting to the other children's pages. Finally, a tear drops onto his page. A first-grader, head thrust forward slightly, one hand on a hip, the other hand scratching his head, eyes open wide in wonder, and mouth making a little "O" shape, stares at the gorillas in the zoo.

Head scratching, wide eyes, worried looks, tears, twirling, smiling, a red face, and a fist that smashes. Not one of these children uttered a word, but they all communicated eloquently. Their hands, feet, facial expressions, and body movements communicated just as well as words. Of course, young children communicate with words. They are just as likely, though, to tell us what they are experiencing, how they feel, and what they think with behavior.

Perceptive teachers know that behavior has meaning and that observing behavior is an essential skill in teaching.

Example: Mr. Thompson, the toddlers' teacher, observed that Paul reached over and touched Alissa's curly red hair very gently with one finger, much like a person who gingerly touches wet paint. Paul pulled his hand back and looked at his finger, eyebrows and forehead knitted in puzzlement.

Example: Ms. Vargas, the preschool teacher, observed Chelsea motion to her dad to bend down. Chelsea (one of the case study children) then spoke very softly into her dad's ear while Dad helped her take her coat off at arrival. She smiled and then gave her dad a hug before going off to play. Dad turned to the teacher: "Birthday party for her older brother this afternoon. Looks like she's a little excited."

Example: Philip, a 7-year-old in Mr. Nellis's class, had moved to this new school in September and had become good friends with two other boys. He usually approached school enthusiastically, but one Monday morning in March, Mr. Nellis watched Philip walk slowly into the classroom. The second grader moved listlessly and hung his head. He said nothing and responded with an uncharacteristically quiet "Hi" to greetings from other children. The teacher asked if something was wrong. Philip slowly lifted his eyes, looked at his teacher, and then looked away. "We're going to move—again," he whispered.

Paul, Chelsea, and Philip all communicated mainly with their bodies and behavior. Paul seemed to be curious, but certainly not malicious, about Alissa's red hair. Chelsea's behavior and facial expression told us that she seemed excited and happy. Philip's behavior and body language spoke of heavy sadness.

Behavior is a code much like the code that whales use in their beautiful and exotic language. Scientists have worked for a long time on cracking the code in whale sounds. A scientist who wants to decipher the whale's coded message has to understand the code to know what the signals mean.

A child's behavior is also a code: his way of communicating what he needs or wants. Having greater responsibility in interaction with children requires teachers to do **code switching.** They must switch their focus from the adult-like code of using words to communicate feelings and thoughts to a child's code of using behavior to communicate feelings and thoughts. Early childhood teachers take this part of their job seriously: to observe a child's behavioral code and then to decode it as accurately as possible.

Observe Behavior to Discover and Build on Children's Strengths

One goal in observing, decoding, and then reflecting on and interpreting behavior should be to discover and build on children's strengths—always. It is unethical to observe any child with the intention of manipulating his behavior. Ethical authoritative professionals observe behavior to discover what children like to do or can do with success. This is especially important to keep in mind when observing challenging behavior or behavior brought on by stress.

Example: Using the anecdotal record method,[2] Mr. Lee, the third- and fourth-grade teacher, documented third-grader Jim's difficulty concentrating on things during large-group instruction in class. Mr. Lee also documented Jim's ability to concentrate much better when working either alone or in small groups. He also noticed that Jim seemed to be a natural leader in the small groups. Having identified two strengths—the ability to concentrate in small groups and the ability to lead—the teacher developed a plan to build on Jim's strengths.

Example: Mr. Nellis had recorded anecdotal record observations of Sandi's (age 6 years, 10 months) behavior in interaction with groups of two or three other children. The

---

[2]Chapter 3 describes, explains, and gives examples of the anecdotal record method of observing.

Jim's teacher discovered by observing that one of Jim's strengths is that this child is a natural leader in small groups (Jim is the second child from the left).

teacher concluded that Sandi, intelligent, cheerful, well liked, and observant, was remarkably good at dealing in a positive way with almost any child in the class. She seemed to have good interpersonal intelligence (Gardner, 1993).

For instance, Mr. Nellis observed as Sandi prevented an argument in a small reading group. Bert finished reading, Sara started her turn, and Dave yelled, "It's my turn!" Sandi looked at each child in the group as if figuring something out and then said, pointing at Bert, "Uh-oh! Look, Dave. Bert just read. Sara is sitting next to Bert, so it's Sara's turn next." Then Sandi fairly beamed at Dave and chirped, "You go right after Sara!" Dave nodded and simply said, "Oh, yeah. OK."

Observe Behavior to Assess Special Needs

Observing behavior plays a major role in assessing special needs that children might have. For example, Landau and McAninch (1997) advocate a multidimensional approach to assessing ADHD (attention-deficit hyperactivity disorder) including systematic observation of a child's behavior in the classroom or play setting, that is, assessment in a naturalistic setting. The teacher's assessment of a child's time spent engaged in on-task or in off-task behaviors yields direct information about how a child functions. Please see Figure 7.1 for behavioral indicators of ADHD.

We need to be extremely careful about tossing around labels like "ADHD." Teachers can observe behaviors, but we are not really qualified or licensed to make a diagnosis of ADHD in any child. We have to pay attention to how our classrooms are set up and how the curriculum is structured, because a developmentally inappropriate setting can bring out behaviors like those in ADHD. We can, however, work with those charged in officially diagnosing special needs by observing and recording a child's behavior.

The following lists some of the behaviors that children with ADHD typically show. Early childhood teachers are well aware that the part of the brain controlling attention is not fully developed until later in childhood (Shaffer, 1996) and therefore that young children typically have difficulty paying attention or are easily distracted.

Children with ADHD, however, show these behaviors much more frequently and much more severely than do other children the same age and developmental level. We can expect to see ADHD in only 3 to 5% of school-age children.

- Blurts out answers[1]
- Very easily distracted
- Fidgets or squirms
- Talks too much and has difficulty playing quietly
- Has trouble paying attention
- Makes careless mistakes. Does not pay attention to details
- Has trouble listening and following directions
- Interrupts others or intrudes on others
- Impatient

Figure 7.1
Behavioral Indicators of ADHD

Sources: AACAP (1999). Children who can't pay attention/ADHD. *AACAP facts for families,* Fact Sheet #6. http://www.aacap.org/publications/factsfam/noattent.htm; Landau and McAninch (1993/1997).

[1]*Frequency count:* Some observers like to get a tally of the number of times that a behavior, a clearly defined behavior, such as blurting out answers, occurs. The observer writes the behavior on a sheet of paper and then makes a mark every time he sees the behavior. For example, an observer might record five tally marks next to "blurts out answers," meaning that the child has shown this behavior five times.

Observing behavior in the naturalistic setting of a classroom is an excellent way to get data on current behavior and then combine that information with data from other sources, such as parent reports. The authors also advocate observing the behavior of same-sex classmates of the child. For example, "Joe (with symptoms of ADHD) spends 20% of the time in on-task behavior during math, while the other boys spend almost 90% of the time in on-task behavior during math."

Even if a child shows these behaviors, it does not automatically mean that he has ADHD. There are always a number of explanations for behavior. For example, this child's ability to integrate information from his senses might be impaired (AACAP, www.aacap.org.). Only licensed psychologists or psychiatrists are qualified to make an official diagnosis.

Observe Behavior as the First Step in Dealing with Challenging Behavior

Early childhood professionals deal with normal *discipline encounters* on a daily basis (Marion, 2003). They also confront what they classify as difficult or challenging behavior (Kaiser & Rasminsky, 1999; Marion & Swim, 2001). If challenging behavior involves hurting others or damaging property, then a teacher is clearly responsible for stopping the behavior and ending the threat. Therefore, a short-term goal with challenging behavior is to protect children and to communicate expectations.

Teachers also have a long-term goal to help children with challenging behavior learn a more positive way of interacting with others. Teachers observe a child with challenging behavior, as Ms. Vargas did with Calvin (case study child), as the starting point in supporting that child.

Supportive teachers understand that challenging behavior is complex and puzzling and has no easy solutions. They do not engage in knee-jerk reactions to misbehavior, such as automatically using some sort of punishment at the first sign of a challenging behavior. Instead, they observe challenging or difficult behavior carefully to determine factors contributing to the misbehavior. They realize that challenging behavior is the child's voice: his way of telling us what he needs or wants so desperately.

Listen carefully to the voice of challenging or difficult behavior and it will tell how you can help a child. Challenging behavior might well say one of the following three things (Educational Productions, 1998; Kohn, 1996):

- "I have an unmet need. Please help me meet this need."
- "There is a skill that I need but don't have. Please teach this skill to me."
- "There is a mismatch between me and something in our classroom or in the schedule or in the curriculum. Can you please fix things to help me?"

Example of a Mismatch Between Child and Environment.   Mr. Lee had realized that there was a mismatch between some of the children and the schedule in his classroom. The teacher had then examined his own instructional practices and rearranged the schedule and adjusted his instructional methods (Kohn, 1996).

Mr. Lee's new schedule enabled his children to do their work at their own pace. The children realized that they had to complete a menu of curriculum assignments within a specified time, but they chose the order in which they completed their work and where to work in the classroom (Pelander, 1997). This method seemed to be more developmentally appropriate to Mr. Lee and helped a number of children, including Jim, who concentrated poorly when the teacher had all children doing the same thing at the same time.

Example of a Child Lacking a Specific Skill.   In spite of a developmentally appropriate new schedule, Mr. Lee realized that one of the boys had a problem connected to the new arrangement. Rory, a very capable and bright third grader, zoomed through his work. He got along well with the other children, engaging in friendly interaction while working, causing no disruptions while he worked. However, the teacher noticed that Rory did not seem to know what to do after completing an assignment. Instead of just going on to choose the next thing, Rory darted around the classroom, good-naturedly creating chaos.

Mr. Lee decided, after observing Rory's behavior, that this child lacked a specific skill. Rory did not seem to know how to stop, look at his menu of choices, and then choose the next thing to do. Mr. Lee decided to simply teach this skill to Rory (Marion, 2003). He taught him how to *stop* (and cross off what he has just finished), *look* (at choices remaining), and *choose* (the next activity). Mr. Lee coached Rory through this process the first few times that Rory used it.

Example of a Child's Unmet Need.   It had been raining all day, and Ms. Vargas's preschool children had not been able to get out to the playground. Because the children seemed unusually restless in a large group, the teacher changed the group time to include some marching, jumping in place, and running in place. Then Ms. Vargas moved her group time to the library so that the children had a chance to get a short walk. Later that day, the children did four simple yoga stretches to soft music.

The teacher realized that her children had an unmet need for exercise. Adding well-supervised physical activity to the group time, going on a walk in the building, and yoga stretches helped to meet that need. Children have many basic needs—for example, rest, food, security, play, acceptance, love, and exercise. Authoritative (highly responsive) adults make a real effort to tune into those needs by observing a child's behavior. Then, as much as is possible, an authoritative adult supports a child in meeting the need.

Observe Behavior to Recognize Children's Feelings, Signs of Stress, or Signs of Child Abuse and Neglect

Use Observation to Pick Up on Children's Feelings.   Authoritative adults understand child development and realize that even young infants have emotions, and that the list of emotions children experience grows during early childhood. Not only that, but teachers who observe behavior will quickly see that different children express the same emotion in different ways (Fabes & Eisenberg, 1992).

Example: Ms. Vargas observed several different reactions to one child's frequent grabbing of things from others. Ralph expressed anger by *actively resisting*, that is, he asserted himself nonaggressively. He simply demanded that Nellie return his magic marker. Cindy's behavior, *venting*, expressed a greater degree of anger when she twisted her face into a frustrated expression, sank to the floor, and cried. Justine revealed anger by *expressing her dislike* of Nellie: "You're mean, Nellie! You can't come to *my* birthday party!"

Ms. Vargas also noticed that her three "withdrawn" children (Calvin, Chelsea, and Jordan, see chapter opener) behaved in ways that told her they all had different feelings

Use observation to discover how children express an emotion such as sadness.

about not playing with others. Calvin's behavior seemed to say that he was relaxed about playing alone. Chelsea's behavior hinted at anxiety about not playing with other children.

Observe Behavior for Signs of Stress.   Figure 7.2 lists several behaviors indicating that a child is probably experiencing some stress. Often, we suspect that something is bothering a child but do not know the source of the worry. What teachers do see, however, is the child's clearly stressed behavior. For instance, Mr. Nellis has observed that one of the boys clenches his jaws together and at the same time squeezes pencils tightly when doing any type of written work. This child also repeatedly rubs

Children show us that they are experiencing stress in a number of ways.

Reactions to stress might be passive
Excessive fatigue
Withdrawing and putting head on table or desk
Excessive fears

Reactions to stress might be more active with behaviors that involve only the child.
Nail biting
Manipulating one's hands or mouth
Repetitive body movements[1]

Reactions to stress might show up when children interact with others.
Stuttering
Bullying, threatening, or hurting others
Nervous, inappropriate laughter

Reactions to stress might show up as children work with objects.
Excessive squeezing or tapping of pencils, markers, crayons
Clumsy or fumbling behavior

Figure 7.2
Behavioral Indicators of Stress in Young Children

Sources: Hart, Burts, Durland, Charlesworth, DeWolf, and Fleege (1998): Brodeur and Monteleone (1994): Selye (1978).

[1]*Time sampling:* Some observers like to find out whether a specific behavior occurs during a specific period. An observer chooses a specific behavior to look for, such as repetitive body movements during a standardized test, a stress-inducing situation for many young children. Observer chooses a specific segment of time, such as 3 minutes. Observer draws this segment on a piece of paper and then marks the 3 minutes off into 15-second intervals (12 intervals). The observer marks "✓" if she sees the behavior during one of the intervals. She marks a "0" if she does not see the behavior. If she had observed a child during 3 minutes of a standardized test and she counted a total of 8 "✓" marks, then she might well conclude that this child was showing clear signs of stress during the test.

one hand with his other hand during large-group instruction. Ms. Vargas has noticed that Chelsea bites her lip when she stands on the edge of playgroups, looking in.

The important thing to remember about a child's stress-induced behavior is that the behavior is a symptom of a problem, a problem that the child did not create. The child who is under stress needs help, not judgment and certainly not punishment. Some teachers who observe behaviors such as aggression (often a sign of stress) might simply punish the child for behaving aggressively. They tend to punish the behavior, but they forget to acknowledge the stress that begets anger that begets aggression.

Other teachers prefer to avoid punishment and instead to take a problem-solving approach with such behavior (Kohn, 1996). Getting to a problem-solving approach and avoiding punishment requires examining behavior which might appear, for example, to be defiant or aggressive.

Behaviors such as bullying or aggression often indicate that a child is under great stress. As usual, authoritative teachers deal with such behaviors by being highly demanding and highly responsive. They do confront an aggressive child, but they use positive discipline strategies. They also respond to an aggressive child's needs by recognizing, acknowledging, and dealing with the stress running like an underground river below the behavior.

Observe Children for Behaviors Signaling Abuse or Neglect.   Finally, conscientious observation can even help teachers identify behavioral indicators of child abuse or neglect. Because there are several forms of child abuse and neglect, there are also many different behavioral indicators, depending on the specific type and the severity of the abuse or neglect. Figure 7.3 lists some of the major behavioral indicators of

---

Infants

- Shrill, high-pitched cry
- Passive watchfulness (excessive amount of lying quietly in crib and observing surroundings intently)
- Show little interest in toys
- Accept losses with little reaction

Beyond infancy

- Seem old for their age
- Lack ability to play
- Temper tantrums beyond what would be expected for age and stage of development
- Low self-esteem—behaves in a way that tells us that he does not feel competent or in control or that he is not worthy of the attention of others
- Withdrawal—can, but does not always indicate abuse
- Chronic aggression or overt hostility against peers, animals, adults, themselves
- Passive watchfulness, an excessive amount
- Compulsivity or efforts to control some small aspect of their lives
- Fearful of failure
- Difficulty listening to or carrying out instructions
- Difficulty organizing thoughts, conceptualizing, and verbalizing
- Regression to an earlier stage of development—bedwetting, thumbsucking, baby talk
- Poor social skills
- Extreme shyness
- Steals or hoards food
- Little or no empathy for others

Figure 7.3

Some Child Behaviors Indicating Abuse or Neglect

Sources: Brodeur & Monteleone (1994); Tower (1999).

child abuse and neglect. Any one indicator does not conclusively indicate abuse or neglect. However, teachers who observe a pattern of behavior, an abrupt change of behavior, or behavioral indicators combined with physical indicators of abuse or neglect (chapter 8 in this text) might well be observing an abused or neglected child.

WHO, WHAT, WHEN, WHERE, WHY: FIVE QUESTIONS ABOUT BEHAVIOR

Background of Michael's Behavior

Michael, a first grader in Mr. Nellis's K–2 class, has always been a happy and well-cared-for child who has lived with his aunt and uncle, who are his foster parents, since the age of 2 months. Michael has had regular visits with his biological mother who, until 3 months ago, was in a residential mental health treatment facility. With the permission of the court, she had taken Michael back to live with her just 1 month ago. Mr. Nellis fully expected a period of adjustment but was particularly concerned about some of Michael's specific behaviors that he recently observed. He made a series of brief anecdotal records over a 2-week period (Michael had been living with his mother for about 2 weeks at the start of that time).

Synopsis of Observations of Michael's Behavior

As he had always done, Michael ate breakfast at school along with all the other children. Mr. Nellis first observed a change in Michael's behavior when Michael had begun, in the previous 2 weeks, to ask for second helpings of breakfast, something he had never done in the past. At lunch, Michael had secretively begun to take whatever food he could off his tray, stuff it in his pockets, and then transfer it to his backpack when they returned to the classroom after lunch. Just the previous Friday, Michael had requested seconds at lunch and then crammed what he could of the extra food in his pocket.

The gradual change in Michael's behavior, at first surprising and confusing to the teacher, changed to alarm that Friday. Mr. Nellis was justifiably concerned about the sudden changes in Michael's behavior: hoarding food. His careful observations, documented in anecdotal records, allowed him to answer five questions about Michael's behavior: Who, what, when, where, and why? These five questions can help authoritative teachers begin to understand any behavior.

Who *Was Involved in This Behavior?*

Was only the one child involved, or were there others? If others were involved, were they adults, children, or both? Even if the child was the only person involved, did the behavior ever involve animals? Who were the others? If this is a recurring behavior, are the same children or adults (or animals) generally involved?

Who Was Involved in Michael's Behavior?   Michael was the only child involved. He never asked others to help him, and he took only his own food. However, he did trade food with other children, food such as applesauce for things like cookies or fruit.

What *Happened?*

The observer carefully notes the precise nature of the behavior. If possible, the observer notes what occurred before the behavior and then what happened after the behavior. It is also helpful to note whether this behavior is new, or whether it is part of a pattern of behavior. Note how long the behavior went on.

What Happened with Michael's Behavior?   Michael asked for seconds at breakfast several times and ate the extra food. He ate very little at lunch and only those things that he could not take home or could not trade, such as milk or soup. He traded what he could at lunch for things that he could take with him. He did not ever bully the other children into trading and accepted "No" for an answer. On Friday he even asked for seconds at lunch and took that with him, too.

When *Did the Behavior Occur?*

Does it always happen when the child arrives at school, during naptime, during large group, at transitions? Does the behavior seem to occur during a variety of activities during the day? Be specific. If it occurred during large group, say whether it occurred at every group time or just some of them. If the behavior happens at arrival time, does it occur, for example, every morning or perhaps on the same 2 or 3 days each week?

Answering this question gives helpful clues to an observer. If a behavior occurs at transitions, then say whether it happens with every transition during the day, only with transitions out of large group, only when specific adults are present, or only when specific children are present. Jordan, for example, the 4-year-old in the chapter opener, behaved in an extremely impulsive way every day. He blurted things out during large and small groups, when he talked with almost any adult, when he talked with other children, and when he played in a variety of centers.

When Did Michael's Behavior Occur?   Mr. Nellis had observed food gathering and hiding at all lunches for the past 9 days. Later, on Friday afternoon, Michael had eaten only one bite of his piece of another child's birthday cake, carefully wrapping the rest of his portion and placing it in his backpack.

Where *Does the Behavior Typically Take Place?*

Does it happen only in certain areas of the classroom or school, or is the behavior likely to occur just about anywhere? For example, a teacher noticed that one of the girls in his class behaved in an extremely agitated way, but only in one place—standing in the line waiting for the school bus at the end of the day. Her father, he discovered, had sexually abused this child for a number of years. School was a safe place for her, and her agitation showed up only while she waited to leave her place of safety.

Where Did Michael's Behavior Occur?   It occurred mainly in the lunchroom, in his locker as he stored his food, and once in the classroom (birthday cake).

Why *Does the Child Behave This Way?*

This requires that the observer interpret the child's behavior, which might be a difficult thing to do in many cases. In answering this question, it helps to look at the answers to the other four questions and then to make some conclusions based on this information. Figure 7.4 lists just a few of the things that asking "who, what, when, and where" might reveal.

Why Did Michael's Behavior Occur?   Mr. Nellis, unable to reach Michael's mother, called Michael's aunt. He discovered that the child's mother had stopped taking her medication, never really cooked regular meals, bought food mainly at fast food restaurants, and kept only snack food in the house. This had been a major change for Michael, who up until now had eaten well. The aunt was also clearly concerned.

Mr. Nellis accurately concluded that Michael had an unmet need for food. Michael's behavior (hoarding food) that had originally stirred the teacher's curiosity was Michael's attempt to meet this need. The teacher also guessed correctly that Michael had spent the whole weekend with little food other than what he had gathered from school. Michael's aunt had been out of town that weekend and figured out that Michael must have been on his own since dinner with his relatives on

A young child's behavior, translated into words, might say,

Behavior $\longrightarrow$	What this behavior might be saying . . .
• Twirling in the snow, smiling	"I'm so happy that it's snowing!"
• Arms folded on chest, mouth closed tightly, chin down	"I think that I am powerless and I'll get some power by being stubborn with you."
• Talking quietly to the gerbil	"I think that loud noise scares the gerbil." (This child is empathic.)
• Stands at edge of playgroup, looks at different children	"I'd like to play."
• Disrupts group time that lasts 40 minutes	"This group time has gone on way too long. Stop!"
• Interrupts frequently	"I have poor social skills."
• Waves at friends when leaving school for the day. Smiles.	"Tom and Kendra are my friends!"

Figure 7.4
Cracking the Code: Children Speak to Us with Behavior

- Help and support from family members
- A naturally stable and happy personality in the child
- Positive self-esteem
- Inner strength and good coping skills in the child
- A strong relationship with a healthy adult
- Friendships and positive peer relationships
- Interest in and success at school
- Help from outside the family to improve the family environment, e.g., parenting classes

These protective or positive factors seem to decrease, but certainly not eliminate, the risk of harm to children who have mentally ill parents.

Figure 7.5

Factors That Might Protect Children with Mentally Ill Parents

Source: AACAP, 2000.

Thursday. The teacher called Social Services and, using his anecdotal records and notes from his conversation with the aunt, reported his suspicion of the behavioral indicators of neglect.

Mr. Nellis acted properly in reporting suspected child neglect. As a teacher, he is a mandated reporter (is required to report). A parent's mental illness often impairs the adult's ability to parent, thus placing children at risk for harm, as Michael's mother placed him at risk by not providing the food that he needed.

Some teachers would merely have stopped Michael the minute they saw him stuff food in his pockets. Some might even have punished him. Mr. Nellis was curious at first and, to his credit, decided to observe this behavior. His observations gave him just the right information that he needed to begin to help Michael. Figure 7.5 describes protective factors for children with mentally ill parents.

Activities to Help You Construct Knowledge and Skills in Observing

ACTIVITY 1

Reflect on a child's unmet needs. For each scenario, a teacher might first see difficult behavior. Please consider the impact on each teacher's perception of the behavior of discovering the child's unmet needs. How might such knowledge change how the teacher interacts with the child?

📖 Caitlin, 4 years old, had been whiny and clingy for almost 3 weeks. Mrs. Vargas was clearly puzzled because this was an abrupt change in behavior for Caitlin. The teacher, in spite of her nonjudgmental ways, did get a little irritated with Caitlin. Then, the teacher discovered that Caitlin's parents had separated and her mother had moved to another state. Caitlin had not seen her mother for the past 2 weeks.

Please state in writing how you think the teacher's knowledge about Caitlin's unmet need for *security* might affect how the teacher deals with her whining and clinging.

📖 Jonathan, in Mr. Nellis's kindergarten, always seems to be tired and groggy when he arrives at school. The teacher has a good relationship with Jonathan's father, a single parent. Jonathan's father said that he now worked the 4 p.m. to midnight shift at the hospital. The hospital provided on-site child care for parents on this shift, but Jonathan's father was worried about interrupting his son's sleep at midnight to take him home and then put him to bed there.

State in writing how you think the knowledge about Jonathan's unmet need for uninterrupted nighttime *rest* might affect how the teacher views and deals with a low-energy child every morning.

📖 Mr. Nellis has noticed how much Jeff, a child new to his class, treasured playground time and play with the other children. Jeff, a second grader, asked the teacher, "Is it almost time to go to the playground?" about five times every morning. Mr. Nellis always said the same thing: "Playground time comes right after lunch."

Then Mr. Nellis met Jeff's mother and father. They had enrolled Jeff in several activities and lessons (French class, swimming, children's theater, origami paper folding, Olympics of the Mind, and piano). Jeff was busy every night of the week except Friday. He had no time after school to play with other children.

Please state in writing how Mr. Nellis's knowledge of the hurried nature of Jeff's life and his unmet need for *play* might affect how he deals with Jeff's questions about playground time.

ACTIVITY 2

Identify the skill that each child lacks. Then say how the teacher can help the child acquire the skill.

📖 The teacher of the 3-year-olds noticed that Samuel, a new child in the class, looked confused at his first group time in her class. The other children knew immediately what the teacher meant by her statement, "Please sit like a pretzel."

The skill that Samuel needs to acquire is _____.

📖 Mrs. Vargas said to Ralph, "Please use words to tell Jake that you are upset." The next day, Ralph did not use words but again pushed Jake when Jake took Ralph's marker.

The skill (related to "using words") that Ralph needs to acquire is _____.

📖 Jordan, one of the children in the case studies at the beginning of the chapter, blurts out questions, comments, and responses in group time.

In this case, the skill that Jordan seems to lack is _____.

ACTIVITY 3

Please read Figure 7.5, which lists factors that might protect children with mentally ill parents. Then reread the section on Michael, who stashed food from school breakfast and lunches in his backpack and took it home. From your perspective, which of the factors from Figure 7.5 seem to be present in Michael's life?

REFERENCES

American Academy of Child and Adolescent Psychiatry (AACAP) (2000). Children of parents with mental illness. AACAP *facts for families*, No. 39. Washington, DC: AACAP. (See Web site listed at end of this chapter.)

Brodeur, A., & Monteleone, J. (1994). *Child maltreatment: A clinical guide and reference*. St. Louis: G.W. Medical Publishing, Inc.

Educational Productions (1998). *Reframing discipline: Dealing with difficult behavior*. Portland, OR: Author.

Fabes, R., & Eisenberg, N. (1992). Young children's coping with interpersonal anger. *Child Development, 63*, 116–128.

Fujiki, M., Brinton, B., Morgan, M., & Hart, C. (1999). Withdrawn and sociable behavior of children with language impairment. *Language, Speech, & Hearing Services in Schools, 30*, 183–195.

Gardner, H. (1993). *Multiple intelligence: The theory in practice*. New York: Basic Books.

Hart, C., Burts, D., Durland, M. A., Charlesworth, R., DeWolf, M., & Fleege, P. (1998). Stress behaviors and activity type participation of preschoolers in more and less developmentally appropriate classrooms: SES and sex differences. *Journal of Research in Childhood Education, 12*(2), 176–196.

Kaiser, B., & Rasminsky, J. (1999). *Meeting the challenge*. Ottawa, Ontario: Canadian Child Care Federation.

Kohn, A. (1996). *Beyond discipline*. Alexandria, VA: ASCD, Association for Supervision and Curriculum Development.

Landau, S., & McAninch, C. (1997). Young children with attention deficits. In E. Junn & C. Boyatzis (Eds.), *Child growth and development* (pp. 232–238). (Reprinted from *Young Children*, May 1993, 49–58.)

Marion, M. (2003). *Guidance of young children* (6th ed.). Upper Saddle River, NJ: Merrill/Prentice Hall.

Marion, M., & Swim, T. (2001, November). *The challenge of dealing with challenging behavior*. Seminar presented at the NAEYC National Conference.

Pelander, J. (1997). My transition from conventional to more developmentally appropriate practices in the primary grades. *Young Children, 52*(7), 19–25.

Selye, H. (1978). *The stress of life* (rev. ed.). New York: McGraw-Hill.

Shaffer, D. (1996). *Developmental psychology* (4th ed.). Pacific Grove, CA: Brooks/Cole Publishing.

Tower, C. (1999). *Understanding child abuse and neglect*. Boston: Allyn & Bacon.

WEB SITES RELATED TO THIS CHAPTER

✓ AACAP (American Academy of Child and Adolescent Psychiatry)

http://www.aacap.org

Check out the "Facts for Families Fact Sheets." They are excellent, are free, and may be reproduced but may not be included in a document for sale. See the entire list of fact sheets at http://www.aacap.org/publications/factsfam/index.htm

✓ CHADD (Children and Adults with Attention-Deficit/Hyperactivity Disorder)

http://www.chadd.org

Go to the link "Frequently Asked Questions" for information about AD/HD or about the organization.

✓ Iowa State University Extension

http://www.exnet.iastate.edu

Go to "Publications." Click on the "child development" link. Look for the article on childhood stress.

✓ New York University Child Study Center

http://www.aboutourkids.org

Provides timely tips and articles on a variety of children's behaviors.

✓ Extension divisions of land grant universities.

Each state has a university with an Extension division, charged with providing information and education for people throughout that state. Extension produces written documents on many topics, including parenting. Here are examples of information on stress management for children from several different extension sources. Check the extension division in your own state, either on the Internet or at your county's extension office (Yellow Pages).

✓ University of Illinois Extension

http://www.urbanext.uiuc.edu

Locate the search box. Type in "children and stress." You will get an extensive list of brief articles on this topic.

✓ University of Minnesota Extension

http://www.extension.umn.edu

Locate the search box. Type in "children and stress" (use the quote marks). You will get two articles on stress.

✓ University of Nevada-Reno

www.unce.unr.edu

This is the main page for the University Cooperative Extension of the University of Nevada-Reno. Click on publications. Then click on Children, Youth and Families. You will get a categorized list of articles. Look for and click on the article "Children and Stress, a Fact Sheet."

CHAPTER 8

Using the Eclectic Approach to Observe

MOTOR AND COGNITIVE DEVELOPMENT

"Well-prepared early childhood professionals understand the purposes of assessment, use effective assessment strategies; and use assessment responsibly, to positively influence children's development and learning."
(NAEYC Standards for Early Childhood Professional Preparation, revised 2001; Hyson, 2002)

Chapter objectives

1. *Explain* the eclectic approach to observing child development.
2. *Describe, explain, and give examples of* different categories of observation and assessment strategies.
3. *Restate* major reasons for observing children's development.
4. *Value* the responsible and ethical use of observation and assessment of young children's development.
5. *Reflect* on your own view of the purposes of observation of children's development.
6. *Apply* knowledge of observation of child development in specific learning activities.

AN OBSERVATION AND ASSESSMENT DILEMMA

The early childhood teachers, Mr. Nellis (K–2), Mrs. Vargas (preschool), Mr. Claiborne (first grade), and Mr. Lee (third grade) met to finalize their assessment plans for the year. This year, for the first time, they face an assessment dilemma. How will they continue to do authentic, play-based observation and assessment in the face of the school district's decision to require a standardized test of large motor skills for all early-childhood children? As you read in chapter 1, this group of teachers believes that standardized tests are not always in the best interests of young children. They had stated their position on standardized testing by appearing before the school board giving the written document "Standardized Testing of Young Children 3 Through 8 Years of Age" to the board. (See the NAEYC Web site at the end of this chapter.) In spite of that, the board went ahead with their decision to mandate a standardized test.

The early childhood teachers in this school favor authentic assessment and particularly favor using informal assessment strategies. Therefore, they have decided to continue using informal ready-made and teacher-made observations of large motor development because they believe that observations will continue to give them good information about children's development. They do not want to ever base decisions on a single test score from any standardized test. These teachers will also continue to use informal anecdotal records and checklists to assess selected aspects of cognitive development. Here is the list that they wrote as their meeting proceeded. It summarizes their plans for observing large motor and cognitive development. They did not include the school board's mandated standardized test on this list because they do not think that it is part of authentic assessment. However, the test will be administered. You will see in this chapter how these teachers come to grips with their dilemma.

We Will "Authentically" Assess Large Motor and Cognitive Development with

- Williams's Preschool Motor Development Checklist (3–6$\frac{1}{2}$-year-old children)
- Obstacle Course: Project Spectrum (all children)
- Anecdotal records: cognitive and motor development
- Checklists: cognitive and motor development

Then, for midyear parent conferences, each teacher would consolidate all the data for motor development (and for other areas of development) and progress of children in their classes with a brief report for the parents.

Every teacher in this group wrote a brief plan for assessment. Figure 8.1 is Mr. Nellis's timeline for assessment in his classroom, his plan incorporating the group's general

Checklist: Timeline for Assessment
Early Childhood Classes: Oaklawn School

Sept. 1–14
___Social Attributes Checklist (existing/ready-made)
___Williams's Motor Development Checklist (existing/ ready-made)
___Explain concept of portfolios to children and parents
___Portfolio items as appropriate: e.g., writing samples from all children

Sept. 15–30
___Portfolio items as appropriate: e.g., art samples for each child
___Anecdotal or running records for 1/3 of the class

Oct. 1–15
___Math skills checklist (all children)
___Portfolio items or other checklists as appropriate for each child
___Anecdotal or running records for 1/3 of the class

Oct. 16–31
___Social Attributes Checklist (second time to administer this)
___Anecdotal or running records for 1/3 of the class
___Begin Project Spectrum Motor Development Assessment Obstacle Course
___Portfolio items as appropriate; writing samples
___Review portfolios for one-half of the class

Nov. 1–15
___Portfolio items as appropriate
___Review portfolios for other half of the class
___Math Skills Checklist

Nov. 15–Dec. 10
___Portfolio items as appropriate
___District administers standardized test for motor skills to all early childhood classes
___Emotional development checklist: two parts
___Rating Scale: How _____ Manages Anger

Dec. 27–Jan. 8
Holidays (work on observation reports and portfolios)
___Consolidate observation data for each child: write reports
___When school starts up again: Portfolio Review and Reflection
___Work with each child to review portfolio's contents
___Organize for parent conferences
___Write helpful comments for parents as appropriate

Jan. 12–14
___Parent conferences
___Portfolios: midyear observation report/analysis of children's work samples

A checklist/timeline: observation and assessment in Mr. Nellis's school for first semester. Mr. Nellis uses this checklist to track assessment activities. He has also made a notation of each item in his day planner.

Figure 8.1

assessment plan. He had made his timeline into a checklist so that he could track tasks completed. Finally, he transferred each task to his day planner.

PURPOSES OF THIS CHAPTER

Explain the Eclectic Approach to Observing Development

Eclectic: Selecting what appears to be the best from several different methods. The eclectic approach is a practical, well-rounded, effective approach that teachers can use both in guiding children (Marion, 2003) and in observing their development. In this approach, a teacher chooses one or more observation strategies most likely to give the most helpful information about a child's development. Our goal is to uncover each child's strengths and abilities, and to do this teachers really do have to get the best information, which comes from multiple sources.

Describe, Explain, and Give Examples of Different Categories of Observation and Assessment Strategies

Teachers interested in responsible observation and assessment strive to choose the most effective and developmentally appropriate tool for getting the information they seek. When planning for assessment, they look to the different categories of assessment strategies. Tools from different categories stress different things and elicit different information. This chapter describes the three major categories of assessment strategies, some of them formal and many informal.

Reiterate Major Reasons for Observing Children's Development

The main goal in observing children's development is to discover their strengths and abilities and to build on those abilities. This enables teachers to begin from a position of strength. Along with that, teachers throughout this text have also observed child development to assess children's needs and interests. They have used the information to plan for that child, to build on the child's strengths.

CATEGORIES OF OBSERVATION AND ASSESSMENT STRATEGIES

This chapter describes three main categories of observation/assessment tools:

- *Standardized assessment instruments* (see NAEYC's position statement with cautions about using standardized testing with young children). These tend to be formal assessment instruments. (See NAEYC's Web site at the end of this chapter.)
- *Teacher-made assessment instruments*. These tend to be informal assessment strategies.
- *Ready-made assessment instruments*. These also tend to be informal assessment strategies.

Teachers can assess any area of development with these categories of instruments. This chapter explains how to use the eclectic approach to assess gross or large motor development and cognitive development as the focus. Chapter 9 uses the eclectic approach to describe observing social and emotional development.

Whatever method chosen, our main goal is to first understand and then to practice responsible assessment (NAEYC, Revised Guidelines for Preparing Early Childhood Professionals, 2001; the NAEYC Web site has the full text: www.naeyc.org).

STANDARDIZED ASSESSMENT INSTRUMENTS

There are many issues swirling around the use of standardized tests with young children (Bracken, 2000; Kelley & Surbeck, 2000; Nagel, 2000). Teachers face decisions about whether they will use standardized tests or, as in Mr. Nellis's situation in the case study, how such standardized tests will fit into their overall assessment plan. Mr. Nellis and his colleagues did not choose the standardized test, but they had to figure out how to deal with the test in their assessment plan. They wanted to do a more authentic assessment than the standardized test allowed. Reflective teachers can make wiser decisions when they understand many types of assessment tools, including even those like standardized tests that early childhood professionals generally resist using.[1]

Description and Purpose: Standardized Tests

Several specific formal, standardized test batteries for assessing motor development exist (Williams & Abernathy, 2000). In terms of motor development, the developers of such tests wanted to determine the *norms*, the typical or average age when most children would perform a skill such as hopping or running. To get this type of information, test developers administered their tests to large groups of children from specific age ranges. From this, they developed the norms of motor development to which their tests refer.

Standardized tests yield quantitative data as numbers. In fact, the goal in using a standardized test is to describe a child's performance on these tests numerically—for example, with a percentile or a standard score. Here is how it works:

- A child takes a standardized test, for example, of motor performance.
- The person administering the test obtains this child's raw score on the test.
- Then the adult compares the child's raw score to a standard score or percentile on this test.
- This tells the adult about the child's mastery of skills. If the standardized test focuses on large motor development, then the scores would refer to skills such as

---

[1]NAEYC's position statement on standardized testing is admirable. Consider getting the statement from the Web site listed at the end of the chapter.

running, hopping, or skipping and how this child compares to other children of the same age.

The real purpose of standardized tests is to compare the child taking the test to other children of the same age statistically (Williams & Abernathy, 2000). Thus, a standardized test is called a norm-referenced test.

Problems with Standardized Tests

There has been quite a bit of debate about whether to use standardized tests with preschool children (Kelley & Surbeck, 2000; Nagel, 2000). The NAEYC has issued guidelines for the preparation of early childhood teachers, and one of the guidelines states that teachers should be able to observe, document, and assess appropriately (Hyson, 2002; NAEYC Web site). NAEYC has also issued position statements about standardized testing (NAEYC Web site, http://www.NAEYC.org. Click on NAEYC Resources. Then click on Position Statements. Then click on Improving Program Practices with Children. Then, open the article "Standardized Testing of Young Children 3 Through 8 Years."

Many early childhood professionals think that standardized tests are not an appropriate way to assess a young child's development or progress (see chapter 1 for a discussion). They prefer developmentally appropriate, authentic assessment strategies over standardized, norm-referenced tests for young children. They prefer direct observation, curriculum based assessment, play-based assessment, and interviews with children and parents (Bagnato & Neisworth, 1991, 1994; Nagel, 2000).

In addition, they caution that norms derived from one group or *population* of children might not really be applicable to groups of children from different populations. It seems unfair to compare a child's score to the norms if researchers obtained the norm from a group of children vastly different from the child taking the test. Teachers would probably not get the most accurate information about a child in this case.

If a person wanted to use a standardized test of motor development, it would be much more helpful to get information from a test whose norms were set from a group of children similar to the children taking the test. Even then, critics of standardized tests see little merit in these tests. For example, Williams and Abernathy (2000) ask what it means when a child has a score above or below the 50th percentile on a standardized test. They note that even experts are not clear about the meaning of such a score.

TEACHER-MADE AND READY-MADE OBSERVATION AND ASSESSMENT TOOLS

These two categories of tools do not try to describe a child's performance statistically. They do, however, in terms of motor skills for example, tell a teacher whether a child can run, hop, or jump and *how* the child carries out these motor skills: that is, does the child run gracefully? Is the child agile as she climbs on the climbing structure?

Teacher-made and ready-made tools can help teachers uncover a child's cognitive strengths (Krechevsky, 1998). They can also tell a teacher whether the child has a developmental lag, although that is not always their purpose. The teacher generally ends up verbally describing a specific child's performance.

Careful observation is essential if schools decide to use any standardized tests with young children. Therefore, in addition to the standardized test for large motor development, the early childhood teachers at Oaklawn (Nellis, Claiborne, Vargas, and Lee) are using other tools for observing this domain. Their observations have always been effective for them and now can be used to support or contradict standardized test findings if necessary (Bracken, 2000).

Ready-Made Assessment Instruments

Ready-made instruments are similar to teacher-made instruments because they include checklists, rating scales, and anecdotal and running records. These two categories are also different from one another because teachers simply purchase or copy the ready-made instruments. Teachers attend workshops to understand how to administer some of these instruments, but need very little training to use others. Existing tools tend to vary in quality, ease of use, affordability, and accessibility (Facts in Action, 2002).

Teacher-Made Observation Instruments

These informal, straightforward methods supply good information that helps identify children's strengths. They are flexible because teachers can use them to observe any area of development: that is, a teacher develops a different checklist for observing each area of development—motor, emotional, social, or cognitive.

A teacher can readily combine two specific teacher-made instruments, such as a checklist and a rating scale, to gather even more powerful information than either tool alone. Finally, teachers use teacher-made checklists or rating scales in the natural setting of a classroom or playground, as children go about their day (Sanders, 2002). This makes assessment seem like a natural part of the day to teachers; it does not feel artificial to teachers and does not produce stress for children.

Example: Mr. Claiborne used his own anecdotal record forms (Figure 8.3) to observe motor development of specific children—for example, to observe Dean, one of his first graders. Mr. Claiborne wanted to get better information than that supplied by the standardized test.

Example: Mr. Nellis used anecdotal records to observe how his students were progressing in the ability to do a conservation task.

OBSERVING AND ASSESSING MOTOR DEVELOPMENT

Definitions

Motor development: occurs when a child gradually gains control of and uses the large and small muscle masses of her body.

Large (or gross) muscle development: gradual control and use of muscles enabling a child to engage in body movements like running, jumping, hopping, and throwing or catching a ball. Large muscles of the body also help children maintain posture (Williams & Abernathy, 2000).

Small (or fine) muscle development: gradual control and use of muscles for picking up and manipulating objects like puzzle pieces, items on a busy board, pencils, or chalk.

Neuromuscular coordination: the intertwined nature of brain development (neurological development) and motor development. Children who have good coordinated movement can explore, try things out, and move, thus advancing their brain development and perception even further (Sporns & Edelman, 1993; Williams & Abernathy, 2000).

Different Children, Different Levels of Motor Development

Children will enter your classes with varied backgrounds and different levels of motor skills. They will also differ in their enjoyment of movement and even in their willingness to try different movements. Observing and assessing motor development is not trivial. Some of the children you teach will be extremely agile and athletic, others less so, and some might even be clumsy (American Psychiatric Association, 1993). Some children will have identified motor problems or disabilities.

Families of some children encourage active play such as taking hikes, riding bicycles, skating, running, or playing ball; activities that build motor skills. Some children are lucky enough to have people teach them specific skills, such as how to catch a ball most effectively or how to get a good start in a race. An activity-rich lifestyle helps children develop good motor skills.

Other families allow hours of television watching or computer play and do not model or encourage active play, thus effectively blocking muscle-building activity. Some parents abuse their children, affecting their children's willingness and ability to play. Other families neglect their children's basic need for enough nutritious food, thus causing catastrophic effects on a child's body.

Observing the Basics About Large Motor Development

Here is the most basic question about a child's large motor development: Can this child climb, run, jump, hop, throw a ball, and catch a ball? Observing to answer this question assesses whether children have basic motor skills. Teachers surely need to assess whether children can indeed perform basic large motor skills because children do acquire the basic collection of manipulative (small muscle) and large-muscle skills during early childhood.

There is a second basic question about large motor development: How does this child perform each of the large motor skills? Observing to answer this question assesses how the child moves. At the most basic level, we need to assess *how* a child runs, throws, or balances. That will tell us whether she runs gracefully or stiffly, whether she catches a ball in a fluid movement or clumsily.

Some families encourage active play, which helps children develop good motor skills.

These first questions are necessary, but offer a somewhat limited perspective for assessing large motor development if they are the only questions that a teacher asks. Often, we need to go beyond observing the basics.

Going Beyond the Basics in Assessing Large Motor Development

Here are some additional questions to ask about a child's large motor development.

- What are this child's strengths in terms of creative movement: Does she have good body control? Can she call forth moods through movement? How rhythmically does she move? Can she come up with ideas for moving? How responsive to music is she? (Krechevsky, 1998)
- What is this child's attitude about large motor activities?
- Does this child show exceptionally good performance in large motor skills?
- Does this child seem to have a developmental lag in large motor skills?

As this list of questions implies, teachers can answer many different questions through observation, questions that go well beyond merely asking whether the child can run or climb. For instance, you could discover that a child is quite good at coming up with or generating great ideas for how to move—as if you were in a cloud, like a rabbit, like a flower just opening.

A child who generates such ideas about movement actually shows good cognitive and creative abilities that show up in relationship to movement (Krechevsky, 1998). Katz (1997) urges teachers to assess a child's dispositions or attitudes, which includes a child's feelings about large motor activities.

Example: Mrs. Vargas had observed that Ralph seemed to enjoy motor activities. She also observed that he was excellent in how he controlled his body. She wrote (anecdotal record), "When I gave the signal to freeze, Ralph stopped quickly and controlled his movements completely."

Example: Mrs. Vargas also observed that Ralph came up with many new ways to move; that is, he was strong in generating movement ideas. She wrote, "When we were thinking of different ways to move from one side of the room to the other, Ralph suggested moving like a robot whose parts needed to be oiled." She has noticed throughout the year that Ralph generates good and creative solutions to many problems.

Identify Developmental Lags in Motor Skills

Teachers might well need to identify developmental lags in a child's motor skills so that they can intervene appropriately (Nagel, 2000). Children who have lags in motor development are more likely than other children the same age to have trouble adapting to play and school. For example, children often exclude from playing games or joining sports teams those children who have difficulty throwing a ball or running. Such children then miss valuable opportunities for personal growth and social interaction (Williams & Abernathy, 2000).

An Example of a Standardized Test for Assessing Motor Development: Cratty's Perceptual-Motor Behaviors Checklist

This is a standardized, norm-referenced test of motor skills (Cratty, 1970, 1986). It is a simple checklist testing a child's ability to perform specific motor (and perceptual) tasks. (Figure 8.2 shows a portion of Cratty's Checklist.) It seems to be useful in identifying children who have not yet mastered specific large motor skills for their age group and who probably need help in acquiring those motor skills.

Seventy to 80 percent of children in the age ranges shown can usually perform the tasks described. Cratty's test was first administered to middle-class Caucasian children. Thus, the motor performance of middle-class Caucasian children established the norms (Williams & Abernathy, 2000). Cratty's test also provides a developmental sequence for large motor skills.

Teacher-Made Observation Instruments for Assessing Motor Development

These are informal tools created by the teacher and include checklists, rating scales, and anecdotal or running records (or other types of instruments). This is a favored method for assessing children's development; teachers tend to like using these

---

2–3 Years
Can walk rhythmically at an even pace
Can step off low object, one foot ahead of the other
Can walk a 2-in.-wide line 10 ft long placed on ground

4–4$\frac{1}{2}$ Years
Can do a forward broad jump, both feet together, and can clear ground at same time.
Can hop 2 or 3 times on one foot without precision or rhythm
Walks and runs with arm action coordinated with leg action
Can walk a circular line a short distance

5–5$\frac{1}{2}$ Years
Runs 30 yd in just over 8 sec
Balances on one foot; girls 6–8 sec; boys 4–6 sec
Catches large playground ball bounced to him or her chest-high from 15 ft, 4 to 5 out of 5 times
Can high-jump 8 in. or more over bar with simultaneous two-foot takeoff
Bounces playground ball using one or two hands a distance of 3–4 ft

6–6$\frac{1}{2}$ Years
Can gallop if it is demonstrated
Can exert 6 lbs or more of pressure in grip strength measures
Can walk a balance beam 2 in. wide, 6 in. high, and 10–12 ft long
Can run 50 ft in about 5 sec
Can arise from ground from backlying position in 2 sec or less

---

Figure 8.2
Examples of Large/Gross Motor Skill Items from the Cratty Perceptual-Motor Behaviors Checklist as Described by Williams and Abernathy (2000)

Sources: Cratty (1970, 1986). *Perceptual and Motor Development in Infants and Young Children;* Williams and Abernathy (2000).
The tasks described above are usually performed by 70–80% of children of ages indicated. This checklist's data was obtained from Caucasian, middle-class children. A child who has not mastered two-thirds of the tasks for the age needs further evaluation (Williams & Abernathy, 2000).

informal strategies because they are easy to develop and to use. The focus teachers in this text rely heavily on teacher-observation instruments to observe both motor and cognitive development.

Example: Dean, 6 years old, transferred to Oaklawn and Mr. Claiborne's first-grade class 3 days before taking the standardized test for motor development. Dean's score showed that he was not doing as well as other children his age taking this test—that his large motor skills were not very good. This bothered Mr. Claiborne, who had observed Dean on the playground for 3 days and knew that Dean had better motor skills than the test indicated.

Anecdotal Record

Goal for this observation: large motor skills
Setting: Playground   **Date/day:** Tuesday, Nov.   **Time of day:** after lunch
Basic activity: variety of playground activities
Focus child: Dean   **Others involved:** several other children

The Anecdote: Dean zoomed over to the main climbing structure, Pae racing with him. Dean grabbed onto the bar and pulled himself up smoothly, gracefully, and quickly. He climbed all over the structure, going over bars, sliding under bars, and hanging on others. He and Pae climbed together, laughing when they did something new like sliding under a bar to grab onto another.

Dean stuck out his leg, pointed his toe and leg in an exaggerated way, and then swung his leg up and over a bar. "Hey, Pae," he said, "I'm in the Olympics!" Pae imitated Dean. "I'm in the Olympics, too!"

The boys got off the climbing structure and ran to the balance beam. Pae walked across easily. Dean started out smoothly but faltered in his balance. Pae responded, "Get back on the beam, Dean." Then Pae said, "Put your hands out like this and then you can balance, OK?" Dean followed this suggestion and his balance improved. The boys then looked at each other and wiggled their eyebrows, which seems to be a funny signal of friendship that these two share.

Reflection/Comment/Interpretation: Dean seems to be agile and strong. He runs smoothly and quickly. He had a little problem with balance, but did not seem unduly upset by this. He seemed perfectly willing to take some advice from a friend, and that seemed to please Pae. Dean seems willing to practice skills in which he is not yet proficient (balance).

Figure 8.3

The teacher observed Dean's motor development, using other more informal assessment strategies to supplement information from the standardized test. For example, Mr. Claiborne also wrote several anecdotal records (teacher-made observation tools) about Dean's motor skills (Figure 8.3).

In addition, he used existing observation tools (ready-made) to get a more authentic picture of Dean's large motor development. These included the Williams's Motor Development Checklist and Project Spectrum's ready-made instruments. He asked a colleague, Mrs. Vargas, to observe as Dean went through the Obstacle Course (Krechevsky, 1998) because Mr. Claiborne wanted another teacher's input.

A Ready-Made Informal Observation Instrument for Assessing Motor Development: Williams's Preschool Motor Development Checklist

The Williams's Checklist (Williams, 1995) is a ready-made observation instrument, a checklist focusing on six gross motor skills in children 3 to 6 years old. Thus, this ready-made test is used with some but not all children during the early childhood years. The Williams's checklist assesses four locomotor skills; running, jumping, skipping, and hopping, and assesses two ball-handling skills; throwing and catching.

It is useful in assessing the *way* a child performs each of the skills, that is, the quality of the child's performance in running, jumping, and so forth. It is also useful in identifying developmental lags in motor development.

The Williams's Checklist is written in question format: "Does the child experience difficulty in starting, stopping, or making sudden turns?" Teachers answer *yes* or *no* to each question. Figure 8.4 shows how a teacher interprets the checklist results.

This is the ready-made instrument, a checklist, that Mr. Nellis and the other teachers had been using to assess large motor skills for many of their students. They have found the nicely detailed information from this checklist to be helpful in a number of ways (Williams & Abernathy, 2000).

It Can Be Used to Help Children Reach Even Higher Levels of Mastery in Motor Development.

Example: Mr. Nellis found that Andy had no lags in motor development. He planned a few enrichment activities for this child so skilled in motor development—sprinting through the obstacle course and running to a target, hitting it, and turning to run back to the starting point. See Figure 8.4.

Observe large motor development in regular classroom and playground activities.

Directions: Carefully observe the child perform each skill several times in different settings. Ask the following questions about the way the young child performs each motor skill. Try to answer *Yes* or *No* to each question.

Child's Name: Andy (Kindergarten)

Skill: Running

1. Does the child experience difficulty in starting, stopping, or making sudden turns?
   Yes (No)
2. Does the child run using a flatfoot; that is, does he or she receive the body weight on the whole foot?
   Yes (No)
3. Does the child run with toes pointed outward?
   Yes (No)
4. Do the arms move back and forth in a sideways motion across the body?
   Yes (No)

Interpretation: Running

If three of the four questions are answered yes, there might be a developmental lag in running. (*No developmental lag in running for Andy*)

Skill: Catching

1. Does the child attempt to catch the ball with arms outstretched and straight?
   Yes (No)
2. Does the child use the arms, hands, and body as a single unit to trap the ball?
   Yes (No)
3. Does the child turn his or her head away from the ball as he or she catches it?
   Yes (No)
4. Does the child seem to let the ball bounce off the outstretched arms?
   Yes (No)
5. Does the child only catch balls bounced from close distances (5 ft or less)?
   Yes (No)
6. Does the child fail to watch or track the flight of the ball?
   Yes (No)

Interpretation: Catching

If the child is 3 years old, and the answer to questions 2, 3, 4, and 5 is yes, keep a watchful eye on this aspect of motor development. If the child is 5 years old, and the answer to any question is yes, there may be a developmental lag in catching. (*No developmental lag in catching for Andy*)

Figure 8.4

Example from the Williams's Preschool Motor Development Checklist

Source: Williams's Preschool Motor Development Checklist, by H. Williams, 1995. The Perceptual-Motor Development Laboratory Protocols, University of South Carolina-Columbia. Used and adapted with permission.

Use the Williams's Checklist When Deciding on Referring a Child for Additional Professional Help.

Example: Mr. Nellis had answered *Yes* to every question about running on the Williams's Checklist for one kindergarten boy, meaning that the child probably had a developmental lag in running. The teacher put this information together with that from some teacher-made anecdotal records and decided to consult with the principal and the child's parents about getting this child some help from a specialist.

Use in Modifying Tasks So That a Child Can Be Successful.

Example: The teacher had answered *Yes* to only one question about catching for Janet, a first-grade girl, failing to watch or track the flight of the ball. Mr. Nellis decided to help her with the one difficulty in catching a ball. He modified the task by using a larger ball and showed her how to watch the ball while waiting to catch it.

Can Be Used to Clarify or Extend a Teacher's Own Observations.

Example: Mr. Nellis had noticed a kindergarten boy's problem with running during the first week of school. Consequently, he wrote several anecdotal records. The Williams's Checklist validated and strengthened his original observations. He used the results of both observation instruments when he talked with the child's parents and with the principal.

A Ready-Made Observation Instrument: Project Spectrum

Project Spectrum (Krechevsky, 1998) is a unique approach to assessing children's development and progress. It provides existing or ready-made instruments for assessing development. Project Spectrum was a joint research and curriculum development project between Harvard and Tufts Universities. One of the main goals of the first phase of this 9-year-long project was to develop a new method of assessing the cognitive strengths of young children. The project resulted in three volumes, the third of which describes Spectrum's set of assessment instruments. See the Harvard Web site listed in "Web Sites Related to This Chapter."

Project Spectrum is a ready-made assessment system examining seven areas of knowledge: movement (creative movement and athletic ability), language, mathematics, science, social, visual arts, music, and working styles. Flexibility is the key, with developers urging teachers to use as much of Project Spectrum's assessment and activities as they wish. Developers realize that some teachers will want to use the Spectrum assessment strategies as a whole unit, but that others might want to start by using only part of Project Spectrum's assessment strategy.

Example: Mr. Nellis and his colleagues (chapter opening case study) have decided to use Project Spectrum to assess only the movement domain. Specifically, they chose to use one part of the movement assessment section, the Obstacle Course, which assesses four large or gross motor skills. They are particularly interested in Spectrum's approach and want to compare the results from Spectrum's assessment with the standardized test of motor development that the district now requires.

Most of the teachers in this group, Mr. Nellis included, decided not to adopt the "Creative Movement Curriculum" part of the movement domain assessment, although Mr. Vargas had used it informally for a couple of years. They are starting to use this program gradually and have chosen to use only one small section this year. They plan to use selected other sections in subsequent years.

Project Spectrum's Obstacle Course.   Project Spectrum uses the Obstacle Course to assess a limited number of motor skills—power, agility, speed, and balance. Figure 8.5 shows the obstacle course as a series of stations, each meant to assess one or more of these four targeted gross motor skills. Teachers demonstrate the skill at each station. The obstacle course can be set up in the classroom or on the playground. A teacher can observe a child at each station on the entire course or can set up discrete sections of the course. Project Spectrum developers encourage teachers to reformat the scoring sheet if they emphasize specific skills such as agility or balance rather than all the stations.

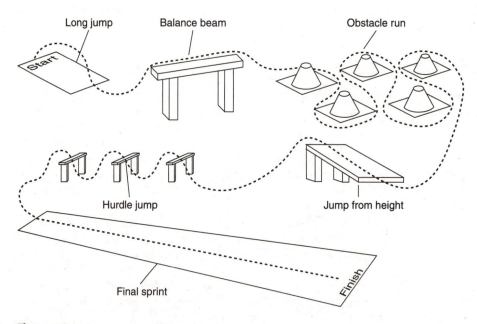

Figure 8.5
Obstacle Course from Project Spectrum

Source: Used by permission of the publisher from Krechevsky, M. *Project Spectrum: Preschool Assessment Handbook* (p. 25). New York: Teachers College Press. Copyright © 1998 by Teachers College, Columbia University. All rights reserved.

CHILD'S NAME: Andy
Station 2/Balance Beam
1 =   has difficulty maintaining balance; frequently slips or steps off beam; needs to hold adult's hand; seems hesitant and tentative; may only shuffle feet; body tends to be rigid
(2 =)   has some trouble balancing; approach is tentative, but uses strategies to regain balance; *may step off beam to prevent falling;* wobbles; alternates or shuffles feet, or both
3 =   moves forward while maintaining balance; walks straight across without hesitating; looks ahead; alternates feet; body is relatively relaxed

Station 3/Obstacle Run
1 =   hesitates before running around obstacles; is not able to maneuver close to obstacle or touches and knocks obstacles over, or both; poor control of limbs; change of direction is awkward and slow
2 =   runs at a moderate speed around obstacles with some hesitation; tries to stay close to obstacles, but may touch or knock them over; some lack of control of limbs
(3 =)   runs quickly around obstacles without hesitation; stays close to obstacles without touching them or knocking them over; keeps limbs close to body; makes quick and accurate shifts in body position and direction of movement

---

Figure 8.6
Project Spectrum's Obstacle Course: Example of Scoring Criteria*

Source: From M. Krechevsky (1998). *Project Spectrum: Preschool Assessment Handbook.* New York: Teachers College Press. Copyright © 1998 by the President and Fellows of Harvard College. Adapted with permission.

*Teachers advised to model the skill at each station before observing children.
See Krechevsky, 1998, pp. 31–33, for entire set of scoring criteria

A teacher begins scoring a child's performance on the obstacle course by reading the criteria for scoring (Figure 8.6). There are three skill levels given for each item. The teacher observes as a child goes through the Obstacle Course and uses a separate sheet for scoring each child. The teacher rates each child's skill level as Level 1, Level 2, or Level 3 for each station in the Obstacle Course and can also make written comments.

Example: Mr. Nellis completed the Obstacle Course Observation Sheet for each child, and Figure 8.7 shows how he assessed Andy's performance.

Teachers are encouraged to observe other outdoor play, noting skills children show and rating them on the skills using same criteria as above, and using the same levels—Levels 1, 2, and 3. The Obstacle Course incorporates assessment in daily life

Child: Andy
Age: Kindergarten: 5 years 5 months
Date: Sept. 18
Observer: Sean Nellis (K–2 teacher, Oaklawn School)

1. Long jump	Power	____3_____	
2. Balance beam	Balance	____2_____	Stepped off beam to keep from falling
3. Obstacle run	Agility	____3*____	Nimble and quick; graceful
4. Jump from height	Balance	____3_____	
5. Hurdle jump	Power/ Agility	____3_____	
6. Final sprint	Speed	____3*_____	Very fast

General Notes: This observation backs up information about Andy's motor skills from other sources. He is one of the fastest, most nimble/agile children in the class, including all of the first and second graders.

Figure 8.7
Project Spectrum Obstacle Course Observation Sheet

*Demonstrates exceptional ability
Source: From M. Krechevsky (1998). *Project Spectrum: Preschool Assessment Handbook,* New York: Teachers College Press. Copyright © 1998 by the President and Fellows of Harvard College. Adapted with permission.

and curriculum of the classroom. Teachers are encouraged to reconfigure the Obstacle Course throughout the year to give children opportunities to demonstrate motor skills in a variety of settings.

Example: In April, Mr. Nellis (K–2) and Mr. Claiborne (first grade), set up the Obstacle Course outside. They put the stations in a different order than had been used inside. They also each observed the children in their classes on the playground's regular climbing structure to rate the child's strength (when doing pulling up) and agility (when they moved around the structure).

Authentic Assessment of Motor Skill

Authentic assessment involves multiple points of assessment—different types of observation done in real-world, everyday play-based settings. This yields the most helpful information to teachers. Mr. Claiborne, from earlier sections and examples, steadfastly refused to rely on only the standardized test score of large motor development for one of his students. He insisted on using other observational methods and got a much better picture of that child's motor development. He used both existing and teacher-made tools to arrive at his conclusion.

He used the Williams's Checklist, anecdotal records, and Project Spectrum's Obstacle Course. Using all of these informal sources of information, Mr. Claiborne analyzed Dean's skills as being very good, quite a different picture from that given by the standardized test.

He wrote a report, attaching the original anecdotal records, the Williams's Checklist, and the score sheet from the Obstacle Course (completed by a person who knew nothing about the standardized score). He met with Mrs. LeBlanc, the principal, and presented the other data. The principal agreed that the standardized score might not have given the whole picture and that the other observation instruments gave a much better picture of this first grader's large motor scores.

Williams and Abernathy (2000) offer practical suggestions for making observations most useful. Their recommendations are in keeping with the early childhood profession's preference for authentic assessment. Figure 8.8 lists the suggestions.

Wise Use of Observations in Action

In January, the early childhood teachers (Nellis, Lee, Vargas, and Claiborne) from the Oaklawn School met to evaluate the assessment plan. Specifically, they voted to continue using the Project Spectrum Obstacle Course, the anecdotal records, and the Williams's Checklist. Mr. Lee, who teaches the oldest early childhood children in the school, does not use the Williams's Checklist because it is designed for assessing motor skills of younger early childhood children. Mr. Nellis does not use it with his second graders.

They were particularly concerned about the standardized test administered in November. Mr. Claiborne wanted to describe the problem that had arisen with Dean's

---

Williams and Abernathy (2000) offer practical suggestions for making observations and assessment of motor development most useful.

- *Observe:* Observe children in naturalistic play settings.
- *Screen:* Screen all children in gross motor development.
- *Screen:* Screen all children in fine motor control (e.g., manipulating pegs, cutting, using markers or pencils). Screen all children for simple perceptual skills (e.g., color matching, visual, verbal, and tactile discrimination of shapes and sizes.
- *Reflect:* Reflect on both sets of information.
- *Choose activities:* If the child has only gross motor problems (and no other sensory or motor problems), then choose activities to help the child develop the missing skill.
- *Refer:* If the child has both gross motor problems and other sensory or perceptual problems, then discuss the issue with parents and principal or director and together consider referring the child to an appropriately trained professional for additional observation.

Figure 8.8
Practical Suggestions: Responsible Use of Information from Observations of Motor Development

score and so obtained written permission from Dean's parents to discuss the incident with Dean's score with the other early childhood faculty. This incident encouraged the teachers to request a reevaluation of how their school would use that standardized test score.

They requested a meeting with their principal, who respected and supported her faculty. Before the meeting, everyone reread NAEYC's 1987 Position Statement on Standardized Testing of Young Children 3 Through 8 Years of Age. The teachers also made a brief PowerPoint presentation of the major points from NAEYC's 1996 Position Statement "Guidelines for Decisions About Developmentally Appropriate Practice," highlighting the section on "Assessing Children's Learning and Development."

The school district would continue to require the standardized test. However, the Oaklawn group worked out a plan so that Oaklawn would never use the standardized test score alone to make any decisions in their school. They also decided that they would never give out numbers from standardized tests. This group decided to emphasize the teachers' ongoing, purposeful observations of the children in their classes.

They decided to summarize each child's strengths in large motor skills in the form of a narrative and to share the summary with parents. They then used the information in planning the movement curriculum. The score from the standardized test would never appear. Neither would they share any score from the Project Spectrum assessment. They reasoned that the written narrative would be much more helpful than a number. Figure 8.9 is Mr. Claiborne's statement about Dean's motor development.

Large Motor Development: Summary Statement[1]

Child's Name: Dean
Date: January, 2003

   "Dean really seems to enjoy school, whether it's the computers or outdoor play. In the short time that he has been with us, I have noticed how strong he is and how much he loves to run and climb. He has very good motor skills; in fact, he is quite a speedy and agile fellow when he runs and he throws and catches a ball with ease.

   "He tries all activities, showing no hesitation. He likes to practice, too! He is working on balancing with more ease and walks the balance beam almost every day. We are planning additional activities focusing on balance for him and the other children.

   "Dean gets along with other children very well, and this is especially noteworthy during large motor activities. His fun-loving approach to activities attracts other children to him, which seems to only increase his willingness to try everything and to become ever more skillful."

[1]Dean's teacher was able to write this summary statement because he had observed Dean several times in real-life situations. His observations have given him much more information that he would have obtained from the standardized test of motor skills alone.

Figure 8.9

Notice how the teacher emphasizes Dean's strengths. Even when describing areas in which Dean needs help, Mr. Claiborne has been positive.

OBSERVING COGNITIVE DEVELOPMENT

There is a strong link between a child's cognitive and social development. Teachers are most effective with children when they consider how a specific child thinks, whether he can understand what the adult says, whether he can take somebody else's perspective, and whether he can even remember what another person said.

The teachers at Oaklawn use informal, teacher-made observation instruments to observe and assess specific areas of cognitive development. They want to document children's strengths while acknowledging the limitations on thinking during early childhood. They use the information for help in instruction and curriculum decisions, to determine progress on developmental achievements, and for help in developing guidance plans for the children in their classes (Katz, 1997; Marion, 2003).

This section of the chapter, like the section on large motor development, briefly describes selected aspects of cognitive development and explains how to use informal teacher-made instruments to observe and assess these parts of the cognitive domain. The emphasis is on ages 2 to 6 in Piaget's framework (Piaget, 1968).

Major Cognitive Ability: 2- to 6-Year-Olds Can Represent Experiences

Two- to 6-year-old children *can use symbols to represent* (*stand for*) their experiences through deferred imitation, with language, and by using a variety of art media or technology.

Deferred Imitation.   Young children learn from many different models and then often, but not always, imitate the model. They learn from real people in everyday life, real people on any type of screen (movie, video, computer), models in audio recordings or on computers, and reading material such as books, pamphlets, or even billboards. Children observe events, form and hold a visual image of the event, and then often defer, or put off, imitating the action until some later date.

Example: Six-year-old Dean, in Mr. Claiborne's first-grade class, watched as Pae dropped the container of snap-together blocks, spilling blocks on the table, chairs, and floor. Dean helped his friend pick the blocks up. Dean's model was his father, who helped his mother pick up gardening equipment that she had dropped.

Language.   Children also represent experiences by talking about them. The major cognitive accomplishment of this stage is that children can use a symbol to stand for something else, and words are the symbols through which children represent experiences, both good and bad.

Examples: Dean used words to tell Mr. Claiborne that he and his family had moved to their new house. Ralph used words to tell Mrs. Vargas that his cat had been taken to the emergency veterinary hospital.

Use of Art Media or Technology.   Children also record their experiences through art media such as painting, drawing, or playdough. They use chalk, paint, playdough, markers, pencils, computers, and other media or technology to create an artistic expression that symbolizes, represents, or stands for an experience that they have had.

Example: The kindergarten children in Mr. Nellis's class recorded their experiences at the zoo by drawing pictures of their favorite zoo animal. Mr. Nellis helped them to scan their pictures into the computer and to narrate a story about each animal.

Limitations on Preoperational Thinking

Some of the funny and charming things that children say and do are a direct result of limitations on their thinking. Young children who are 2 to 6 years old tend to:

- View things from a somewhat egocentric perspective
- Judge things by how they look
- Focus on the before-and-after and ignore how things change (transformations)
- Have trouble reversing a process

Preoperational thinkers tend to be somewhat egocentric.

Observe a preschool child and you will quickly see some of these limitations.

Example:
Mrs. Vargas (adult):   "Nellie, Sara was using the marbles. You cannot take them from her."
Nellie: "I need the marbles."
Mrs. Vargas: "Yes, you do need some marbles, but Sara was working with these marbles. Tell me another way to get the marbles that you need."
Nellie: (looked puzzled) "You can take all the marbles and give them to me!"

The teacher has appropriately restated a limit. She also attempted to help Nellie do some problem solving, but Nellie's egocentricity has gotten in the way of her understanding the limit. Nellie's idea of solving the problem also reflects her inability to take Sara's perspective.

Preoperational Thinkers Have Difficulty with Perspective Taking.   *Perspective taking*: a cognitive developmental skill; the ability to understand how another person views a situation; takes several years to develop; first evident at the end of early childhood (Dixon & Soto, 1990). Selman (1980) described an orderly series of levels in perspective taking (Figure 8.10).

In the previous example, Nellie's ability to take Sara's perspective simply does not exist, largely because Nellie is somewhat egocentric. Egocentric thinkers center on themselves and what they want, but this is not the same thing as being selfish. A selfish person understands somebody else's perspective and chooses to ignore it, but an egocentric thinker like Nellie cannot take the other person's perspective. A preoperational thinker like Nellie believes that everyone, Sara and the teacher in this case, thinks the same way she does.

Age in Years	Level	Perspective-Taking Ability
2–6	Level 0	• Egocentric perspective • No distinction between own and another's perspective
6–8	Level 1	• Still not able to take another's perspective • Believes that another, if in the same situation, will respond just as the target child would respond
8–10	Level 2	• Can take another's perspective • Sees self as others do • Not everyone reaches this level
10–12	Level 3	• Can take another's perspective but in a more sophisticated way than at Level 2 • Now aware of recursive nature of different perspectives: "Mom thinks that I think she wants me to." • Not everyone reaches this level
Adolescence and Adulthood	Level 4	• Very sophisticated perspective-taking ability • Has conceptualized society's viewpoints on legal/moral issues • Not everyone reaches this level

Figure 8.10
Levels in Perspective Taking

Sources: Selman (1976; 1980). Figure from Marion (2003), p. 38. Adapted with permission.

A child has to get older before perspective taking can ever take place; that is, getting older is necessary to perspective taking. However, getting older is, by itself, not a sufficient condition, that is, it is not enough by itself, for getting better at taking another's perspective. Some people never go beyond Levels 0 or 1. They never learn to take the perspective of others and have a great deal of trouble in their lives because they are so deficient in perspective taking. For example, many, but not all, abusive parents cannot take their child's perspective.

Preoperational Thinkers Focus on the Before and After, Ignoring How Things Change.
Preoperational thinkers ignore the process through which something is transformed or changed. Do the classic conservation experiment to get a sense of how children focus on the before and after but not how things change. Show the child two short glasses of the same size with the same volume of water in each. Then, *as the child watches you,* pour water from one of the glasses into a taller, thinner glass. A preoperational thinker focuses first on water in the two short glasses (the *before* state). Then he focuses on

water in one short glass and one tall glass (the *after* state). He tends to ignore the pouring of the water from the short glass to the tall glass (the transformation). An older child, adolescent, or adult, aware of the pouring, would explain things by saying, "All you did was pour water from one container to another."

This cognitive limitation affects how young children operate in their social world, as the following example shows. Mrs. Vargas, the preschool teacher, used a teacher-made anecdotal record to document 4-year-old Jordan's inability to **conserve**, or see the equivalence in two sets of items in spite of apparent change (Figure 8.11).

Preoperational Thinkers Tend to Judge Things by How They Look.   In any conservation experiment, such as the pouring of the water, preoperational thinkers typically assert that the tall container has more water in it "because it looks like it has more." Similarly, Jordan asserted that Chelsea had more fries because her line of fries simply looked like more. Appearances tend to deceive preschool children because they tend to judge something by how it appears on the surface.

Preoperational Thinkers Have Difficulty Reversing a Process.   Preoperational thinkers focus on one thing at a time, either the *before* or the *after* in any action. An older child, who can think about a couple of things at once, is not deceived by how things look. Adults and older children realize that they could quickly show that the volume of liquid in the tall glass is equivalent to that in the short glass. They would simply pour the contents of the tall glass back into the short glass—they can reverse the process. Young children, however, would not think so logically.

Anecdotal Record

Goal for this observation: cognition/conservation
Setting: lunch table   **Date/day:** Tuesday, Sept. 12   **Time of day:** lunch
Basic activity: serving/eating lunch
Focus child: Jordan   **Others involved:** Chelsea, Ralph, Justine, and I

The Anecdote: I placed a small pile of eight french fries (I counted them out for each child as a part of a math lesson) on each child's plate. They counted with me. We chanted, "Jordan has eight fries, Chelsea has eight fries . . . ," and so on. Then, Chelsea lined up her fries end-to-end, creating a long line on her place mat. Jordan had watched as she had lined up the fries. Jordan said, "Mrs. Vargas, you gave Chelsea more french fries than you gave to me. I need more."

Reflection/Comment/Interpretation: Chelsea transformed her pile of eight fries into a line, creating the illusion of many more fries. Jordon demonstrated that he does not understand conservation when he ignored the process of lining up or *transforming* the pile into the line of fries. He focused on the before (the pile) and the after (the line), but ignored the transformation.

Figure 8.11

Concrete Operational Stage: Major Changes in Cognition

Children in this stage of cognitive development are usually between the ages of about 6 and 11 and in primary (first, second, third grade) or elementary school (grades four, five, six). Some of the cognitive skills of the concrete operational child include the ability to:

- Distinguish reality from appearances.
- More easily detect apparent changes. They pay attention consistently to both relevant dimensions (height and width) in the standard conservation task. A concrete operational thinker uses this information about dimensions to arrive at an understanding of conservation.
- Pay attention to how things change—transformations—even in standard conservation experiments.

These are changes representative of a qualitative shift in the type of thinking that a child this age can do. A primary or elementary school child shows evidence of the further development of skills that emerged during the preschool years. Mr. Nellis decided to use an episode like the french fry incident to assess his first and second graders' ability to conserve. Figure 8.12 is a teacher-made anecdotal record that he used to document his observation of one of the second graders, Willis.

Anecdotal Record

Goal for this observation: cognition/conservation
Setting: lunch table   **Date/day:** Thursday, Sept. 14   **Time of day:** work period
Basic activity: different work centers
Focus child: Willis   **Others involved:** me (the teacher)

The Anecdote: I placed two small piles of poker chips on the table. Willis counted them out with me and we agreed that the piles had the same number of poker chips. Then, I lined up one of the piles of poker chips end-to-end on the table. Willis had watched as I lined up the chips from the one pile. "Willis," I said, "Are the pile and the line of chips the same, or does one have more chips?" Willis turned to me and just stared for about 5 seconds. Then he spoke: "They're exactly the same, Mr. Nellis. All you did was put one pile in a line and you can just put the line back into a pile to show that they're the same. Besides, you can count them. I watched you move the chips and you didn't add any to the line. So, they're the same."

Reflection/Comment/Interpretation: Willis has made the move to Piaget's third stage. Willis is a concrete operational thinker and demonstrated his ability to conserve in this observation. He even seemed a little exasperated by the process because it appeared so simple to him. He was not deceived by the transformation. He took the length of the line of chips and the volume of the pile of chips into account in his reasoning.

Figure 8.12

MEMORY

A child's memory affects his interactions in so many ways that it is a good idea to assess this part of a child's cognition (Marion, 2003).

Example: Mr. Nellis has been working with all of the children in his class on using words when they are angry, and he has seen some good progress toward that goal. Willis, whom you have just seen demonstrate the ability to conserve and thus his developing cognitive skills, seems to have understood the information. Willis, as you will discover in chapter 9, gets angry quite often but has recently demonstrated that he can use words when he is angry. Mr. Nellis was surprised and somewhat disappointed when Willis went right back to using his fists instead of his words when he was angry.

Some adults might see this behavior as defiant, but the teacher suspected that it was really Willis's memory development in action. During early childhood, children like Willis who have used aggression for a long time to get what they need or want have strong memories of the ineffective method. The dry facts of their aggressive interactions are stored in the hippocampus of the brain. Then, the emotional quality of each of those interactions is stored in a different part of the brain called the amygdala. These memories are so strong that they can easily override our good teaching. Knowing this about memory and then assessing this aspect of cognition will help us to help the child.

Definitions

- 📖 *Memory*: basic cognitive process by which we store information and then later retrieve it.
- 📖 *Long-term memory*: storage for the information that we perceive and then learn. We collect such information and then store it as a permanent record. Most of us can call up information from our long-term memory because we often have stored the memory as a strong sensory image of places and events, sometimes from years or even decades ago.
- 📖 *Short-term memory or working memory*: storage site for temporarily storing new information or well-known information to which we need access. A child's space for short-term memory increases with age, allowing him to work with and process more information for longer periods of time (Case, 1992).
- 📖 *Recognition memory*: the realization that we have seen or experienced some information that we now encounter (Shaffer, 1996). Ask a child, for example, to pick out pictures of her dog and the cat who lives next door from a small group of photos of cats and dogs. She probably will easily recognize her pet and the pet from next door.
- 📖 *Recall memory*: used when a person has to retrieve or call up some information. There are different types of recall memory, and these are important when we look at the memory capacity of infants and young children.
- 📖 *Cued recall memory*: memory prompted by a cue or reminder.

Example: Mr. Nellis made a list of the names of trees that the children have studied. He posted the list (the cue) at the children's level in the area where they worked on the tree project.

- **Pure recall memory**: a memory that does not require prompting with any cue or reminder. A child actively retrieves information from memory with no cues involved, as Willis did when he recited the names of all the children in his class.
- **Metamemory**: a person's overall knowledge about memory. Metamemory improves during childhood: Older children realize that they have different types of memory and know that they can use memory strategies, and they understand why memory strategies work. Willis, for example, said that it was

---

Checklist: Milestones in Memory Development in Early Childhood

Child's Name/Age: Willis (second grade/7 years old)
Date: October 8

Birth to approximately 5 months (birth to 5 months)
____ Recognizes familiar objects; *Habituates to*—becomes accustomed to or bored with—a stimulus, such as a toy put in front of him several times
____ Can recall a memory but must get a **cue or reminder**

5 months to 1 year (5 to 12 months)
____ Recognizes objects after seeing them only a few times
____ Remembers an object for several weeks
____ Actively recalls (needs fewer cues) events from the recent past

12 to 36 months (1 year to 3 years old)
____ After about age 2, recalls events that happened quite some time before
____ Occasionally tells about the memory in the form of a story
____ 3-year-olds recall events from 1 or 2 years before

4 years to 12 years (all of the above plus . . .)
____ 4-year-olds can recognize an array (group) of items
____ 4-year-olds recall only 3 or 4 of a group of 12 items
✓ Third graders able to recognize all of an array of 12 items
✓ Third graders can recall about 8 of the items

Comment: Willis has excellent recognition and recall memory. This makes me wonder about his behavior last week when he screamed at and then hit another child when he had become angry with that child even after he had learned about using words when angry. Do additional brief observations.

Figure 8.13

Sources: Baker-Ward, Gordon, Ornstein, Larus, and Clubb, 1993; Howe and Courage, 1993.

easier to remember all the names of the children in the class if he divided the group into two smaller groups of boys and girls when he was trying to remember the names.

Figure 8.13 is an informal teacher-made checklist showing some major milestones in memory development. Mr. Nellis used this checklist to assess the memory development of the children in his K–2 classroom. He was particularly intrigued with the information that he gleaned about Willis, a second grader who has problems with anger and aggression.

Mr. Nellis decided to talk with Willis about how he could help Willis to remember to use words instead of hitting someone. The teacher had documented Willis's excellent recall memory and knew that Willis should indeed be able to recall the lesson on using words. Mr. Nellis also took Willis's behavior of hitting as a signal that Willis needed more help in recalling this important lesson. The teacher decided to help Willis by using cued recall with Willis, that is, by giving Willis a cue when Willis should remember to use words. They decided that Mr. Nellis would use the signs from sign language as a quiet cue to Willis. Mr. Nellis taught the appropriate signs to Willis.

Figure 8.14 is the anecdotal record that Mr. Nellis used.

Anecdotal Record

Goal for this observation: Memory development/Observe Willis's ability to use **a cue** to help him recall and use responsible anger management skills
Setting: computer lab   **Date/day:** Oct. 10   **Time of day:** morning
Basic activity: choosing where they would sit
Focus child: Willis   **Others involved:** Andy (kindergarten)

The Anecdote: Andy sat at a computer which, as we found out, was Willis's favorite computer. I could see Willis's anger starting when he blew out air and closed his eyes. Before he did anything else, I moved over to where he was standing and gave him our prearranged sign for "use words." Willis looked confused at first, but then blinked. He looked sideways and bent his head down a bit (looked a lot like concentration to me). Then he said to Andy, "I wanted to sit there, Andy. When you're done, I'll move to that computer."

Reflection/Comment/Interpretation: Mission accomplished. Willis already has excellent recall memory and usually does not need to use cues. When he is angry, though, he still needs help, and using a cue to remind him of our lessons on using words seems to work. This should also help him to remember to take somebody else's perspective, which he is capable of doing, but forgets to do because he has not practiced it enough.

Figure 8.14

Activities to Help You Construct Knowledge and Skills in Observing

ACTIVITY 1

Analyze a teacher's narrative about a child's motor skills. Reread Figure 8.9, Large Motor Development: Summary Statement. Point out the statements Mr. Claiborne used to describe Dean's strengths in large motor development. Point out the statements in which he described the areas in which Dean needed help.

ACTIVITY 2

Journal writing: Please continue to focus on the summary statement of Dean's motor development written by his teacher (Figure 8.9). Suppose that you were Dean's mother or father. Describe how you might have felt if you had read this statement. Describe how you might have felt if, instead of that statement, you had only read, "Dean falls below the 50th percentile in motor skills."

Explain how the two types of statements are different. Say which you would rather read if you were a parent.

ACTIVITY 3

Conservation experiment: Reread the french fry and poker chip episodes, which was merely an assessment of a 4-year-old's and a 7-year-old's ability to conserve. Do a similar experiment with either one or both of these ages. Use pieces of paper or poker chips. Start out by gathering two piles of paper squares of the same size. Use the same number of squares. Count out the squares as you place them into the piles. The child watches you. Then move the squares from one pile into a long line. Ask, "Are the line and the pile the same, or does one have more squares?" Record the child's response. Then ask the child to explain his response. Record that answer. Decide whether the child can conserve.

REFERENCES

American Psychiatric Association (1993). DSM-IV, *diagnostic and statistical manual of mental disorders*. Washington, DC: Author.

Bagnato, S. J., & Neisworth, J. T. (1991). *Assessment for early intervention: Best practices for professionals*. New York: Guilford.

Bagnato, S. J., & Neisworth, J. T. (1994). A national study of the social and treatment "invalidity" of intelligence testing for early intervention. *School Psychology Quarterly*, 9(2), 81–102.

Baker-Ward, L., Gordon, B. N., Ornstein, P. A., Larus, D. M., & Clubb, P. A. (1993). Young children's long-term retention of a pediatric examination. *Child Development*, 64, 1519–1533.

Bracken, B. A. (2000). Clinical observation of preschool assessment behavior. In B. Bracken (Ed.), *The psychoeducational assessment of preschool children* (3rd ed., pp. 45–56). Boston: Allyn & Bacon.

Case, R. (1992). *The mind's staircase: Exploring the conceptual underpinnings of children's thought and knowledge*. Hillsdale, NJ: Erlbaum.

Cratty, B. J. (1970). *Perceptual and motor development in infants and young children*. New York: Macmillan.

Cratty, B. J. (1986). *Perceptual and motor development in infants and young children*. Boston: Allyn & Bacon.

Dixon, J. A., & Soto, C. F. (1990). The development of perspective taking: Understanding differences in information and weighting. *Child Development, 61*, 1502–1513.

Facts in Action. (2002, June). Making it count: Online resources for outcome measurement tools. Boston, MA: Early Education Clearinghouse/Associated Early Care and Education, Inc.

High/Scope Educational Research Foundation. (2003). Descriptions of preschool COR and COR for infants and toddlers. Ypsilanti, MI: High/Scope Foundation. www.Highscope.org (then go to Assessment link). October, 2002

Howe, M. L., & Courage, M. L. (1993). On resolving the enigma of infantile amnesia. *Psychological Bulletin, 113*, 305–326.

Hyson, M. (2002). Preparing tomorrow's teachers: NAEYC announces new standards. *Young Children, 57*(2), 78–79.

Katz, L. (1997, April). A developmental approach to assessment of young children, an ERIC DIGEST. View this DIGEST under the "Ds." www.ericeece.org/pubs/digests/by title.html October, 2002

Kelley, M. F., & Surbeck, E. (2000). History of preschool assessment. In B. Bracken (Ed.), *The psychoeducational assessment of preschool children* (pp. 1–18). Boston: Allyn & Bacon.

Krechevsky, M. (1998). *Project spectrum: Preschool assessment handbook: Vol. 3 in H. Gardner, D. H. Feldman, & M. Krechevsky (Eds.), Project zero frameworks for early childhood education*. New York: Teachers College Press.

Marion, M. (2003). *Guidance of young children* (6th ed.). Upper Saddle River, NJ: Merrill/Prentice Hall.

Nagel, R. J. (2000). Issues in preschool assessment. In Bruce Bracken (Ed.), *The psychoeducational assessment of preschool children* (3rd ed., pp. 19–32). Boston: Allyn & Bacon.

Piaget, J. (1968). *Six psychological studies*. New York: Random House.

Sanders, S. W. (2002). *Active for life: Developmentally appropriate movement programs for young children*. Washington, DC: NAEYC in cooperation with Human Kinetics Publishers, Champaign, IL.

Selman, R. L. (1980). *The growth of interpersonal understanding: Developmental and clinical analysis*. New York: Academic Press.

Shaffer, D. R. (1996). *Developmental psychology* (4th ed.). Pacific Grove, CA: Brooks/Cole.

Sporns, O., & Edelman, G. (1993). Solving Bernstein's problem: A proposal for the development of coordinated movement by selection. *Child Development, 64*, 960–981.

Williams, H. (1995). *The perceptual-motor development laboratory protocols*. Columbia, SC: University of South Carolina.

Williams, H., & Abernathy, D. (2000). Assessment of gross motor development. In Bruce Bracken (Ed.), *The psychoeducational assessment of preschool children* (3rd ed., pp. 204–233). Boston: Allyn & Bacon.

WEB SITES RELATED TO THIS CHAPTER

✓ Facts in Action

http://factsinaction.org

Go to 123 Making It Count, then to Measuring Program Outcomes, to June 2002 "Online Resources for Outcome Measurement Tools." This issue describes several resources for existing assessment tools.

✓ Harvard University's Project Spectrum

www.Harvard.edu

Homepage of Harvard. Click on the search box. Using quote marks, type in "Project Spectrum." You will get a list of relevant articles. Read the one called "Project Spectrum."

✓ High/Scope Foundation

www.highscope.org

Homepage for High/Scope. Many links including one for assessment, for ordering materials for the COR, infant and toddler or preschool, or for information on registering for training at High/Scope. Postal mail address: High/Scope Foundation, 600 N. River Street, Ypsilanti, MI 48198-2898. Telephone: 1-734-485-2000. The COR reportedly can be used to assess and report Head Start outcomes.

✓ NAEYC, National Association for the Education of Young Children

www.naeyc.org

Homepage for NAEYC. Go to NAEYC Resources, and then Position Statements link. Find specific position papers, such as, "Standardized Testing of Young Children 3 Through 8 Years of Age."

www.naeyc.org/profdev

The "Professional Development" link with the complete document on NAEYC's revised Standards for preparing early childhood professionals. Contains detailed explanations and references. Standard 3 deals with observation and assessment.

CHAPTER 9

Using the Eclectic Approach to Observe Emotional and Social Development

"Observation gives insight into how young children develop, and how they respond to opportunities and obstacles in their lives."
(NAEYC, Standards for Early Childhood Professional Preparation, revised 2001; Hyson, 2002)

Chapter objectives

1. *Describe and explain* selected aspects of children's emotional development.
2. *Summarize* information on anger triggers for young children and on how children express anger.
3. *Comprehend and demonstrate appreciation* of the connection between a child's emotional development and social development.
4. *Describe and explain* selected aspects of children's peer interactions.
5. *Explain* how teachers can observe emotional and social development with informal, ready-made and teacher-made observation instruments.

NAEYC's standards ensure that well-prepared early childhood professionals understand child development and know how to observe and assess development. Knowledge about child development in general is the foundation for developmentally appropriate practices in curriculum, instruction, guidance, interaction with parents, and policy decisions.

Chapter 8 illustrated the eclectic approach to observation and focused on two domains—motor and cognitive development. The current chapter continues this work by describing and explaining salient features of emotional and social development during early childhood. The second major goal in this chapter is to illustrate the eclectic approach in observing emotional and social development. Mindful of the many problems associated with using standardized tests with young children, it emphasizes using *informal* instruments, both teacher-made and ready-made, to observe children's peer relationships and children's feelings.

CHILDREN'S FEELINGS: EMOTIONAL DEVELOPMENT

Emotions play a central role in a child's development, with a child's emotions affecting, for example, whether she likes herself, how she deals with other people, and how she resolves conflict (Eisenberg & Fabes, 1998). Knowledge about emotional and social development enhances a teacher's ability to help children appropriately regulate emotions and make their way in a world filled with people.

Definition of Emotion

Emotion[1]: a child's attempt to establish, maintain, or change the relation between herself and her environment concerning things that are important to the child (Saarni, Mumme, & Campos, 1998). This is a **functional definition** because it focuses on the *function of* or what a child tries to do when she feels a specific emotion.

Example: As first-grader Sandi sat near the gerbil house listening to music on a portable CD, she unwisely hit the volume button too many times. The resulting noise frightened the gerbils. Sandi herself jumped when the volume exploded and then saw her two friends run for cover. Sandi, a very kind person, then felt *guilt,* an emotion whose goal is to maintain a person's own standards. Sandi realized that she had done something contrary to those standards, even if it had been an accident. Sandi's guilt motivated her to repair the damage that she had done (talk softly to the gerbils), communicate remorse ("Uh-oh! I really did scare you") and her intention to behave prosocially ("I'd better pay attention when I turn up the sound").

Basic Emotions

Infants show **basic emotions**—contentment, distress, joy, anger, and fear. Newborns show contentment and distress. Between 6 weeks and 14 months of age, infants' joy,

---

[1]See Figure 9.1 for a list of major definitions used in this chapter.

Anger: basic (unpleasant) emotion elicited when goals are blocked

Basic emotions: emotions present at birth or within the first year or so of life; contentment, distress, joy, anger, and fear

Complex, self-conscious emotions: emotions that evolve after a child has developed a sense of self; pride, hubris (conceit, arrogance), shame, embarrassment, guilt

Emotion: a child's attempt to establish, maintain, or change the relation between her and her environment about things that are important to the child

Emotional intelligence: ability to motivate oneself, hope, empathize, regulate moods, focus in spite of distress, and persist when facing frustrations

Emotional regulation: the ability to appropriately manage emotions, their strength, and how long we will feel them

Friendship: voluntary relationship recognized by both children, characterized by positive affect

Group: a collection of individuals who influence each other in some way

Interaction: social give-and-take resulting from an exchange of behavior between two individuals (children)

Relationship: when two children who know each other have a series of interactions

Social competence in a peer group: a child's ability to operate effectively at all three levels of peer relationships: interaction, relationship, and group level

Social skills: observable behaviors through which a child demonstrates that he can regulate thoughts and emotions

---

Figure 9.1
Selected Definitions from This Chapter

anger, and fear emerge. Infants feel and express these basic emotions, but they do not understand them, and they cannot manage them. As children get older, they develop another set of more complex emotions: self-conscious emotions.

Self-Conscious Emotions

Self-conscious emotions: pride, hubris (conceit, smugness, arrogance), shame, embarrassment, and guilt. You will see self-conscious emotions only when children refer to themselves and show that they know that other people are separate from themselves. Self-conscious emotions make their debut late in infancy and continue to evolve during the preschool years.

Children grow in the ability to show self-conscious emotions when they can do three things (Saarni, Mumme, & Campos, 1998):

📖 Recognize that they must meet standards (e.g., show respect to classroom animals).

📖 Evaluate how they themselves meet these standards (e.g., I usually show respect but did not show respect toward the gerbils when I played loud music).

📖 Show willingness to take responsibility for meeting or not meeting the standards (e.g., I was the one who hit the volume button, and I'd better be more careful about playing the music so loudly).

Emotional Regulation

One of the major accomplishments of the preschool years is that children can begin to regulate their emotions. For example, 6-year-old children are much better than are 2-year-olds at regulating how long they stay angry and how intensely they show anger. However, there is great variation in how children of the same age are able to regulate their emotions appropriately. Some 6-year-olds, for example, are simply better at regulating their emotions than are others.

Emotional regulation consists of three things:

📖 The capacity to manage the strength of our emotions.

Example: Eight-year-old Jose, his mother, father, and grandparents were on an Alaskan cruise with Glacier Bay being one of the major stops. Jose expressed the basic emotion of *joy* when he first glimpsed the glaciers: "Grandpa! Look! There it *is!*" Then Jose stood by Grandpa, holding his hand. Jose had expressed this basic emotion calmly yet enthusiastically.

📖 The ability to manage how long our emotions last.

Example: Jose had written three haiku poems with his teacher, who then read one of the poems to the class. The warm glow of success and a healthy sense of quiet *pride* (but not arrogance or smugness) washed over this third grader. When his father asked about school, Jose simply said, "The teacher read one of my poems to the class." His father replied, "How did you feel when he did that?" Jose said, "Pretty good," and let it go. Jose's family has taught him to feel good about his accomplishments, but to be humble at the same time.

📖 Appropriately changing our reaction (intensifying or restraining the reaction) to an emotion when it is stirred up so that we can accomplish our goals (Eisenberg et al., 1997; Brenner & Salovey, 1997).

Example: Jose wore his new Glacier Bay sweatshirt to school and brushed up against the chalk mural as he headed toward his portfolio box. His mild distress (emotion stirred up) was evident when he said, "Oh, no! Purple chalk." He showed evidence of having restrained this emotion when he took a slow breath and brushed off as much of the purple powder as possible. He then went on and continued with filing portfolio items (completed his task because he changed his reaction to the new emotion).

Emotional Intelligence

Emotional intelligence (often referred to as "EQ"): the ability to motivate oneself, to hope, to be empathic, to regulate moods, to keep distress from drowning a person's ability to focus and to think, and to persist in the face of frustrations.

Goleman (1995) believes that emotional intelligence is essential to a person's success in life—that it is probably as powerful, and perhaps more powerful, compared to traditional measures of intelligence. An intellectually gifted teacher education student, for example, might get a teaching position, but keeping that job depends as much on her EQ (emotional intelligence) as it does on her intellectual powers. If she cannot regulate her moods, or if she is not empathic, then her work relationships will suffer. She might write great lesson plans, but probably would not be a good colleague.

Building Blocks of Emotional Intelligence.   An important component of EQ is a sense of emotional self-awareness or awareness of one's moods as the moods strike, an awareness making us "smart about how we feel" (Gibbs, 1995, 1997). The second major building block of emotional intelligence is the ability to shake off a bad mood. A person can pull himself together if he is aware of how he feels and can come up with a helpful way to cope. Goleman urges teachers and parents to help children develop emotional intelligence.

Example: Jose has a good model in his father, who has said things like, "I could feel myself getting nervous about the presentation (aware of his mood). I did my deep breathing and then went for a walk and that seemed to help" (used a good coping mechanism). Jose imitated his father's style when the purple chalk landed on his new sweatshirt (acknowledged his distress and then pulled himself together with a deep breath, getting on with his work).

The Brain's Role in Emotional Regulation and Emotional Intelligence

Look to the role of different parts of the human brain to get some insight about how children gradually develop the ability to regulate emotions. This section briefly explains the role of three parts of the brain in emotional regulation:

- 📖 The limbic system, including the amygdala
- 📖 The neocortex, especially the prefrontal cortex
- 📖 The connection, or pathway, between the prefrontal cortex and the amygdala

The Limbic System, Including the Amydgala.   The limbic system is the emotional center in the brain and was one of the first parts of the human brain ever to develop. The **amygdala** (Greek word for *almond*) is one part of the limbic system. This almond-shaped structure lies at the top of the brain stem. The human amygdala is near full formation at birth.

The amygdala's function is to store the memory of the emotional quality of all our experiences. For example, it stores the contented, joyful quality of your relationship with a beloved pet from when you were a child. Your amygdala would also preserve the memory of fear when someone followed you out of a store and into a parking lot. The amygdala watches, scans, and monitors every new experience to spot new dangers and to remind you of previously stored episodes of danger.

Example: Suppose that a car had been following you for ten blocks; your amygdala connects this and the parking lot incident. Your amygdala, always alert, signals danger and arouses the emotions of anxiety and fear. It screams "Danger! Danger!" You are afraid, and you act on orders from your amygdala. You act quickly, even before you get much of a chance to analyze the incident. You flash your lights and lean on the car's horn, all the time fumbling for your cell phone so that you can dial 911.

A child's amygdala works the same way. A child's amygdala can seize or hijack a child's brain by short circuiting or doing an end run around the more rational part of the brain. Children, like adults, act before they think when strong emotions hit them like a wall of water. This is the root of a lot of aggressive behavior in classrooms. We teachers want children to think before acting and to use words. But, a child's amygdala often takes over and keeps signals from getting to the part of the brain that can help a child do that thinking or use those words.

Neocortex, Including the Prefrontal Cortex.   The *neocortex* developed much later than did the limbic system. The neocortex makes it possible for humans to think, to remember, and to plan. It is the rational part of the brain. The ***prefrontal cortex*** (part of the neocortex) is located at the very front of the human brain. The prefrontal cortex helps us to choose how we respond by helping us analyze information and stimuli.

A major part of the job description of the prefrontal cortex is to balance the amygdala's purely emotional response. The prefrontal cortex does so by helping us analyze information that enters our brain. The prefrontal cortex, connected to the limbic system, receives and processes emotional signals from the amygdala. This gives people a chance to handle an emotion appropriately by thinking about the situation sensibly and shifting from a potentially stressful emotional state such as anger or anxiety to a more relaxed state.

Example: Willis, a second grader in Mr. Nellis's K–2 class, is not very emotionally intelligent. He does not seem to be aware of his feelings of anger or sadness, and he does not know how to snap out of a funky mood. On Wednesday, Willis watched Phillip take the last soccer ball from a large basket. Willis, who gets angry easily, yelled out, "Hey, Phillip! Drop that ball. I want it." With that order, he ran over to Phillip and grabbed the ball. Willis's angry impulse reared its head because he thought that Phillip was robbing him of the ball. Children who are quick to anger often misread cues and misinterpret the behavior of others. They need our help.

A teacher's assistant saw the incident and said to Willis, "Whoa . . . slow down, Willis. I'll hold the ball for now." The teacher set the ball down and said to Willis, who was clearly agitated, "Just sit here next to me for a minute so that you can slow down a little. Then we can talk." The teacher was helping Willis to move from an agitated state of arousal to a more relaxed state because Willis cannot yet do this for himself.

A child's prefrontal cortex shows some growth at around ages 3 to 4, and this partly accounts for a typically developing child's growing ability in self-control and later in emotional regulation. The human prefrontal cortex does not fully develop, however, until adolescence, explaining the long, long process of developing good emotional regulation. By age 6, however, and for some children by ages 4 or 5, the prefrontal cortex has developed to the point that the child can show real progress in emotional regulation. Willis at age 7, however, does not show this progress and needs help from his teachers.

Connection Between Prefrontal Cortex and Amygdala in the Limbic System.   The prefrontal cortex has to get information about emotional states in order to make sense of the information. Consequently, its connection to the emotional center of the brain is important. Think of the prefrontal cortex-amygdala connection as a cable carrying signals between the two parts of the brain. A weak, underdeveloped, or damaged cable slows or obstructs passage of signals. A child with weak connections between these two parts of the brain is at a disadvantage when it comes to managing emotions because his brain is not wired for the prefrontal cortex to communicate with the amygdala.

Example: Willis, 7 years old, is a good example. He misreads signals from others and has a short fuse; that is, he is quick to anger. He rarely labels a feeling, seems unaware of feelings in general, and gets in trouble with peers because of his poor social skills.

A strong, well-developed cable or pathway lets those bits of information pass quickly between the amygdala and the prefrontal cortex. This sets the stage for better analysis and management of emotions because the child's brain is wired for it, meaning the hardware is installed that allows the prefrontal cortex to get the information it needs about emotions. Jose, in previous examples, seems to have developed this strong connection.

Helping Children Build the Connection.   Use the concept of *attunement*, awareness of, and appropriate attention to a child's emotional needs to install the hardware: to build the pathway between the prefrontal cortex and the amygdala. At times, we make a conscious effort to help a child make these connections, as Willis's teacher did. At other times, we might not even realize that our positive interactions are helping a child develop the wiring and connections, the essential hardware for managing his feelings. For example:

📖 Tell a child that hitting somebody hurts the other person—Whoosh!—a connection, a line added to the cable!

📕 Say to a preschooler who has hit somebody, "Jordan, I want you to use words to tell Sean that you are angry." Whoosh!—a connection.

📕 Give the words to the child, that is; tell him the words to use instead of expecting him to come up with the words. "Jordan, you can say, 'I am using the tape recorder, Sean. It's not your turn yet.'" Whiz!—another connection.

📕 Comfort an anxious or fearful child. Connection.

📕 Help a child calm down when he gets agitated. Connection.

📕 Let a child know unequivocally that her needs are important and worthy of attention. Connection.

📕 Model self-control. Manage your own emotions well. Help the child learn how to manage her anger, anxiety, sadness, or even joy. Whoosh! Whoosh! Whoosh!

You have helped to install several lines in the hidden pathway. You have helped the child to develop a good strong cable or circuit connecting the prefrontal cortex and amygdala.

Benefits of Good Emotional Regulation and Emotional Intelligence.   Children who manage emotions and who are emotionally intelligent tend to feel more connected to others. They also tend to get along with others better than children who do not have these abilities. They feel competent and capable, both components of positive self-esteem. They experience a general sense of balance in their emotions (Skinner & Wellborn, 1994).

Children are in a good position to solve problems and deal with conflicts constructively when they can regulate whirling and swirling emotions. They are better able to focus on a problem or conflict and not so much on their anger or embarrassment or guilt.

A CHILD'S FEELINGS: ANGER AS AN EXAMPLE

Anger Is a Basic Emotion, Perceived as Unpleasant

Anger: a basic emotion first evident in early infancy; elicited when a goal of some sort is blocked; expressed in a variety of ways. Anger is a basic emotion, and every person has felt anger's companion—the surge of energy that goes along with this powerful feeling. Whirring anger energy results from the rush of neurotransmitters released in the body when a person feels angry. Indicators of emotional turmoil often include a racing heartbeat, a hot, reddening face, sweaty palms, and an increase in blood pressure.

Anger and anxiety are among the most difficult emotions to manage, even for adults. Imagine how difficult it is for children. Children feel anger, and they certainly express it, but they cannot understand their anger and cannot manage it on their own. It is difficult for both adults and children to manage everyday irritation or anger. It is even tougher to manage anger if a person is already under stress or stirred up about something else.

Example: Andy, usually a hearty eater, only picked at the peas and took one sip of milk at lunch. Ned, another kindergarten child in this K–2 classroom and Andy's friend, reached across Andy's food on the table to get another napkin. Andy, especially quiet throughout the morning and during lunch, clenched fists as he glanced sideways at his friend Ned, a hard frown beginning to crease his face. Andy startled his friend when he barked his command, "Get *away* from my food, Ned!" Stressed and angry, Andy stopped eating altogether and cried.

Andy, the focus child in this chapter's observations, expresses emotions appropriately, as you will see from Mr. Nellis's checklists later in the chapter. When his parents took Andy's favorite horse to the veterinary hospital for surgery, however, Andy appeared to be under stress, something that was unusual for him. Consequently, his teacher was not surprised when Andy reacted more forcefully than he ever had to a mildly anger-arousing interaction in the lunchroom. The teacher realized that Andy typically expressed irritation much less forcefully.

What Causes Anger for Children?

The first component of any emotion, including anger, is the *feeling* of the emotion. It is the feeling that washes over us as the emotion arises. Fabes and Eisenberg (1992) observed and documented typical social interactions that elicit anger in young children. The anger-arousing social interactions are listed below and explained further in Figure 9.8.

- Conflict over possessions
- Physical assault
- Verbal assault
- Rejection
- Issues of compliance

How Do Children Express Anger?

The second component of anger (or any emotion) is the expression of that emotion (Kuebli, 1994; Marion, 1997). Children first feel this basic emotion when they are infants. Anger triggers primarily include having someone or something block us from reaching a goal. Even young infants encounter many events that elicit the feeling of anger which they express with their faces and voices (Stenberg, 1982).

Early childhood teachers are likely to observe that children express anger with one or more of the following behavioral coping strategies (Fabes & Eisenberg, 1992). The examples are from Marion (2003).

 Venting. Expressing anger through facial expressions, crying, sulking, or complaining. Little is done to try to solve a problem or confront the agitator. Some people think of venting as "blowing off steam," which is considered an unhealthy way to express anger if this is all that the person does, that is, if she does nothing to solve the problem that caused the anger.

Example: Jake and Jim, 8 years old, were angry about the number of math problems that they had to do for homework and vented their anger by complaining all the way home from school.

📖 *Active resistance.* Expressing anger by physically or verbally defending their position, self-esteem, or possessions in nonaggressive ways. Considered a healthy way to express anger.

Example: Ralph expressed his anger with active resistance when Nellie tried to take the scoop from him as he worked at the sand table: "That's mine. You can't have it, Nellie!"

📖 *Express dislike.* Expressing anger by telling the offender that he or she cannot play or is not liked because of an incident.

Example: Justine was angry when Jordan pushed her. Later, when Jordan wanted to sit at her table for snack, she said, "You can't sit here, Jordan. We don't like you."

📖 *Aggressive revenge.* Expressing anger by physically or verbally retaliating against the provocateur with no other purpose evident—name-calling, pinching, hitting, or threatening to express their feelings. Considered a negative way of expressing anger. Seen frequently in children who are physically assaulted or rejected.

Example: After snacktime, the children went to the playground. Jordan, steaming from Justine's comment at snack, was hanging from the climbing gym when Justine rode by on her trike. He sang out, "Justine is stupid. Justine is stupid."

📖 *Avoidance.* Expressing anger by trying to escape from or evade the person with whom the child is angry.

Example: Justine, mildly irritated by the name-calling, walked away and played on the other side of the playground.

📖 *Adult-seeking.* Expressing anger by telling an adult about an incident or by looking for comfort from the teacher.

Early childhood teachers see the whole range of possible responses. Most young children express anger nonaggressively through active resistance, but some children express their anger aggressively. Children who hurt others when angry, *learned* their aggressive approach to managing anger (Hennessy, Rabideau, Cummings, & Cicchetti, 1994). These children then resort to using aggression when they face normal everyday conflicts at school, on the playground, or at home.

Teachers face a challenge. On one hand, we want to encourage children to acknowledge angry feelings, and on the other hand, we want to help children express anger in a positive and effective way. The key to helping children learn to manage anger is to observe the sorts of things that touch off a child's anger and then observe how he typically expresses anger.

CHILDREN'S PEER RELATIONSHIPS: THEIR ROLE IN SOCIAL DEVELOPMENT

Early childhood teachers are justifiably concerned about children's social development. We are concerned about how well children interact with others, how they play, participate in relationships, and how they fit into groups. We want to help them develop friendships and develop social skills. In short, we want to help children become socially competent.

This section of the chapter, therefore, focuses on how children's peer relationships affect social development. A child's peer group, along with school, family, and community, affects social as well as all other areas of a child's development. The literature review of peer interactions by Rubin et al. (1998) gives a full account of this complex but highly useful area of social development. I have followed their lead in describing peer interactions at three levels.

THREE LEVELS OF PEER EXPERIENCES: INTERACTIONS, RELATIONSHIPS, GROUPS

Helping children become socially competent requires that we observe a child's experiences at three different levels—the child's interactions, his relationships, and how he functions in groups to which he belongs. Socially competent children function well at each of these levels.

Children's Interactions

Jordan: "Give me that marker, Ralph!"
Ralph: "No, I had it first."

Jordan reached over and grabbed for the marker.

Ralph, surprised, held on to the marker, getting green ink on his hands.
Ralph: "Stop it Jordan. It's *my* marker."

Jordan and Ralph's exchange is typical of a classic *interaction*.

Interaction: social give and take resulting from an exchange of behavior of two individuals (children in this case). Each person responds to the other and each person elicits behavior from the other.

It is helpful to think about the variety of peer interactions that you will see in a classroom and to realize that the list of possibilities is long. Infants gaze longingly at other infants, waving at and trying to make contact. Children can fight, or argue, or even tell jokes. They can sing silly songs to one another in an interaction. Child-child interactions include greetings, departures or saying good-bye, negotiating, rough-and-tumble play, threatening one another on occasion, showing compassion, helping the other child, cooperating, lying, sharing, and engaging in dramatic play.

Rubin et al. (1998) suggested using three categories of peer interactions to organize rather than thinking about the endless list of possibilities. The three major categories are:

- Moving toward others, for example, greeting, showing compassion, helping
- Moving away from others, for example, withdrawing from interaction or contact
- Moving against others, for example, aggression in any form

Several factors affect how any interaction proceeds. For instance, how might the physical setting affect the interaction? Will it make a difference if there are others watching the interaction? How will each child's place in the group affect the interaction? What has the children's culture or community communicated about the way that they should respond to the other child? What are each child's personal goals in the exchange?

As teachers, we need to constantly think about how rich and varied children's *social interactions* are. Children differ in their ability to deal effectively with social interactions, with many children unable to cope well. Other, more socially competent children deal effectively with a wide range of social interactions.

Children's Relationships

This is the second level of thinking about children's peer relationships. **Relationship:** when two individuals (children in this case) who know each other have a series of interactions. Some relationships have existed for quite some time. These can be filled with conflict (children who do not get along well at all) or can be positive and satisfying (classmates who get along well and have been together for an extended period). Other peer relationships are more casual and can be tainted with hostility or can be pleasant (e.g., two children, not friends, who have ridden on the same bus and who, therefore, have many interactions).

Like all of us, children can have different types of relationships. A friendship is a specific type of relationship. **Friendship:** a relationship that:

- Is recognized and acknowledged by both children
- Is characterized by shared liking of one another, that is, shared affection
- Is voluntary. Friendships cannot be ordered or assigned (Rubin et al., 1998)

Children's Groups

This is the third level of thinking about children's peer relationships. **Group:** a collection of individuals (children in this case) who influence each other in some way. As teachers, we are concerned about how each child functions in our classroom group. Teachers want to help children feel comfortable in the group and accepted by the others in their class.

Children in groups show some degree of liking or disliking to each other child in the group. Thus, some children are well liked while others are not. Observing how children view other children in the group is the first step toward helping neglected or rejected children. Figure 9.2 describes popular, average, rejected, and controversial children on a continuum of positive behavior and on a continuum of negative behavior.

Social Competence

Social competence in a peer group: a child's ability to operate effectively at all three levels of peer relations: interaction, relationship, and the group levels. He would be able to meet his own needs but also have primarily positive interactions under many different conditions. He would also be able to initiate and sustain good relationships. Other children would act in a friendly way toward him and would invite him to play and work with them.

Example: Andy seems to be successful in interactions with other children. Mr. Nellis's observations yield a picture of a socially competent child. Andy has predominately positive interactions, largely because he has good social skills. He has developed a couple of friendships, and his classmates like him.

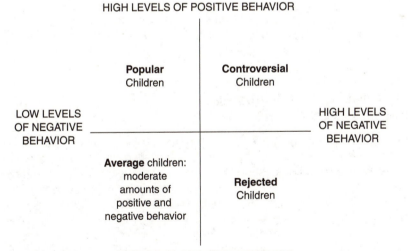

Figure 9.2
Levels of Behavior of Popular, Average, Rejected, and Controversial Children

Chris is a popular child. He has good social skills and knows how to regulate his emotions.

Vygotsky and Piaget: A Constructivist Look at the Value of Peer Relationships

Both Piaget (1932) and Vygotsky (1978) gave us a base for understanding how peer interactions, relationships, and groups can help children achieve higher levels of social competence. Interactions and relationships with peers give children the chance to bump their own ideas against their friend's ideas, to negotiate conflicts, and to accept or reject another child's ideas. Rubin et al. (1998) summarized research based on Piaget's and Vygotsky's constructivist theories. Their review showed that:

    📖 Pairs of children who work together (interact) can solve problems that the children could not have solved by themselves.

Example: Andy and Ned were choosing a library book and chose the same book. "What's the problem?" asked the librarian.

"I want the book about the pandas," said Ned.

"But I saw it first," piped up Andy.

Teacher: "OK, one book and two boys who want it. It looks like you have a problem to figure out. Tell me an idea of how you can fix this problem."

"I could read it first and then Andy could read it."

Teacher: "So . . . you could take turns. How do you like that, Andy?"

Andy: "Hey, Ned. We could read the book together. Want to do that?"

Ned considered this idea. "Yeah, read it together." To the teacher, he said, "Can we sit over on the beanbag together to read?"

📖 Children who talk *cooperatively* rather than argumentatively about their conflicting ideas on a topic make better cognitive advances. Willis is the second grader who has poor social skills and has few friends. In an earlier example, a teacher urged Willis to sit and take deep breaths so that Willis would relax and become less agitated. Here is how his teacher used his expert ability to help Willis make an important cognitive step forward in the ability to take the other child's perspective.

Example: The teacher smiled at Willis and gave him a thumbs up. "OK, I think that we're ready to talk. I'm going to go get Phillip and bring him over here so that we can all talk about what happened." When he returned, he said to the two boys, "We need to talk together about what happened with the soccer balls. Willis, did you want the ball?"

"Yeah, but Phillip was running away with it."

Teacher: "Phillip, please tell Willis why you were running away with the ball."

Phillip: "All I did was get the soccer ball and then I ran to where we kick it."

Teacher: "Willis, please ask Phillip how he felt when you yelled out, 'Drop the ball!'" The teacher nodded encouragingly at Willis, who asked Phillip the question.

Phillip: "I was mad when you screamed at me, Willis. I didn't take the ball from you, I just got to the basket first."

Teacher: "Please tell me what you think about that, Willis."

Willis: "I thought that Phillip was taking the ball from *me,* but he said that he just got to the ball first. I guess that it was his 'turn' first."

📖 Talking out conflicting ideas with a peer who is more skillful or more knowledgeable promotes more conflict within a child. This, in turn, helps the child make better cognitive progress than discussing a conflict with a peer who has less knowledge and fewer skills.

📖 It is more beneficial for children when they exchange conflicting ideas with friends than when they do so with children who are not friends.

Example: Willis and Phillip are not friends, and Phillip is much more socially skilled and competent than Willis. The teacher, therefore, stepped in and mediated their exchange of ideas. He knew that Willis would benefit from an open discussion of the issue with Phillip, but that he had to guide the conversation. Willis was able, for the first time, to recognize another person's viewpoint because the teacher encouraged a conversation between a socially competent and a less socially competent child, but did so respectfully. Phillip might begin to see Willis in a new light, too, because of this conversation.

Social Skills

Good social skills make it easier for children to have good peer interactions and relationships. **Social skills**: observable behaviors through which a child demonstrates that he can regulate thoughts and emotions. Popular, socially competent children have good social skills.

Example: Andy was excited about a movie that he had seen and wanted to tell Mr. Nellis (his thoughts and emotions). When he saw that the teacher was talking with another child, he stopped and stood next to Mr. Nellis without speaking (Mr. Nellis had taught this social skill to the class). Andy waited patiently (Andy regulated his emotions, and this showed up in his waiting behavior). Mr. Nellis spoke with Andy right away after he finished speaking with the other child, first thanking Andy for remembering to wait.

Birth to 12 months
• Facial expressions (smiles or frowns) or gestures (reaching out a hand) directed to play partners
• Showing social interest by watching other babies
• Responding to a play partner's behaviors, such as reaching out to a person who shows interest in playing with the infant

12 to 36 months
• Child is aware that somebody is imitating her
• Can imitate another person's activity
• Turn-taking: Observe peer/Respond to peer/Observe and wait
• Shows helping and sharing behaviors

Preschool, Kindergarten, and Primary Grades
• Able to share meaning in dramatic play and in rough-and-tumble play
• Indicates that they understand a listener's characteristics with forms of speech
• Spontaneous acts of kindness and compassion toward peers
• Appropriately expresses positive emotions
• Can control negative thoughts about social partner
• Knows how to start a conversation and keep one going in an interaction
• Able to "scope out" a setting and a partner in which an interaction might take place
• Can figure out what the consequences of her actions will be for her and for the person on the receiving end of the actions
• Speaks clearly and takes turns speaking when having a conversation; does not interrupt

---

Figure 9.3

Developmental Sequence: A Journey Toward Social Skills

Sources: Rubin, Bukowski, & Parker (1998); Schneider, Rubin, & Ledingham (1985).

Parents have a major impact on a child's social skills.

Several factors affect a child's social skills, with the parent-infant attachment extremely important. Having good models of social skills from parents, teachers, other adults, and the media is an essential element of developing the same skills. A child's developing perception, language skills, cognitive developmental skills such as perspective taking, or cue detection skills also affect social skills. You will witness this journey toward social skills as you observe how different skills emerge in a child. Figure 9.3 is a chart showing the developmental differences in social skills.

PLAY

Reframing Our Perspective on Sequences of Play

Play is a complex phenomenon and such an elemental part of a child's makeup. We do a disservice to children if we do not acknowledge play's complexity and the different ways in which play works for children. We need to go beyond counting how many times a child engages in parallel, or solitary, or cooperative play. We need to observe each child's approach to play and how she uses play to solve problems, move forward in development, and connect with other children.

Parten's Early Work and Interpretation of Sequences of Play.   Parten (1932) observed 40 middle-class children and from those data developed a social participation grouping. She identified six categories of social participation: unoccupied behavior, solitary play, onlooker behavior, paralled play, associative play, and cooperative play. She reasoned that this order described stages of play, with older children showing increasingly greater amounts of cooperative play and showing that solitary play drops out. Teachers have accepted this interpretation, but are beginning to appreciate a refinement of Parten's work.

More Recent Research and Interpretation of Sequences of Play.   Recent research clarifies and extends Parten's work (Rubin et al., 1998), making her categories of interaction

---

Infants
- By 2 months: aroused by presence of peers, engages in mutual gaze
- 6 to 9 months: smiles, vocalizes, directs looks at others
- 9 to 12 months: watches others even more, imitates partner, points at things

Toddlers
- Interactions go on longer and are more complex
- Moves around easily and uses words to communicate in interactions
- Themes or simple games evident for the first time; give-and-take type of imitation, foundation for later pretense play
- Turn taking behaviors evident

Preschool: 2 to 5 years
- Frequency, length, and complexity of peer interaction increases
- All forms of interaction evident: unoccupied, onlooking, solitary, parallel, and group activities
- Frequency of parallel play remains constant from 3 to 5 years
- Solitary sensorimotor play (seemingly aimless repetitive actions) decreases
- Solitary constructive play increases (working alone to build something)
- Sociodramatic play evident: a complex form of group interaction
- Positive interactions more common with increasing age
- Aggression increases with age, but positive behavior predominant
- Directs more speech to peers; linguistically competent children at a clear advantage
- Older preschoolers more socially skilled in making requests

Primary grades
- Generosity, helpfulness, and cooperation increase
- Forms of aggression change from physical to verbal
- Hostile aggression now possible
- Pretend play declines in middle childhood
- Games with or without formal rules evident

Figure 9.4

Development Sequence: Peer Interaction During Early Childhood

Source: Rubin et al. (1998).

and play much more useful for teachers. For example, a more recent analysis of play shows that children of all ages participate in onlooking, unoccupied, solitary, parallel, and group play (Howes & Mathison, 1992). This recent research supports an older study showing that the frequency of parallel play seems to remain constant from 3 to 5 years (Rubin, Watson, & Jambor, 1978).

Figure 9.4 is a chart of the developmental sequence of peer interaction in early childhood. Consider referring to it whenever you observe interactions or play. The developmental sequence will help you figure out how a child of any age is using different types of play.

Snapshots of Play

Different children, different ages, different family backgrounds, and different circumstances yield different types of play. Here are several snapshots of play with comments. Refer to Figure 9.4 as you read through the comments.

Snapshot: Josiah and Andy drove a tricycle onto the grass, parked it next to a table, flipped the trike over, whirled its pedals, and announced the opening of an ice cream store. They pretended to make ice cream with their new pedal-powered ice cream machine. Josiah made the ice cream, after consulting with Andy about ingredients, and Andy sold it at the table (their counter). Other children got into the act by suggesting silly ice cream flavors.

Comments: This is classic **sociodramatic play;** the boys display the remarkable ability to share meaning during this complex play sequence.

Snapshot: Sandi (first grade) stood outside the area where children were building their version of a spaceship. She watched and listened for about 1 minute and then moved into the area, sat with two other children, and tore up bits of paper and placed them in the pile created by the others (paper to cover the rocket). Then Phillip said, "OK, everybody (he included Sandi)! Time to cover the rocket."

Comments: Sandi first shows *onlooker* behavior, considered by Parten (1932) to decrease dramatically during the preschool years. Sandi actually demonstrated a good social skill by scoping out the group's activities before entering the group. Then she engaged in **parallel play** by sitting at the table and doing the same thing that the others were doing. Again, she used parallel play as a good social skill because it opened the way for her to join the group. Her sophisticated method of joining the group met with approval, and she was invited to join the group in the **cooperative play** of working together on a project.

Snapshot: Rhonda, an abused child, smacked her doll on the face and buttocks. "Don't you dare sass me again! Do you hear me?" she hissed. Rhonda does *not* play joyfully, and when she does play, one quickly sees evidence of her harsh treatment.

Comments: Play is supposed to be a joyful experience, but the play of abused children mirrors the harsh realities of their lives. Rhonda's treatment of her doll speaks to us of her stress.

Snapshot: Kenny, who had ridden a ferry to his grandma's, reenacted that trip with himself the captain, at the water table. Other children also played at the table. At times, he invited others to get on board for the trip to the island, and he helped another child play with a boat, too (this play sequence was documented with a running record in chapter 4, Figure 4.2).

Comments: At first, this episode appears to be *parallel play*, but careful observation revealed a greater level of complexity in Kenny's play. It showed his positive interactions, his empathy, and his excellent use of language and speech in making requests. It also revealed that he could reenact an event at a later time.

Snapshot: Willis (second grade), clearly agitated and frustrated, stood still and took a deep breath. He then headed toward the "stress-buster" corner and finger-painted until he calmed himself.

Comments: Mr. Nellis has been working with Willis (several previous examples) to help him learn some of the skills he needs for more positive peer interaction. He is also helping Willis learn how to manage his feelings in more positive and satisfying ways. In this play episode, Willis shows us that he has indeed made good progress. Seven years old, he is using **solitary play** to manage his feelings, to decrease his reaction to stress, and to calm his agitated state.

OBSERVING EMOTIONAL AND SOCIAL DEVELOPMENT

In the following section, Mr. Nellis observes and documents emotional and social development with a variety of informal observation tools (Figure 9.5). First, he used an *existing checklist*, the "Social Attributes Checklist" (SAC). He also used **teacher-made observation tools** to illustrate specific points from the checklist.

Social Attributes Checklist: A Ready-Made Instrument

Teachers use this existing or ready-made checklist developed by McClellan and Katz (1992, 2001) to assess young children's social development. This checklist does *not*

TEACHER-MADE OBSERVATION TOOLS

- Anecdotal Records: Social Development, Social Skills, and Play
- Checklist: Causes of Anger in Early Childhood Classrooms
- Checklist: How Children Express Anger
- Graphic Rating Scale: How _____ Manages Anger
- Digital Photographs of Social Interaction

READY-MADE OBSERVATION TOOL: Social Attributes Checklist

Figure 9.5
Informal Observations Instruments Mr. Nellis Used to Assess Emotional and Social Development

compare one child with others statistically. The authors caution that there is no "correct social behavior;" but that teachers should use this checklist to "observe, understand, and support children as they grow in social skillfulness." For example, the developers of the checklist emphasize that some children are simply shyer than others. They note that forcing a shy child into social relationships might well be quite uncomfortable and stressful for that child.

There are three parts to this checklist (Figure 9.6). There are sections on:

- Individual attributes
- Social skill attributes
- Peer relationship attributes

The developers urge teachers to use the checklist not just once, but a couple of times over a period to observe how a child functions in each set of attributes. This, they believe, will yield a more accurate and reliable picture of the child's social development than using the checklist only once.

Figure 9.6 shows that Mr. Nellis had used the Social Attributes Checklist for the second time to assess Andy's social development. He checked all but one of the attributes. The teacher will combine this information with that from the observation tools when he writes a narrative or summary of Andy's development for the midterm meeting with Andy's parents.

Mr. Nellis has observed that Andy usually is appropriately assertive in anger-arousing situations. He has noticed that Andy, like many of the younger children, seems to be scared and anxious when one of the fourth-grade children who bullies younger children is on the playground.

The developers believe that a child's social development is adequate if he *usually* exhibits many of the attributes in the checklist, as in Andy's case. Children, however, encounter short-term difficulties that might affect their social development temporarily, even if they usually show a particular attribute. Early childhood teachers must be able to recognize temporary problems and to look beyond them to discern an overall pattern in a child's social functioning.

Social Attributes Checklist

Child's Name: *Andy (kindergarten)*
Date: October 21
Observation #: 1 ② 3 4

I. INDIVIDUAL ATTRIBUTES

The child:

✓ is usually in a positive mood

✓ is not excessively dependent on adults

✓ usually comes to the program willingly

✓ usually copes with rebuffs adequately

✓ shows the capacity to empathize

✓ has positive relationships with one or two peers; shows capacity to really care about them, misses them if they are absent

✓ displays the capacity for humor

✓ does not seem to be acutely lonely

II. SOCIAL SKILLS ATTRIBUTES

The child usually:

✓ approaches others positively

✓ expresses wishes and preferences clearly; gives reasons for actions and positions

✓ asserts own rights and needs appropriately

✓ is not easily intimidated by bullies

✓ expresses frustrations and anger effectively and without escalating disagreements or harming others

✓ gains access to ongoing groups at play and work

✓ enters ongoing discussion on the subject; makes relevant contributions to ongoing activities

✓ takes turns fairly easily

✓ shows interest in others; exchanges information with and requests information from others appropriately

✓ negotiates and compromises with others appropriately

✓ does not draw inappropriate attention to self

✓ accepts and enjoys peers and adults of ethnic groups other than his or her own

✓ interacts nonverbally with other children with smiles, waves, nods, and so forth

III. PEER RELATIONSHIP ATTRIBUTES

The child:

✓ is usually accepted versus neglected or rejected by other children

✓ is sometimes invited by other children to join them in play, friendship, and work

✓ is named by other children as someone they are friends with or like to play and work with

Figure 9.6

Source: McClellan and Katz (1992, 2001).

Example: For Andy, Mr. Nellis had checked the item *usually comes to the program will-ingly* both times that he used the Social Attributes Checklist. On the day that Andy's horse was at the vet school hospital having surgery, the teacher understood Andy's reluctance to come to school.

Teacher-Made Instruments: Mr. Nellis Uses Checklists, Anecdotal Records, and Photographs

In addition to the Social Attributes Checklist, Mr. Nellis used anecdotal records to observe and document Andy's social skills and play (Figures 9.7A and 9.7B). This is an efficient method for busy teachers, and it yields good information.

Anecdotal Record

Goal for this observation: observe social development and play
Setting: indoors/work period
Date/day: Tuesday, Oct. 10
Time of day: morning
Basic activity: math manipulatives/small group/table
Focus child: Andy (kindergarten)
Others involved: Louie and Ned (both also in kindergarten)

The Anecdote: Louie and Ned were already working with the magnetized plastic pieces and individual magnet boards. Andy, just finished with another activity, looked over to the science table and then walked toward it. Andy sat on a chair at the table and pulled the third magnet board toward himself so that it sat directly in front of him. The children shared magnetized pieces from a container set in the middle of the table. Andy looked at both Louie and Ned and then reached for some of the pieces. He dragged them toward himself and started to work. Finally, he spoke: "I have a lot of blue pieces. I'll make a blue picture." Louie: "I have a lot of red pieces." Andy: "I'll make a blue and you make a red picture. Maybe we can make a red and a blue picture together." Then, Andy stopped and smiled broadly: "Hey, Louie . . . if we mix up our red and blue pieces, do you think we'll get purple pieces?" He then laughed at his own joke, which led me to think that he was enjoying himself. Louie sang out, seeming to enjoy composing a jingle, "Purple, purple. Pieces, pieces. Purple pieces, purple pieces."

Reflection/Comment/Interpretation: Andy has a nice way of joining groups; he watches what is going on before entering or speaking. Then he shows interest in what others are doing and converses easily with them. Children seem to appreciate this style and accept Andy as a partner in work and play. In this episode, Andy's developing sense of humor has bubbled up and he had a positive effect on Louie, whose enjoyment of the activity seemed to increase greatly because of Andy's skillful, positive, and funny interaction.

Figure 9.7a

Anecdotal Record

Goal for this observation: observe social skills and play
Setting: indoors
Date/day: Tuesday, Oct. 17
Time of day: morning
Basic activity: work period/group mural
Focus child: Andy
Others involved: Josiah and Jessica (both kindergarten)

The Anecdote: This activity was set up for three children. Andy and Josiah had been working on painting on the long piece of paper taped to the wall. There were three pots of paint, each with three brushes, so that three children could use each color. Andy worked at the center. Josiah was working to Andy's left. When Andy and Josiah both wanted to use yellow paint, Andy and Josiah each waited at least once for the other boy to dip a brush into paint before dipping in his brush himself (turn-taking).

Jessica approached the artists and put on the remaining apron. Then she stopped because the boys were using all three containers of paint set up for the activity (they had moved the pots of paint so that the pots sat between Josiah and Andy). "I need some paint and a brush," said Jessica. Andy and Josiah looked over at her. "Oh, yeah. Hey Josiah, we need to move the pots again so Jessica has paint and brushes, too, OK?" Josiah nodded and grabbed one pot, moving it to the center. Andy moved the second pot and said, ". . . want to slide the yellow paint over here, too, Jessie?"

After moving all the pots, the children resumed painting, with Jessica on the right.

Reflection/Comment/Interpretation: Both Andy and Josiah take turns well and show signs of the growing ability to negotiate and compromise. The boys had arranged the paints between them at the start of the activity and then compromised readily when Jessica joined the group. What might appear to be simple parallel play is really a picture of two boys who take turns, negotiate, communicate effectively, and show a great deal of positive behavior.

Figure 9.7b

Mr. Nellis, realizing that anger is one of the most difficult emotions to control, also developed and used a two-part "Emotional Development Checklist" with all children in the class (Figures 9.8 and 9.9). He was particularly interested in the types of everyday social interactions that aroused his students' anger, that is, what specific situations aroused anger. He was also interested in how each child expressed his or her anger. After completing these brief observations, Mr. Nellis used Figure 9.10, a graphic rating scale, to get an overall picture of how a specific child managed anger.

Checklist: Causes of Anger in Early Childhood Classrooms

Observe this child react to social interactions that typically arouse anger. Check *Yes* if the child reacts with anger; check *No* if s/he does not; check *Not observed* if you have not yet observed the child's reactions to this type of interaction. Write brief comments.

Child's name and age: *Andy: 5 years, 7 months*

Conflict over Possessions. Someone takes or destroys focus child's property or invades their space

__×__ Yes   _____ No   _____ Not observed

Comment/Date: Early in October. He was only mildly irritated

Physical Assault. Something done to a child's body, such as pushing or hitting

__×__ Yes   _____ No   _____ Not observed

Comment/Date: September, playground, incidents with an aggressive fourth-grader

Verbal Assault. Taunting, teasing, insults, degrading or demeaning statements

__×__ Yes   _____ No   _____ Not observed

Comment/Date: Same as physical assault, with same older child

Rejection. Other children either ignore or refuse to allow a child to play

_____ Yes   _____ No   __×__ Not observed

Comment/Date:

Issues of Compliance. Someone asks or forces a child to do something that he does not want to do; almost all anger over issues of compliance occurs between an adult and a child

_____ Yes   __×__ No   _____ Not observed

Comment/Date: All semester. Andy does not seem to have an issue here.

Conclusions: Andy shows anger when somebody takes something from him, which is not at all unusual for a kindergarten child. He seems to feel anger when somebody assaults him, which is also not unusual. Andy's responses to these events are positive, however, which demonstrates good emotional awareness.

Figure 9.8

Source: Fabes and Eisenberg (1992); Marion (2003).

Checklist: How Children Express Anger

Observe how this child reacts to anger-arousing situations. Check *Yes* if s/he expresses anger as described in that method. Check *No* if the child does not express anger that way. Observe over a period of at least several days.
Child's name and age: *Andy; 5 years, 7 months*

Venting. Crying, sulking, or complaining; blowing off steam
_____Yes   _X_No
Comments:

Active resistance. Physically or verbally defends self-esteem or possessions in nonaggressive ways
_X_Yes   _____No
Comments: When somebody takes something from Andy

Express dislike. Tells offender that he or she cannot play or is not liked
_____Yes   _X_No
Comments:

Aggressive revenge. Physically or verbally retaliates against the provocateur with no other purpose evident—name-calling, pinching, hitting, or threatening
_____Yes   _X_No
Comments:

Avoidance. Attempts to escape from or evade the offender
_X_Yes   _____No
Comments: Avoided the fourth grader who hit other children

Adult-seeking. Tells an adult about an incident or looks for comfort from adult
_X_Yes   _____No
Comments: Andy played near me when the aggressive fourth grader was near

Conclusions: Andy typically expresses the emotion of anger in a healthy and positive way, using good social skills. He needs help, as do all of the younger children, in dealing with an older child who is aggressive. The older child also needs help, which the school is providing.

Figure 9.9

Source: Fabes and Eisenberg (1992); Marion (2003).

Graphic Rating Scale: How _Andy_ Manages Anger

Reflecting on your observations of this child, rate how she or he "manages" the emotion of anger. For each statement, choose the rating that best describes this child and circle the appropriate spot on the scale. Write a brief narrative in the "comments" section. Use this information when you write your observation report of this child's development.

Child's Name: _Andy, age 5 years, 7 months_

Date: _November_

	Always	Often	Occasionally	Seldom	Never
Uses words appropriately to express anger	⊙				
Strikes out when angry					⊙
Name calling when upset					⊙
Expresses anger appropriately toward teachers	⊙				
Expresses anger appropriately toward other children		⊙			
Generates word labels for frustration and anger		⊙			

Comment: My overall impression is that Andy, who is only in kindergarten, has learned to regulate anger very well. The only time that I've seen him *not* manage it well was when he was under a great deal of stress about his horse and yelled at his good friend Ned at lunch time. Even then, though, he used "active resistance," a positive strategy, although he used it a bit too forcefully.

Figure 9.10

Mr. Nellis combined information from the various informal assessments along with a set of digital photographs that he took of Andy's social interaction just as he had done for the other children. He used the information to write a narrative of Andy's emotional and social development.

Activities to Help You Construct Knowledge and Skills in Observing

Choose one child to observe over a period of several weeks. Plan on observing and assessing that child's emotional and social development and play by using the same tools used in this chapter.

ACTIVITY 1

Do at least three anecdotal records of your child's emotional and social responses as he or she interacts with other children (blank form in Appendix C).

ACTIVITY 2

Use the two checklists "Causes of Anger in Early Childhood Classrooms" and "How Children Express Anger" (both in Appendix C) to assess your child's experience with the emotion of anger. Again, you will get a more complete picture if you observe over a period of a couple of weeks. Write brief comments to clarify each item checked. Use the rating scale "How _____ Manages Anger" (Appendix C) to assess the child's overall ability to manage anger.

ACTIVITY 3

Use the ready-made "Social Attributes Checklist" (Appendix C) to record your observations of his or her individual, social skills and peer relationship attributes.

ACTIVITY 4

Reflection. Review the information that you have collected in the anecdotal records, the two anger checklists, and the Social Attributes Checklist. Reflect on what you have observed and write a narrative or summary of your child's emotional and social development. (Consider using Appendix A and Appendix B as a guide.)

REFERENCES

Brenner, E., & Salovey, P. (1997). Emotion regulation during childhood: Developmental, interpersonal, and individual considerations. In P. Salovey & D. Sluyter (Eds.), *Emotional literacy and emotional development* (pp. 169–192). New York: Basic Books.

Eisenberg, N., & Fabes, R. A. (1998). Prosocial development. In W. Damon & N. Eisenberg (Eds.), *Handbook of child psychology* Vol. 3; *Social, emotional, and personality development* (5th ed., pp. 701–778). New York: John Wiley & Sons.

Eisenberg, N., Guthrie, I. K., Fabes, R. A., Reiser, M., Murphy, B. C., Holmgren, R., Maszk, P., & Losoya, S. (1997). The relations of regulation and emotionality to resiliency and competent social functioning in elementary school children. *Child Development, 68,* 295–311.

Fabes, R. A., & Eisenberg, N. (1992). Young children's coping with interpersonal anger. *Child Development, 63,* 116–128.

Gibbs, N. (1995, October 2). The EQ factor. *Time,* 60–66, 68.

Gibbs, N. (1997). Reprint of "The EQ factor" from *Time,* October 2, 1995. In E. N. Junn & C. J. Boyatzis (Eds.), *Annual editions: Child growth and development 97/98* (4th ed., pp. 114–120). New York: McGraw-Hill/Dushkin.

Goleman, D. (1995). *Emotional development.* New York: Bantam Books.

Hennessy, K., Rabideau, G., Cummings, E. M., & Cicchetti, D. (1994). Responses of physically abused and nonabused children to different forms of interadult anger. *Child Development, 65*(3), 815–829.

Howes, C., & Mathison, C. C. (1992). Sequences in the development of competent play with peers: Social and social-pretend play. *Developmental Psychology, 28*, 961–974.

Hyson, M. (2002). Preparing tomorrow's teachers: NAEYC announces new standards. *Young Children, 57*(2), 78–79.

Kuebli, J. (1994). Young children's understanding of everyday emotions. *Young Children, 49*, 36–47.

Marion, M. (1997). Research in review: Guiding young children's understanding and management of anger. *Young Children, 52*(7), 62–68.

Marion, M. (2003). *Guidance of young children* (6th ed.). Upper Saddle River, NJ: Merrill/Prentice Hall.

McClellan, D., & Katz, L. G. (1992). Assessing the social development of young children: A checklist of social attributes. *Dimensions of Early Childhood,* Fall, 9–10.

McClellan, D., & Katz, L. G. (2001, March). *Assessing young children's social competence.* ERIC/EECE Publications-Digests, EDO-PS-01-2.

Parten., M. B. (1932). Social participation among preschool children. *Journal of Abnormal and Social Psychology, 27*, 243–269.

Piaget, J. (1932). *The moral judgment of the child.* Glencoe, IL: Free Press.

Rubin, K. H., Bukowski, W., & Parker, J. G. (1998). Peer interactions, relationships, and groups. In W. Damon & N. Eisenberg (Eds.), *Handbook of child psychology: Vol. 3; Social, emotional, and personality development* (5th ed., pp. 619–700). New York: John Wiley & Sons.

Rubin, K. H., Watson, K., & Jambor, T. (1978). Free play behaviors in preschool and kindergarten children. *Child Development, 49*, 534–536.

Saarni, C., Mumme, D. L., & Campos, J. J. (1998). Emotional development: Action, communication, and understanding. In W. Damon & N. Eisenberg (Eds.), *Handbook of child psychology: Vol. 3; Social, emotional, and personality development* (5th ed., pp. 237–309). New York: John Wiley & Sons.

Schneider, B. H., Rubin, K. H., & Ledingham, J. E. (Eds.). (1985). *Children's peer relations: Issues in assessment and intervention.* New York: Springer-Verlag.

Skinner, E., & Wellborn, J. (1994). Coping during childhood and adolescence: A motivational perspective. In R. Lerner (Ed.), *Life-span development and behavior* (pp. 91–133). Hillsdale, NJ: Erlbaum.

Stenberg, C. (1982). *The development of anger facial expressions in infancy.* Unpublished doctoral dissertation, University of Denver.

Vygotsky, L. S. (1978). *Mind in society: The development of higher psychological processes.* Cambridge, MA: Harvard University Press.

WEB SITES RELATED TO THIS CHAPTER[2]

✓ Cornell University Extension

www.cce.cornell.edu/publications/children.cfm

Resources on children. For example, "Terrific and Terrible Two-Year-Olds" and "The World of the Five-Year-Old" are inexpensive and useful fact sheets with information on child development, including social and emotional development.

[2]Navigating sites: If you type in a site's address and it has several links, for example, www.cce.cornell.edu/publications/children.cfm, you might not get to the site. Try this if you have this difficulty. Type in a smaller amount of information, such as, www.cce.cornell.edu/publications. Then follow links to the exact resource that you need.

✓ ERIC-EECE

www.ericeece.org/pubs/digests/byyear.html#1997

and the updated version of 2001. An ERIC D*igest* by Lillian Katz and Diane McClellan. A developmental approach to assessment of young children, ERIC Digest, ERIC-EECE, March. Go to the 2001 list to view the updated version.

✓ University of Wisconsin Extension

In cooperation with other state university extension divisions, the UW Extension has produced newsletters on child development and parenting for the early childhood years. Research-based. Reader friendly. Well-written. The newsletters are widely available. Hard copy available from addresses listed on the Web site. Full text of every newsletter on the Web site. Superb resources.

http://www1.uwex.edu/ces/pubs/

The publication page for the extension division. Click on "Home & family" and then on "Human Development and Family Relations." Scroll to "Parenting Infants and Pre-Schoolers." You will see "Parenting the First Year," a series of multipage newsletters on infant development and parenting issues. See also "Parenting the Second and Third Years," a series of multipage newsletters on toddler development. Publications on older children also available.

CHAPTER 10

Using Observation to Prevent and Solve Problems

Problem: a source of perplexity or distress
Prevent: to keep from happening
Solve: to find a solution for

Chapter objectives

1. *Explain* the value in a problem-solving perspective.
2. *Summarize* the characteristics of teachers who have a problem-solving perspective.
3. *Explain* how to use observation strategies to prevent or solve problems.
4. *Reflect* on one's experience in preventing or solving problems when working with children.

ADOPTING A PROBLEM-SOLVING PERSPECTIVE

In the novel *East of Eden*, John Steinbeck said that the beauty of being human is that we have choices. As adult humans, we certainly do have the capacity to make active conscious choices and decisions. Reflective teachers use their capacity to make wise choices every day

All teachers have to deal with issues, dilemmas, and problems. The problems will differ from classroom to classroom, but every teacher must deal with problems. Alfie Kohn (1996) urges teachers to make active conscious decisions about normal, every-day problems and especially about problems that are more serious.

Specifically, Kohn described two paths that teachers can take when problems arise. One path leads to reactions to problems—reactions that often seem irrational and illogical. This is the path of unthinking and impulsive reactions. For instance, a teacher who perceives a problem with discipline and who reacts impulsively might well punish a child instead of thinking the problem through. The other path leads to rational, conscious solutions to problems. This is the path of problem solving.

Kohn was urging teachers to consider adopting a disposition or attitude toward preventing problems or solving problems when presented with a distressing or confus-ing situation. Reflective teachers who adopt a problem-solving or prevention attitude share some common characteristics.

Reflective Teachers Acknowledge That Problems Exist

Reflective teachers tend to be realistic. They do not deny that a problem is staring them in the face. They realize that acknowledging a problem's existence is the first step in solving it, even if it means quite a bit of thought and work. They also realize that there are many potential problems, and fortunately, they believe that they can prevent at least some of them.

Example: Mr. Claiborne realized almost immediately that Sam was afraid of the rabbit that the class spotted on a walk. He did not deny that the fear was real, but treated it as a problem, knowing that he could help.

Example: Robert had been a student in Mrs. Vargas's preschool class 2 years before. Robert's father had physically abused him, and consequently, Mrs. Vargas had known that Robert had several potential problems.

Reflective Teachers Are Professional and Act Ethically When Solving Problems

The goal of reflective teachers is to solve a problem, not to gossip or gripe. They do think about a problem, but they do not waste time going over and over it. They avoid blaming anyone for the problem, although they seek information about its context.

Although they might seek advice or counsel about the issue from a colleague, reflective teachers do not gossip about children, the child's family, or a specific problem. They do not judge the child or her family. Their conversations center on how they can help the child or family.

Reflective teachers radiate an attitude that says, "This is a problem, and I can search for a solution."

Example: Mrs. Vargas, in dealing with Robert and the aftermath of his abuse, talked with the guidance counselor about the problem. Together, they reviewed the potential problems that abused children are very likely to have. The counselor also offered some suggestions. Neither Mrs. Vargas nor Mr. Santini, the counselor, talked about this problem with others. Both professionals consider their conversation confidential and not to be repeated even to other teachers.

Reflective Teachers Responsibly Manage Emotions When Solving Problems

An important part of staying focused when dealing with problems is the ability to manage emotions that crop up as we tackle the dilemma. Some teachers are particularly adept at responsibly managing their unpleasant emotions.

There Are Three Components to All Emotions (Kuebli, 1994; Marion, 1997).

- 📖 Feeling the emotion
- 📖 Expressing the emotion
- 📖 Understanding the emotion (ability to interpret and evaluate the emotion)

Children and Adults Differ in Dealing with Emotions.   Young children feel emotions, and they express them in a number of ways (Fabes & Eisenberg, 1992; Marion, 2003). However, young children are not able to interpret or evaluate their feelings and, consequently, are not able to understand feelings. For instance, a 2½-year-old who feels angry when somebody snatches a toy from her might express this anger quite loudly by screaming. Most likely, she would not even be able to name the emotion, let alone explain it.

A person must be able to evaluate and interpret (understand) her emotions before she can manage those feelings. Therefore, young children cannot manage their feelings on their own.

Adults also feel and express emotions. Many adults can also clearly evaluate and then interpret their emotions; they understand their emotions. This ability makes it possible for them to manage feelings of anger, shame, guilt, joy, or any other emotion responsibly. Unfortunately, other adults manage emotions irresponsibly or gracelessly, hurting, embarrassing, or degrading themselves, other people, and animals, or damaging property.

Emotions Are Aroused When Teachers Face Problems.   Even the most responsible and reflective teachers feel emotions wash over them when they encounter problems.

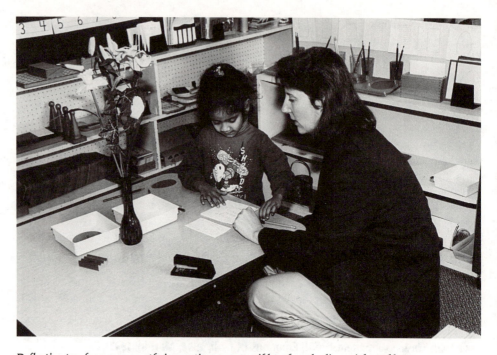

Reflective teachers manage their emotions responsibly when dealing with problems.

They tend to feel distressed or even angry when they encounter abuse or neglect. They might feel frustrated and irritated when a child is aggressive, or feel confused and frustrated when a child's parents fail to pick their child up on time.

Reflective teachers understand and then responsibly manage their emotions, serving as a model for children and parents. They realize that their main responsibility is to think about the problem or potential problem clearly so that they can help a child. They retain the ability to reason in spite of feeling normal emotions.

Example: Mr. Lee winced when he heard Jessie, one of his third graders, say to a child who had just gotten glasses, "Hey, let me count your eyes! Looky here, four eyes." Then, in a sing-song rhythm, the same child sang out, "Four-eyes, four-eyes, four-eyes." He was surprised when Jessie said this because he knew Jessie to be an amiable and kind-hearted child.

To himself, Mr. Lee said, "I feel upset when I hear things like that. Somebody called me four-eyes when I first got my glasses in fifth grade, and I remember how angry I felt then, too." He had interpreted his feelings and understood the root of his upset with what Jessie had said. Mr. Lee was then better able to think through how to help Jessie understand how name-calling hurts other people. The teacher zeroed in on Jessie's customary kindness and helped him focus on taking the other child's perspective. Mr. Lee would not have been able to do this had he remained upset.

Reflective Teachers Value Observation as a Tool in Problem Solving

Reflective teachers use the Decision-Making Model of Child Guidance (Marion, 2003) when dealing with guidance issues and problems. The four steps in the Decision-Making Model (Figure 1.2 in chapter 1) are:

- Observe
- Decide
- Take action
- Reflect

The first step in wise decision making about guidance issues, then, is observation. Teachers make guidance decisions more rationally when they gather helpful information by observing well.

Reflective teachers also commit themselves to observing when they plunge into problem solving. They tend to value observation for its power to give good information. They are skilled observers, choosing the most efficient and effective method to get the information needed for preventing or solving problems. They fully understand that they cannot make good decisions about a problem unless they observe first. Observation is the foundation for building a workable solution for problems or, in many cases, for preventing them.

PROBLEM SOLVING IN ACTION

This section of the chapter focuses on how observation for problem solving or preventing problems might look in a real classroom for busy teachers. You will read about how the four early childhood teachers used observation to prevent or solve problems.

- Mrs. Vargas (preschool) realized that an abused and neglected child has potential problems.
- Mr. Claiborne (first grade) had to decide on how to deal with a child's fear.
- Mr. Nellis (K–2) wanted to help a kindergarten child who dealt with frustration by angrily striking out.
- Mr. Lee (third grade) wanted to minimize the potential stress that often accompanies a child's move to a new school.

PROBLEM SOLVING IN ACTION: MRS. VARGAS (PRESCHOOL)

The Problem: Child Abuse and Neglect

Specifically, Mrs. Vargas had squarely faced several potential problems in her classroom because one of her preschool students had been physically abused by his father. She immediately thought about the effects that the abuse might have had on this child. She considered how the effect of Robert's abuse would show up in the classroom because she had had other abused and neglected children in classes over the years. Teachers worry about the effect of child abuse because they know that child abuse, even in its mildest forms, does harm to children. Its most severe forms threaten children's lives.

Teachers notice physical or behavioral indicators, or a combination of the two, in abused children (Tower, 1999). Aware of their state statutes (laws) about child abuse (each state's law defines abuse and lists indicators of each type of abuse), teachers protect children by following school policies on reporting suspected abuse. Ethical early childhood professionals are acutely aware of and never try to avoid their responsibility to report. They make a good-faith effort to identify physical and behavioral indicators of abuse or neglect.

Teachers see firsthand the behaviors that abused children show in a classroom, and an abused child's behavior often challenges a teacher. Teachers can use observation to get a clear picture of how a child's abuse has affected him. Then the teacher can proceed to plan for helping the child.

How Mrs. Vargas Used Observation: Checklist and Anecdotal Records

This teacher was proactive. She decided to try to identify the issues that Robert faced as he worked and played with other children. Consequently, she reflected on the most efficient observational strategies that would give information on the possible effects of Robert's abuse. She decided to combine two different strategies—a checklist and anecdotal records.

Checklist.   The guidance counselor, in his meeting with Mrs. Vargas about Robert's past abuse, gave her a list of behaviors that abused and neglected children typically display (Figure 7.3 in chapter 7). Mrs. Vargas decided to turn the list into a checklist and to observe Robert with it.

Mrs. Vargas, always careful with observation notes, was probably even more cautious with this checklist. She consulted again with Mr. Santini, the counselor, after using the checklist to get the information that she needed, and then she shredded the list (Figure 10.1).

Anecdotal Records.   After using the checklist, a teacher would have a good idea about the major effects that the abuse had on the child observed. The teacher could easily observe these specific items with brief notes recorded over time: anecdotal records, an efficient and relatively easy observational strategy.

Example: Mrs. Vargas had checked two items—an excessive degree of passive watchfulness and extreme shyness. She noted that she needed more information, and so she decided to do anecdotal records on both items for the next couple of months. She usually wrote anecdotal records on forms first seen in chapter 3 (Figure 10.2). Here is an example of one of her anecdotal records in which she observed Robert's shyness. Please note that the teacher never uses the term *child abuse*. Instead, she focuses on Robert's ability to join a group.

Checklist: Characteristics of Abused or Neglected Children

- ☐ Seems old for their age
- ☐ Lacks ability to play
- ☐ Temper tantrums beyond that expected for age and stage of development
- ☐ Low self-esteem—behaves in a way that tells us that he does not feel competent or in control or that he is not worthy of the attention of others
- ☐ Withdrawal—can, but does not always indicate abuse
- ☐ Chronic aggression or overt hostility against peers, animals, adults, themselves
- ☑ Passive watchfulness, an excessive amount
- ☐ Compulsivity or efforts to control some small aspect of their lives
- ☐ Fearful of failure
- ☐ Difficulty listening to or carrying out instructions
- ☐ Difficulty organizing thoughts, conceptualizing, and verbalizing
- ☐ Regression to an earlier stage of development—bedwetting, thumbsucking, baby talk
- ☐ Poor social skills
- ☑ Extreme shyness
- ☐ Steals or hoards food
- ☐ Little or no empathy for others

Notes/Comments:
Robert shows no aggression so far. He seems to watch others almost all the time, for example; even when he is doing artwork or playing in water. My impression is that he is also shy, almost extremely so. But I need more information on these two things.

Figure 10.1

Sources: See Figure 7.3, chapter 7 of this text.

Anecdotal Record

Goal for this observation: observe Robert as he joins a group for play/work
Setting: block corner
Date/day: 10-22
Time of day: early morning
Basic activity: building with blocks
Focus child: Robert
Others involved: one boy, one girl

The Anecdote: Robert stood at the edge of the block area, looking in, never speaking to the others working. Other boy asked R to play, but R turned his head away with his body still planted at the edge of the block center. He did not look at the other boy, who finally went back to play. R then turned his head back to watch again.

Reflection/Comment/Interpretation: This is the third observation where I've noticed Robert watching in a somewhat wistful way. He is never aggressive and seems to want to play. But he has such a hard time connecting with another child, even when invited to play.

Figure 10.2

PROBLEM SOLVING IN ACTION: MR. CLAIBORNE (FIRST GRADE)

The Problem: A Child's Fear

Mr. Claiborne witnessed Sam's fear when the class saw a very large brownish rabbit scurrying across a field when the class had taken a walk. Specifically, the teacher's dilemma was to try to understand Sam's fear.

Fear is a basic emotion that emerges between 2½ and 7 months of age. It appears that fear and the other basic emotions of anger, sadness, joy, and surprise are biologically programmed. That is, theorists believe that the basic emotions are hardwired into humans. Therefore, the basic emotions emerge at approximately the same time and are shown in much the same way by young children from all cultures (Shaffer, 1996).

Mr. Claiborne has seen the basic emotion *fear* displayed many times by children in his teaching career. He considers emotions natural and normal and fully expects young children to be sad, angry, happy, or afraid. He also knows that it is possible, as children grow older, for them to learn to fear specific situations and objects.

He suspects that Sam, for some reason, has learned to fear rabbits, but he cannot be sure until he gathers a little more information. He had seen what appeared to be fear of the living, breathing, hopping rabbit. Nevertheless, Mr. Claiborne needed to know and document whether he would also see Sam's apparent fear of rabbits displayed in other "rabbit" situations.

This teacher is on the right track in thinking that he needs several observations before he can be reasonably sure that his initial ideas are correct. Observers should *not* make judgments too quickly and should *not* jump to conclusions. Observers can make reasonable and fair conclusions only after they have gathered enough information or data. After they have gathered information through observing, then they can begin to see patterns, and it is the patterns over time that give the most helpful information.

How Mr. Claiborne Used Observation: Running Record and Anecdotal Records

Running Record.   "It's at times like this," Mr. Claiborne commented, "that I wish that we had a cameraperson following us around to film things like the rabbit episode." Because he wanted as accurate a record of the event as possible, the teacher decided that the next best thing to a video would be to make a good written record of the incident.

He worked with the student teacher to write a brief **running record,** with Mr. Claiborne taking the lead in writing. The student teacher commented that she felt like a detective writing notes on a case. They recorded their memory of only a segment of the walk that the class took, a segment dealing with their specific problem. Figure 10.3 shows their running record.[1]

This running record did two things. First, it recorded the rabbit incident so that the teachers could reflect on it more easily. They had thought through the episode,

---

[1]This is a developmental running record. Many teachers also use running records to observe children's progress in reading.

Running Record
"The Pickup Truck Dog and the Rabbit"

Context/Background	Intensive Observation	Comment/Interpretation
Approximately 10:15 a.m. The class went on a walk around the block to check the progress of the construction of the baseball field for the school. **All the children were here, along with the teacher and student teacher.** **Sam walked next to Clay.**	We left school through the main door after checking out with the office. I was in the front and the student teacher brought up the rear with the children walking between us, walking side-by-side with another child. Sam walked along, engaging in the usual chitchat with the children around him. He called out to me, "Hey, Mr. Claiborne. The yellow light (traffic signal) is blinking. What does that mean? Is it broken?" Just as he finished this sentence, a large red pickup screeched to a slow crawl at the light. The dog in the back of the pickup saw the children and started twirling around, whining softly at first and then a little more loudly. The children all noticed the dog and pointed to it, turning to the teachers and urging us to look as well. The student teacher said quietly and firmly, "Thanks for pointing out the dog. Now, look at me." She put her finger to her lips and said, "Sh-h-h. Let's be quiet and not scare him." She put her hands on her face and said again, "Look at my face. Good. Let's turn back now to the field." The children looked at Theresa as she talked, some looking back at the dog, but nobody said anything else.	Sam was relaxed and inquisitive, as usual. Sam looked at the dog but did not seem to be excessively nervous or afraid. Sam looked at Theresa.

Figure 10.3

(continued)

	We got the children moving again and came to the field quickly, but some of the children were still watching the truck as it pulled away, the dog still turned toward the class.	
	Just as everybody moved in the same direction, Jessica screeched, "A bunny! Look, a bunny!" Every pair of eyes swiveled to where Jessica pointed. Children squealed, pointed, and jumped up and down as the rabbit hopped quickly across the field.	Sam did not react as the others did.
	Sam, however, had stopped, squeezed his eyes shut tightly, rolled both hands into fists, brought them up to his face, and covered his eyes with them, the palms toward his eyes. He tightened his face as he forcefully said, "NO!"	This could have been fear for Sam, but the children were in a state of heightened emotional arousal, that is, they were primed and ready to feel many different emotions. *Sam could have been afraid, but he could also have been stressed from the pickup truck dog incident.*
		I think that we need to check this out by using some other form of observation.

Figure 10.3   *(continued)*

recalling critical elements that they would likely have never thought about or would have forgotten had they not recorded them.

Second, the running record revealed a critical question: Was Sam really showing fear? The excitement generated by the dog in the truck might have played an important role in Sam's reaction to the rabbit. His reaction seemed to be fear, but could just as easily have been stress. The teachers would have to use observation again.

Anecdotal Record.   Because they both had questions about whether Sam was afraid of rabbits, Mr. Claiborne asked his student teacher to write four to five anecdotal records about Sam's reactions to rabbits in other situations. She observed as Sam

---

Anecdotal Record

Goal for this observation: observe Sam with rabbits (fear of rabbits?)
Setting: large group area
Date/day: October 7/Wednesday
Time of day: after lunch
Basic activity: guests (vet tech and rabbit)
Focus child: Sam
Others involved: entire class

The Anecdote: Sam sat in his usual spot, right next to Clay. The vet tech had the rabbit in a little house decorated with drawings of rabbits. Sam leaned forward, his arms crossed casually across his knees, his head thrust forward slightly. Sam listened to the guest, his face scrunched up in a questioning look. About halfway through the activity, Sam said, "My friend Jennie has a rabbit. He (the rabbit) eats rabbit food. Does this rabbit have to eat special food?"

Reflection/Comment/Interpretation: This is my fifth observation of Sam and rabbits. Other than that first incident in the field, he has never shown fear when the topic of rabbits comes up. I've observed as he looked at pictures of rabbits, as he watched rabbits and their babies in a video, and as he saw *two* rabbits in that field next to our school (location of the original fear episode). Together with the visit from the real rabbit and Sam's calm demeanor, my conclusion is that Sam is *not afraid* of rabbits. These data lead me to conclude that Sam was overwhelmed with general excitement when we all saw the first rabbit.

Figure 10.4

looked at rabbits in photographs, videos, or books. She wrote anecdotal records when the children sighted two rabbits in the same field. She also observed and recorded his reaction to the rabbit who visited with a veterinary technician. Figure 10.4 shows her last observation in this series, along with her conclusion that she shared with Mr. Claiborne.

Mr. Claiborne reviewed the student teacher's original anecdotal records and concurred with her, based on her observations. The running record and the short, carefully targeted series of anecdotal records gave them the information that they needed.

PROBLEM SOLVING IN ACTION: MR. NELLIS (K–2)

The Problem: Child Hurts Others When She Is Angry

You read in chapter 6 about using periodic observation reports to let parents know about their children's development and progress. Mr. Nellis knows that parents need to know about problems that their child has, and he does not hesitate to bring up such problems.

Janna is a kindergarten child in his class. He noticed that she had difficulty dealing with frustration and irritation or anger. He decided to deal with this problem by observing Janna more closely in this area.

How Mr. Nellis Used Observation: Anecdotal Records and a Rating Scale

Anecdotal Records.   Mr. Nellis combined two teacher-made observation instruments. The first, anecdotal records, is a part of his overall assessment plan. His plan called for completing five or six anecdotal records per semester for each child. Like the other early childhood teachers at his school, he believes that this is an excellent method for getting information about a specific area of development for each individual child. So, each child's anecdotal records target an area of development specific to that child.

For Janna, Mr. Nellis decided to use anecdotal records to assess the area of emotional development. Specifically, he wanted to know how Janna expressed anger and frustration. Figure 10.5 shows one of the anecdotal records.

Rating Scale.   Mr. Nellis, worried about Janna's problem after reviewing the information, used the data gleaned from the anecdotal records to complete the rating scale. He first designed the rating scale to use only with Janna, but then decided to keep a master so that he could use it again when needed.

Figure 10.6 is the rating scale that he developed. He circled his rating of each item, and he wrote a brief summary comment. This is the same comment that he included in the observation report that he wrote when preparing for a meeting with Janna's parents (chapter 6).

Anecdotal Record

Goal for this observation: observe how a child manages frustration or irritation
Setting: gym
Date/day: October 12/Monday
Time of day: 2 p.m.
Basic activity: pairs of children practice ball throwing skills
Focus child: Janna
Others involved: John, Stephen (both in kindergarten)

The Anecdote: Janna and John were partners, throwing the ball as the student teacher demonstrated. As Janna waited for John to throw the ball, Stephen threw his ball, and it ended up bouncing off Janna's leg. Janna looked over at Stephen and said, "Stop it, Stephen! Stop hitting me! You're so stupid."

Reflection/Comment/Interpretation: I have observed three times for how Janna reacts to frustration and irritation when other children are involved. Each time she has used name-calling when another child does something that irritates her.

Figure 10.5

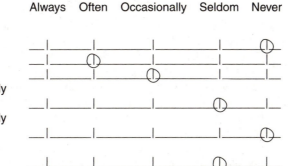

Graphic Rating Scale: How Janna Manages Anger

Child's Name: Janna
Date: December 10
This semester I have been observing how Janna manages anger and have used anecdotal records. One week ago, I used information gathered from the anecdotal records to complete this rating scale to evaluate Janna's ability to deal appropriately with normal feelings of frustration and irritation. I have circled the appropriate spot on the line next to each phrase.

	Always	Often	Occasionally	Seldom	Never
Uses words appropriately to express anger					◯
Strikes out when angry		◯			
Name-calling when upset			◯		
Expresses anger appropriately toward teachers				◯	
Expresses anger appropriately toward other children					◯
Generates word labels for frustration and anger				◯	

Comment: "Janna is having a difficult time with managing her feelings. My observations show that she needs us to help her learn to use words to label angry or sad or disappointed feelings. She now strikes out when angry or tends to yell or do name-calling when she is sad or disappointed or frustrated. We are working on teaching her to use more appropriate words when normal but unpleasant feelings wash over her."

Figure 10.6

Note: You have also read this summary statement in chapter 6, in the section on observation reports.

PROBLEM SOLVING IN ACTION: MR. LEE (THIRD AND FOURTH GRADES)
The Problem: Minimize Stress for a Child Who Moves to a New School

Specifically, Mr. Lee had found out on November 1 that Dean, a third grader, would be moving to the neighborhood and would be in Mr. Lee's class. Mr. Lee had always suspected that moving was stress inducing, but had recently read about the stress of moving as a part of a seminar on reducing stress in children's lives. Mr. Lee wanted to prevent some of the stress of moving for Dean. He also wanted to give Dean's parents information and support as needed.[2]

---

[2]See Marion (2003) for the "list" as well as for detailed information on buffering the effects of moving on children.

How Mr. Lee Used Observation: Checklist

Mr. Lee could have chosen from among several good observational strategies. He based his decision on the one strategy that would best help him prevent as much stress as possible. Therefore, he chose to focus on keeping track of his own practices and his responsibilities relating to this issue.

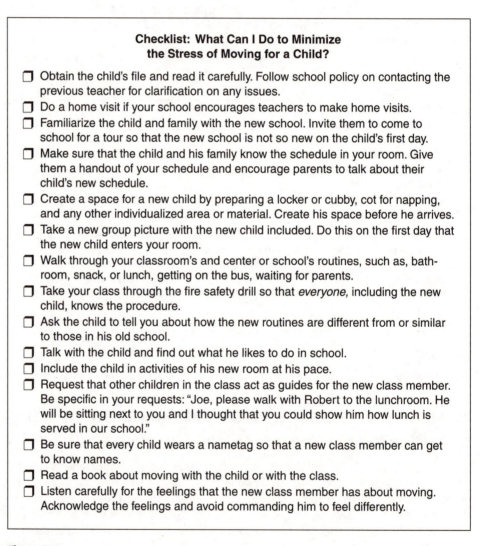

**Checklist: What Can I Do to Minimize
the Stress of Moving for a Child?**

☐ Obtain the child's file and read it carefully. Follow school policy on contacting the previous teacher for clarification on any issues.

☐ Do a home visit if your school encourages teachers to make home visits.

☐ Familiarize the child and family with the new school. Invite them to come to school for a tour so that the new school is not so new on the child's first day.

☐ Make sure that the child and his family know the schedule in your room. Give them a handout of your schedule and encourage parents to talk about their child's new schedule.

☐ Create a space for a new child by preparing a locker or cubby, cot for napping, and any other individualized area or material. Create his space before he arrives.

☐ Take a new group picture with the new child included. Do this on the first day that the new child enters your room.

☐ Walk through your classroom's and center or school's routines, such as, bathroom, snack, or lunch, getting on the bus, waiting for parents.

☐ Take your class through the fire safety drill so that *everyone,* including the new child, knows the procedure.

☐ Ask the child to tell you about how the new routines are different from or similar to those in his old school.

☐ Talk with the child and find out what he likes to do in school.

☐ Include the child in activities of his new room at his pace.

☐ Request that other children in the class act as guides for the new class member. Be specific in your requests: "Joe, please walk with Robert to the lunchroom. He will be sitting next to you and I thought that you could show him how lunch is served in our school."

☐ Be sure that every child wears a nametag so that a new class member can get to know names.

☐ Read a book about moving with the child or with the class.

☐ Listen carefully for the feelings that the new class member has about moving. Acknowledge the feelings and avoid commanding him to feel differently.

Figure 10.7

Source: From Marion, M. (2003). *Guidance of young children* (6th ed.). Upper Saddle River, NJ: Merrill/Prentice-Hall. Adapted with permission.

To focus squarely on his own practices, he designed a teacher-made checklist, which he then used as a guide through the process of helping Dean. He had a list of things that teachers could do to minimize the stress of moving for children. He converted the list into a checklist so that he could make sure that he had not forgotten anything that might help Dean. He did not use every one of the ideas on the checklist, but chose the ones that he thought would help Dean and his family the most. Figure 10.7 is the checklist.

Activities to Help You Construct Knowledge and Skills in Observing

ACTIVITY 1

Journal writing: Reflect on your own experience. Describe a specific problem that you have encountered in working with young children. From your perspective, were you successful in dealing with the problem? If yes, why? If no, please explain.

Choose one observational strategy that you think might have helped you solve the problem even more effectively. Why do you think that using observation in this way would have helped you?

ACTIVITY 2

Choose one of the four major examples of how the early childhood teachers at the Oaklawn School used observation to solve or prevent a problem. Explain why the observation strategies that the teacher used would have been helpful in solving the problem described.

REFERENCES

Fabes, R., & Eisenberg, N. (1992). Young children's coping with interpersonal anger. *Child Development*, 63, 116–128.

Kohn, A. (1996). *Beyond discipline*. Alexandria, VA.: ASCD, Association for Supervision and Curriculum Development.

Kuebli, J. (1994). Research in review: Young children's understanding of everyday emotions. *Young Children*, 49, 36–47.

Marion, M. (1997). Research in review: Guiding young children's understanding and management of anger. *Young Children*, 52(7), 62–68.

Marion, M. (2003). *Guidance of young children* (6th ed.). Upper Saddle River, NJ: Merrill/Prentice Hall.

Shaffer, D. (1996). *Developmental psychology*. Pacific Grove, CA: Brooks/Cole.

Tower, C. (1999). *Understanding child abuse and neglect*. Boston, MA: Allyn & Bacon.

WEB SITES RELATED TO THIS CHAPTER

✓ AACAP (American Academy of Child and Adolescent Psychiatry):

http://www.aacap.org

This is the home page for AACAP. Many of the links are useful to parents and teachers. The fact sheets might help you deal with some typical problems faced by teachers and parents.

http://www.aacap.org/publications/factsfam/index

See the entire list of fact sheets at this link. If this longer address does not work, then just type in the root, www.aacap.org. Then click on "publications" and then on "Family Fact Sheets." The Fact Sheets are listed two ways, alphabetically and by number.

CHAPTER 11

Using Observation to Become a Reflective Practitioner

"We must create school environments that support those educators who are willing to invest the energy required to grow professionally."

(ASCD, 2000)

Chapter objectives

1. *Explain* the meaning and value of reflective teaching.
2. *Summarize* the levels of reflection in teaching.
3. *Assess* your own ability to reflect on your practices.
4. *Value* observation as the key to self-reflection in teaching.
5. *Explain* how to use different observation instruments to reflect on teaching practices.

PROFESSIONAL DEVELOPMENT PLANS: OAKLAWN SCHOOL (CASE STUDY)

The teachers at the Oaklawn School had decided to emphasize *reflective teaching* in their faculty development plans for the year, and "Operation Self-Reflection" was under way. One of the major parts of the plan was for every teacher to take the same online course, "The Reflective Educator" (ASCD, 2000). The goal was for teachers to use the knowledge from this course to increase their ability to reflect on their teaching practices.

Part two of the plan encouraged each teacher to develop a professional development plan focusing on reflection in teaching. The early childhood teachers, Mr. Lee, Mr. Nellis, Mr. Claiborne, and Mrs. Vargas, decided as a group that a logical follow-up to the course would be to do a self-assessment of their classroom practices. They chose two existing, published instruments, one designed specifically for preschool and the other for the primary grades. The primary-grade teachers (Nellis, Claiborne, and Lee) used the APEEC (Hemmeter, Maxwell, Ault, & Schuster, 2001) and the preschool teacher, Mrs. Vargas, used the ECERS (Harms, Clifford, & Cryer, 1998) to observe and assess teaching practices.

From these self-assessments, each early childhood teacher identified several of their practices that were developmentally appropriate. Each teacher also identified two areas of his or her teaching practices in which the teacher wanted to improve. Each teacher then outlined specific requests for faculty development that he or she identified in the course and from the classroom assessment. Their principal approved the following plans for reflection and faculty development.

- All of the early childhood teachers discovered that they needed to reflect on how they used media in their classes (TV, video, and/or computers).
- Mrs. Vargas (preschool) wanted to reflect on math in her class, that is, how the environment could develop even further mathematics-related materials, setup, and activities.
- Mr. Claiborne (first grade) wanted to reflect on how he displayed children's products.
- Mr. Nellis (K–2) wanted to reflect on how he involved families.
- Mr. Lee (third grade) wanted to reflect on child guidance, with an emphasis on teaching conflict resolution.

REFLECTION IN TEACHING

What Is Reflection in Teaching?

Reflection: contemplation, examination, thinking, and consideration. Reflection involves observation and assessment or evaluation by teachers. Effective teachers reflect on their own teaching practices, and they reflect on the teaching practices of others. For instance, they might reflect on how they have set up their classroom, on how the daily schedule is working, on whether they observe children sufficiently, or even on their relationships with other adults and with children. Effective teachers often observe the teaching practices of other teachers, not to criticize, but with an eye to deciding whether that other person's strategies would work in their own classrooms.

Shon (1987) used the term ***reflective practitioner*** to describe teachers who examine and analyze their practices. A reflective practitioner (also called teacher or professional in this chapter) observes and assesses, that is, reflects, to make teaching practices even stronger and more effective.

All teachers would benefit from using reflection to enhance their professional practices. Kohn (1996) urges teachers to examine their own practices and to reflect consciously on them. Reflection supports teachers in making wise decisions and in justifying decisions and choices.

Reflection: A Professional Responsibility

Professional organizations such as the National Council for the Accreditation of Teacher Education (NCATE) and the National Association for the Education of Young Children (NAEYC) are concerned with the preparation of teacher educators. These organizations write guidelines for teacher education programs, guidelines helping institutions focus on what graduates of their programs should know and be able to do.

Guideline 5 in the NAEYC standards addresses the skills and knowledge associated with professionalism. One aspect of professionalism is the ability to engage in self-assessment and self-evaluation. Therefore, NAEYC specifically addresses this ability in Guideline 5.1:

> *Programs prepare early childhood professionals who reflect on their practices . . . continually self-assess and evaluate the effects of their choices and actions on others (young children, parents, and other professionals) as a basis for program planning and modification, and continuing professional development.*

Different Teachers, Different Beliefs About Self-Reflection

The journey of self-reflection is different for everyone: Each teacher has her own style of reflection and her own ability to reflect. Every teacher's beliefs about reflection affect her willingness to reflect on practices. If, for example, a teacher holds strong beliefs that she should think about her professional practices with the intent to change them when indicated, then that teacher will very likely reflect on her practices. On the other hand, if a teacher believes that she should not have to assess her practices, then she will indeed not examine or reflect on those practices.

Some teachers might actually resist the idea of reflection; others simply do not yet recognize that they should reflect on their practices. Many teachers enjoy the whole process of reflection and show no fear or anxiety about it.

Some teachers operate at a high level in terms of reflection, that is, they engage in "meta" reflection. They reflect or think about the topic of reflection: They not only reflect on their own practices, but also get others involved in reflection. They might write about reflection, as Frank (1999) did in a brief article. Teachers at this level might develop workshops or learning circles in which others have a chance to learn about reflection.

Levels of Reflection in Teaching

Lambert (2000) developed a rubric describing four levels of reflection for teachers (Figure 11.1). It describes a range in the ability or willingness to reflect on one's practices, from little or no reflection to the higher level of encouraging reflection in others.

Level 1. Little or No Self-Reflection.   There are many reasons why a teacher might not reflect on practices. A person at this level might actually refuse to do much reflection or self-assessment because she believes that she should not have to reflect or that reflection is pointless.

Example: One of the fifth-grade teachers openly stated his opposition to self-reflection. He also commented about the Oaklawn early childhood teachers' plan to evaluate their classroom practices: "This whole thing (the evaluation of classroom practices) . . . what's the point?"

If administrators do not value or if they punish self-reflection, then many teachers would likely hesitate to reflect, even if their natural inclination would be to think about their practices. This would be a system problem, with the teacher confused and anxious about the best course of action.

Example: The director of a preschool controlled the instructional practices of the staff. He dictated how the teachers were to do their circle time and would not allow a teacher to make any changes in managing circle time. He ridiculed a teacher who said that she had thought about a new seating arrangement for reading group stories.

It is also possible that a person with this style of reflection does not even recognize the need for self-reflection. In this case, telling the person about the need to reflect would likely be effective.

Example: A teacher used circle time because she had seen it used dozens of times in student teaching. However, she managed circle time without regard to the children's needs or abilities and failed to reflect on how her circle times were going. She did not contemplate changes that would help children enjoy circle time more, until a colleague suggested that she might want to consider a different seating arrangement for reading stories so that all the children could see the book.

Level 2. Self-Reflection/Little or No Sharing.   At this level a teacher does reflect on some practices, but usually does not share reflections with other teachers. The teacher might not know that sharing ideas is good, might not want to share ideas, or might not have the skills for sharing ideas.

Example: A teacher discovered that she had a problem with circle time and thought about (reflected on) the possible reasons for the difficulty. She discovered that she had not thought through the seating arrangement very clearly. She changed the seating arrangement, but did not talk about it at all to her colleagues because she thought that they would consider her incompetent.

Level 3. Self-Reflection Combined with Sharing.   At this level, a teacher consciously and willingly reflects on her own practices in order to improve practices. She also shares reflections with others. A teacher has to feel safe with colleagues before she will be willing to share ideas with them.

Example: A teacher discovered a problem with circle time, reflected on the possible causes, and concluded that the seating arrangement made it difficult for some children to see the book. She changed her practice, that is, she rearranged the carpet squares. She made a diagram of the before and after seating arrangement, posted it to the teachers' computer discussion group, and asked teachers to comment on the best arrangement for story reading.

Level 4. Assess Own Practices and Encourages Self-Reflection in Others.   A person operating at this level not only assesses his own practices but also supports an environment of reflection. He might get other teachers together to plan things together or to do peer coaching, or he might write about being a reflective teacher.

Example: Mr. Nellis (K–2 teacher at Oaklawn) seems to operate at this level. He and one of the fifth-grade teachers came up with the idea of "Operation Self-Reflection" for the school and proposed the idea first to the principal and then to all of the teachers. He led the group of early childhood teachers in planning their division's role in "Operation Self-Reflection." The early childhood group already engages in peer coaching, and their evaluation of their classrooms with published instruments is a good example of collaborative planning.

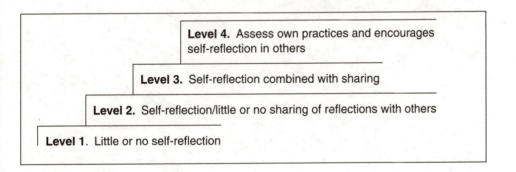

Figure 11.1
Levels of Reflection for Teachers
Source: L. Lambert (2000).

School Environments That Encourage Reflective Teaching

Teachers are much more likely to be reflective when they work in a school that encourages self-reflection. This is a setting where teachers are not afraid to examine their own practices. Teachers feel safe; the climate of the school is nonthreatening and does not create tension for teachers. They are not afraid that their administrator will think badly of or punish them if they identify areas for improvement.

On the contrary: The early childhood teachers at Oaklawn school work in an environment that encourages reflective teaching. They know that their principal or director wants to facilitate their professional growth because professional growth ultimately benefits children and families.

Example: The principal wholeheartedly supported the teachers at Oaklawn School (chapter opener vignette) in their quest to sharpen their self-reflection skills. The principal never demanded that anyone participate. Instead, she asked what she could do to help the teachers with their proposal "Operation Self-Reflection."

This principal writes performance evaluations that highlight a teacher's strengths. She commends and encourages teachers who identify areas for growth and who take action steps to develop new skills. This principal prizes reflective teaching. She is the person who wrote the grant proposal that obtained money for her teachers to take the online course on reflective teaching from ASCD.

Teachers are much more likely to be reflective when they work in a school that encourages self-reflection.

OBSERVATION: THE FOUNDATION OF REFLECTION IN TEACHING

Observation is the cornerstone of authentic assessment of young children. Likewise, observation is the foundation of self-reflection for early childhood professionals. Teachers can use many observation instruments, including checklists, rating scales, anecdotal records, or even running records, either teacher-made or ready-made, for observing.

This chapter explains how to use specific observation strategies and instruments to observe and refine professional practices.

ECERS-R (EARLY CHILDHOOD ENVIRONMENT RATING SCALE–REVISED)

This is the instrument that Mrs. Vargas, the preschool teacher, used to evaluate several parts of her program. After completing this observation, she had a much better picture of things that she might change so that her teaching practices would be even more effective.

Description

The Early Childhood Environment Rating Scale, revised edition (ECERS-R) (Harms et al., 1998) is an observation tool. It was specifically designed as either a research instrument or as a tool for evaluating program quality in preschool classrooms for children ages $2\frac{1}{2}$–5 years of age. Teachers use it to assess seven areas of program quality. These areas appear as subscales on the instrument, each subscale including several items.

- *Space and furnishings* (*the subscale*): The items for this subscale are indoor space, furniture for routine care, furnishings for relaxation and comfort, room arrangement for play, space for privacy, child-related display, space for gross motor play, and gross motor equipment.
- *Personal care routines*: Items in this subscale are greeting/departing, meals/snacks, nap/rest, toileting/diapering, health practices, and safety practices.
- *Language-reasoning*: Items in this subscale are books and pictures, encouraging children to communicate, using language to develop reasoning skills, and informal use of language.
- *Activities*: Items include fine motor, art, music/movement, blocks, sand/water, dramatic play, nature/science, math/number, use of TV, video, and/or computers, and promoting acceptance of diversity.
- *Interaction*: Items include supervision of gross motor activities, general supervision of children (other than gross motor), discipline, staff-child interactions, and interactions among children.
- *Program structure*: Items include schedule, free play, group time, and provisions for children with disabilities.
- *Parents and staff*: Items include provisions for parents, provisions for personal needs of staff, provisions for professional needs of staff, staff interaction and cooperation, supervision and evaluation of staff, and opportunities for professional growth.

Administration and Scoring of ECERS-R

The ECERS-R is a **rating scale.** There are several indicators for each item. Observers rate each item in each subscale. Observers read the indicators and check each as *Yes* or *No* on a separate score sheet. Observers determine the rating for a specific item based on the number of items checked *Yes* or *No*. Ratings range from the numeral 1 (inadequate) to 3 (minimal) to 5 (good) to 7 (excellent).

Example: Mrs. Vargas scored Math/Number under the Activities subscale. She rated her classroom as a 5 for Math/Number because all of the items under 5 were scored *Yes*. Mrs. Vargas decided to reflect further on this area of her program and on increasing the quality of her math/number activities.

   Mrs. Vargas then examined the scores for every item and decided which other item or items to target for improvement. She had scored the item *Use of TV, Video, and/or Computers* as a 4 and was extremely embarrassed about it, until she talked with Mr. Claiborne. He said that the K–primary teachers had rated themselves at about this level for the same item on their observation instrument. Mrs. Vargas, along with her colleagues in the K–primary grades, therefore also decided to reflect further and to focus on the item scored at 4, "Use of TV, Video, and/or Computers." You will read a description of their group action plan further along in this chapter.

   A teacher can do a self-assessment using this tool, as Mrs. Vargas did, or an outside observer may do the assessment. Observers can attend a workshop, watch a training video, or carefully read instructions prior to doing an observation. Developers recommend a minimum of 2 hours, but preferably more time, for the observation.

APEEC (ASSESSMENT OF PRACTICES IN EARLY ELEMENTARY CLASSROOMS)

This is the instrument that the K–primary grade teachers at Oaklawn used to evaluate their programs. This self-assessment gave these teachers a good idea of areas for further reflection and possible change.

Description

Assessment of Practices in Early Elementary Classrooms (APEEC) (Hemmeter et al., 2001) is an observation tool. It measures how well the classroom uses Developmentally Appropriate Practices (DAP). Its structure is similar to that of the ECERS-R. Teachers or researchers can use the APEEC to assess program quality in general education classrooms for K–3 children. These classes might include children with disabilities for at least part of the day. Teachers may also use the APEEC to assess classrooms in which there are only typically developing children.

   A teacher would assess three broad domains of classroom practice. This instrument does not measure the broader school environment such as art or music classes or even the playground environment. The APEEC relies on observation for gathering data. APEEC also provides interview questions, but developers make it clear that "observation data are always preferable to interview data."

There are three broad domains measured by the APEEC. Each domain contains several specific items.

- 📖 *Physical environment (the broad domain)*: The items for this domain are room arrangement, display of child products, classroom accessibility, and health and classroom safety.
- 📖 *Instructional context (the broad domain)*: The items for this domain are use of materials, use of computers, monitoring child progress, teacher-child language, instructional methods, and integration and breadth of subjects.
- 📖 *Social context (the broad domain)*: The items for this domain include children's role in decision-making, participation of children with disabilities in classroom activities, social skills, diversity, appropriate transitions, and family involvement.

Administration and Scoring of APEEC

The APEEC can be scored in two different ways, as a **rating scale** or as a **checklist**.

Scoring APEEC as a Checklist.   There are several indicators for each item within a domain. There are 135 indicators altogether. An observer reads the indicators for each item and marks it as T for true or NT for not true. Scoring APEEC as a checklist takes longer but gives the observer more information about classroom practices.

Example: Mr. Nellis scored the APEEC as a checklist, because he wanted to check every possible indicator for his classroom. For the item "Family Involvement" under the Social Context domain, he marked every one of the 11 indicators as either *T* or *NT*. Mr. Nellis chose this item as the area on which he wants to reflect further.

Scoring APEEC as a Rating Scale.   This is the standard scoring method for the APEEC. The goal is to get an item-level score for each item in the domains. The items are laid out on a numerical scale from 1 to 7. Specific indicators are listed under 1, 3, 5, and 7. A score of 1 indicates inadequacy in terms of DAP. A score of 3 indicates minimally appropriate practices, and a score of 5 indicates that the classroom practices are good in terms of DAP. A score of 7 shows that the classroom is excellent in terms of DAP for that item.

Example: Mr. Lee (third-grade teacher) scored the APEEC as a rating scale and scored the item "Social Skills" as a 6, indicating that his classroom practices approach excellence for this item. He had read and then scored all indicators under 5 as *True*. Therefore, he started reading indicators under 7. He found that one of the two indicators under 7 was *True*. In this case APEEC says that the score should be 6. Although he had an excellent score, Mr. Lee decided that he needed to focus specifically on conflict resolution, the indicator that he marked *Not True*.

REFLECTION IN ACTION

The goal of reflection in teaching is to strengthen professional practices. Observation is the main tool for gathering information about existing practices. The observation points the way for any changes teachers might consider making.

This section of the chapter will focus on how reflection in teaching might look in a real classroom for busy teachers. You will read three examples of reflection in teaching.

- The group of early childhood teachers reflects on improving their use of TV, videos, and computers.
- Mr. Lee reflects on teaching conflict resolution to his students.
- Mr. Nellis reflects on improving involvement of families.

Operation Self-Reflection
EC Teachers: Action Plan—Using Media Even More Effectively

We are working on these goals:
- Teachers being more actively involved in using media with children
- Using materials that encourage active involvement
- Using materials that support and extend classroom themes, projects, and activities
- Primary children using computers for at least three purposes, for example, word processing, drawing or designing, teaching a new skill, practicing a new skill
- Primary children using computers for research (CD-ROM encyclopedia or the Internet)
- Using the Internet more often at school

To reach these goals we will:
- Plan lessons and activities with the goals in mind
- Use *anecdotal records* to document progress toward the goals
- Meet as a group to reflect on our progress
- Use the ECERS-R and the APEEC in 6 weeks to rate this item
- Write a brief report and send a copy to Mrs. LeBlanc (the principal)

Figure 11.2

The early childhood teachers at this school focus on children using computers for several different purposes—word processing, drawing and designing, learning, and practicing new skills.

Group Action Plan

All of the early childhood teachers at Oaklawn School had completed the self-assessment with either the ECERS-R or the APEEC. Mr. Nellis suggested that the group meet to develop an action plan based on each teacher's self-assessment.

Mr. Lee: "Doing the APEEC really took a lot of my time, but I now know what is developmentally appropriate. I was shocked to find out that I don't use computers and TV or videos as well as I could."

"Ditto," said Mrs. Vargas, and she saw that her three colleagues all nodded in agreement. "This looks like something that we could all work on together."

The group then developed their "Action Plan for Strengthening Use of Media" (Figure 11.2). Each teacher would use **anecdotal records** to document changes in how they used media. They sent a copy of the action plan to the principal.

Mr. Lee: Reflecting on Conflict Resolution

Improving Teaching Practices.   Mr. Lee wanted to reflect on teaching conflict resolution skills to his third-graders. First, he decided to rate each child's ability and willingness to use conflict resolution skills and decided to use a rating scale as his observation tool. Figure 11.3 is his ***teacher-made graphic rating scale.***

Second, he used a ***teacher-made checklist*** in his mission to upgrade his classroom practices on conflict resolution. He gave a copy of each of the documents to his three colleagues and requested their input. Figure 11.4 shows the checklist.

Mr. Nellis's Action Plan

Mr. Nellis wanted to make some changes in how he involves families in the classroom.

Refining a Practice That Is Already Good.   Mr. Nellis wanted to refine a couple of indicators, although he had marked them as *True*. He thought that he could increase parent participation if he offered parents even more options.

📖 *True*. "A communication system is present so that families and teachers can communicate easily and in a timely manner."

He currently used voice mail, a telephone in his classroom, and a classroom Web site to communicate with families. He decided to create a distribution list of families

---

Rating Scale: Conflict Resolution Skills

Child's Name:_____

Date:_____

Place an X on the line at the spot indicating the child's ability to use conflict resolution skills.

First, does this child seem to understand how to resolve conflicts? Yes   No

Second, how does this child use conflict resolution skills?

	Always	Often	Occasionally	Seldom	Never
1. Uses appropriate conflict resolution skills					
2. Uses *in*appropriate conflict resolution skills					
3. Uses conflict resolution skills only if T firmly requests					
4. Uses conflict resolution skills only with T guidance					
5. Uses conflict resolution skills without teacher guidance					

Recommendation for helping this child:

Figure 11.3

Operation Self-Reflection
Action Plan on Conflict Resolution
Checklist

__ Rate each child's ability to solve conflicts (use teacher-made rating scale)
__ Invite guidance counselor to do three sessions on conflict resolution
__ Use the thinking puppets to reinforce guidance counselor's lessons
__ Read story about children who resolve a conflict to class
__ Make poster on how to solve problems; hang on wall near group area
__ Give on-the-spot guidance to children about resolving conflict; remind them about how to resolve conflict; remind them about negotiation
__ Designate a special spot in our classroom for resolving conflicts
__ Rate our classroom in 6 weeks on how we have changed in conflict resolution

Reflection:

Figure 11.4

who used e-mail, because over 85% of his families said that they preferred getting information via e-mail or the Internet.

   📖 *True.* "Families are given a variety of options for involvement in classroom-related activities."

He currently encourages parents to observe, to serve as tutors, and to prepare materials. He decided to add the options of selecting curriculum, supervising field trips, being a guest speaker, and arranging classroom celebrations.

Improving Classroom Practices.   Mr. Nellis had marked two indicators as *Not true* in the "Family Involvement" item.

   📖 *Not true.* "The teacher communicates with families at least once a month concerning each child's overall progress at school."
   📖 *Not true.* "The school or teacher asks families how they want to be involved in classroom-related activities."

He thought about effective and efficient ways to accomplish his goals. He decided to work on both items by using the same technique. Figure 11.5 is Mr. Nellis's action plan.

Mr. Nellis Reflects

Asking Families How They Want to Be Involved.   Mr. Nellis realized for the first time that he had never asked parents to give their own ideas about how they prefer to participate and how they wanted him to contact them (Hemmeter, Maxwell, Ault, &

Operation Self-Reflection
Action Plan for Improving Family Involvement

I am working on these goals:
1. To communicate with families at least once each month concerning each child's overall progress at school
2. To ask families how they want to be involved in classroom-related activities

To achieve these goals I will:
1. Contact each family. Either interview them about these two issues or ask them to fill out a survey
2. Develop and use a simple, teacher-made checklist about communicating progress and about involvement in the classroom (Figure 11.6)
3. Write a brief report, share it with early childhood colleagues, and submit a copy to the principal

---

Figure 11.5

Schuster, 2001). Therefore, one of the first things that he did was to contact every family and ask them directly.

Then he had to deal with the rather delicate issue of parents who had never been to school. He had never judged these parents, because judging parents who do not participate is unprofessional. There are many reasons for a parent's lack of participation in a child's classroom.

Some parents have a job far away from home; other parents have had bad experiences with school as a child. Many parents believe that teachers do not need help, and others simply do not understand how much a child benefits when parents participate. Some parents have poor time management skills, might be shy, or might think that their clothing is not good enough. Still others think that they have nothing to offer, but others fear any authority figure and perceive teachers as authority figures. Finally, some parents are overwhelmed with the other parts of their role as parents.

Example: One of the parents in his classroom had talked to Mr. Nellis early in the year and said that she would not be able to come to school very often. The parent of a kindergarten child, she is a single mother, designs Web pages for a living, and is in graduate school. She told Mr. Nellis, long before he ever did the survey, that she regretted having no time to be physically present in the classroom, but that she could easily design and maintain a classroom Web page. Her classroom participation as webmaster might seem unusual and unconventional, but she has been one of the most active parents in Mr. Nellis's class.

Mr. Campbell, one of the fathers, lived in the next town and had joint custody of a child in Mr. Nellis's class, but had never been to school. Mr. Nellis had been sending information to the mom, but not to the dad. So, the teacher contacted the father and asked how the dad would like to participate. The father wanted to get all the information about his child and wanted to find out about coaching softball.

Mr. Nellis promptly added the father's name to the e-mail distribution list and to the list in the school office from which mailing labels were generated. He also added the dad's name to his checklist (Figure 11.6). All information concerning this child now goes to both parents.

The third parent, Mr. Wallace, who also had never visited the school, is an officer on a Navy ship and is away on the ship for several months at a time. When asked how he would

---

Operation Self-Reflection
Checklist: Family Involvement

Month: December, January, *February*, March, April, May, June (indicate month)

Family Name	Communicated with each family this month about child's progress in school		
	Yes	No	Comment about their child:
Hennessy	✓		phone/described science experiment
Thomas	✓		e-mail/sent attachment with poem
Vang	✓		face-to-face/math and motor development checklists
Thao	✓		e-mail/attachment: math checklist
Jorgensen	✓		phone/progress in oral reading
Logan-North	✓		e-mail/attachment: Andy's motor dev. checklist
Mrs. Wallace	✓		e-mail/scanned in Jake's two writing samples
Captain Wallace	✓		e-mail/scanned in Jake's two writing samples
Verden	✓		e-mail/child zooms through math
Kahll	✓		face-to-face/attachment: math checklist
Bocov	✓		e-mail/progress in reading
Martinez	✓		e-mail/described science project
Ramos	✓		e-mail/likes library books about animals
Washington	✓		phone + e-mail/adv. reading group
Bjornrud	✓		e-mail/interest in plants
Capelli	✓		e-mail/leadership ability
Gardner	✓		phone/approaches others, shyness diminishing
Mrs. Campbell	✓		e-mail/excellent reading skills
Mr. Campbell	✓		e-mail/excellent reading skills
Scheff	✓		e-mail/attachment: math checklist

Reflection: The anecdotal records and portfolios helped me stay on track with contacting all parents. It only took 1 hour to complete all the contacts. The Ramos and Capelli families were pleased about the reports. The Ramos family did not know that their child likes to read about animals, and the Capellis said that I validated their own observations about Tony's leadership ability.

This is a very good investment of my time.

Figure 11.6

prefer to participate, he surprised Mr. Nellis by saying, "Well, I can't come to school because I'm out here on this ship. I do read the Web page and get the homework assignments so that my wife and I can both help Jake with homework. What I'd really like to do is to send one e-mail message to Jake's whole class every week. I'm an amateur photographer and bird watcher. I would like to send digital photographs of the birds that I see to the class along with a description."

Mr. Nellis also added Captain Wallace's name to his e-mail distribution list and to his checklist (Figure 11.6).

Communicate with Each Family at Least Once Each Month About Their Child's Overall Progress.   Mr. Nellis enjoys contact with families. He developed and explained portfolios well (chapter 6). He has always had face-to-face family conferences with every family in January and May and will continue using this formal method. However, he wants to contact each family once per month about their child's progress and wants to do this efficiently. Figure 11.6 is the teacher-made checklist that he will use to ensure that he meets this goal.

He will make less formal contacts with each family about their child's progress each month. He plans to make phone calls to those who prefer calls, meet with a few parents at school, and send e-mail messages to the majority who prefer that method; he also plans to send examples of each child's progress when possible.

Example: Mr. Nellis sent an e-mail to Jake's parents and described Jake's progress in writing. With Jake's help in choosing writing samples, the teacher scanned two of Jake's writing samples into the computer and attached them to the e-mail message along with an explanation of the changes. Jake's mother and father (the father is on the Navy ship) were thus able to talk with their son about his progress long before the mother attended the conference in May.

Activities to Help You Construct Knowledge and Skills in Observing

ACTIVITY 1

Journal writing: self-reflection. Read the section on the levels of self-reflection. At this point in your teaching career, where would you place yourself in these levels? What is your reason for placing yourself at that level?

Describe the one thing that you think would help you the most to grow in your ability to do self-reflection. Why do you think that this would help you?

ACTIVITY 2

Put yourself in Mrs. Vargas's place as she improves her classroom practices related to math/numbers. Specifically, she discovered that she needed to offer activities that require more input from the teacher much more often. Here are some examples of such activities:

📖 Making a chart to compare children's weight or height
📖 Counting and recording the number of plants in a planting bed
📖 Offering three or four types of bread and recording the number of children who prefer each type

She also discovered that she needs to rotate math materials to maintain interest. Here are some examples:

📖 Different items to count, such as snowpeople counters replaced by ice cream counters replaced by bumblebee counters
📖 Different objects to weigh
📖 Different objects to measure with a measuring stick
📖 Different collections of geometric shapes

Write an *action plan* for Mrs. Vargas. Use the form provided below. Consider patterning your action plan after those in this chapter.

Reread sections of this chapter on how, specifically, the teachers observed/reflected in order to reach their goals. Develop appropriate observation instruments that you would use. Be prepared to give the reason for choosing the form(s) that you chose.

Self-Reflection
Action Plan for Improving Math/Number Activities

I am working on these goals:

To achieve these goals, I will:

REFERENCES

ASCD (2000). The literacy of reflectiveness, Lesson 1, ASCD Online Course. Retrieved March 4, 2003, from www.ascd.org

Frank, P. (1999). Mission possible: Becoming a reflective teacher, *Catalyst*, 8, 1.

Harms, T., Clifford, R. M., & Cryer, D. (1998). *Early childhood environment rating scale* (ECERS) (Rev. ed.). New York: Teachers College Press.

Hemmeter, M. L., Maxwell, K., Ault, M., & Schuster, J. (2001). *Assessment of practices* (APEEC). New York: Teachers College Press.

Kohn, A. (1996). *Beyond discipline*. Alexandria, VA: ASCD (Association for Supervision and Curriculum Development).

Lambert, L. (2000). Self-reflection rubric. In ASCD, *The reflective educator*, an ASCD online course. Retrieved March 4, 2003, from www.ascd.org

Shon, D. (1987). *Educating the reflective practitioner: Toward a new design for teaching and learning in the professions*. San Francisco: Jossey-Bass.

WEB SITES RELATED TO THIS CHAPTER

✓ ASCD/Association for Supervision and Curriculum Development

Cited in other chapters. Good Web site for assessment and professional development.

www.ascd.org

Go to appropriate links for assessment, online courses, or other professional development. Excellent films and books available.

APPENDIX A

SUGGESTIONS FOR ORGANIZING PERIODIC AND FINAL OBSERVATION REPORTS

Early childhood professionals have a firm sense of their history. It has helped them build the present and will remain a strong foundation for the future of the profession. Carbonara's (1961) booklet, *Techniques for Observing Normal Child Behavior*, offered excellent suggestions for organizing periodic and final observation reports.[1]

Consider using her suggestions as you write a midyear or final report for a child. I have taken the liberty of referring to both boys and girls. Gather all of your observations of a child (running records, anecdotal records, checklists, and rating scales) and use these suggestions to write your observation reports.

OUTLINE FOR PERIODIC OR FINAL OBSERVATION REPORTS FOR AN INDIVIDUAL CHILD

1. **Physical appearance**
   - What does the child look like?
   - How is he dressed?
   - Does he seem to be in good physical health, or not?

2. **Body movement and use of body**
   - Are her body movements characteristically quick or slow?
   - Does she seem at home with her body, or stiff, clumsy, unsure?
   - Are her large muscle and small muscle coordination about equally developed, or is one more developed than the other?
   - How much of what she is feeling is expressed through her body?

---

[1]*Source*: Adapted from Carbonara, N. T. (1961). *Techniques for observing normal child behavior*. Pittsburgh, PA: University of Pittsburgh Press. Reprinted by permission of the University of Pittsburgh Press.

3. **Facial expressions**

- How much of what he is feeling is expressed in his facial expressions?
- Do his reactions minute by minute *show* in his face?
- Do they show only when he feels intensely about something?
- Does he characteristically maintain a deadpan expression?

4. **Speech**

- How much of what she is feeling is expressed through her tone of voice? Is her voice generally controlled, or does it express changing moods?
- If she gets upset, does she talk more or less than usual?
- Is this a child to whom speech is an important means of communication, or does she speak rarely, communicating in other ways?
- Does she like to play with speech, making up chants, puns, and stories?
- Is her speech fluent, average, choppy, or inarticulate?

5. **Emotional reactions**

- How and when does he exhibit happiness, anger, sadness, doubt, enthusiasm?
- Does he seem to have too little control over his feelings; too much; a good balance?

6. **Relationships with other children**

- Does she seek out other children? How and when?
- Does she seek only specific children?
- Does she avoid the other children or specific children? How and when?
- Does she wait until someone seeks her out? How does she respond to another child's invitation to play?
- Does she spend a lot of time watching other children; specific children; certain activities?
- Is she generally a leader; follower; sometimes one and sometimes the other?
- Is she comfortable with other children, able to give and take and share ideas and equipment; or does she seem fearful; bossy; unable to share equipment; unhappy unless she gets her own way; unduly inhibited about expressing her own ideas to other children?
- Are her ways of relating to other children age-appropriate; precocious; immature?

7. **Relationships with adults**

- Does he seem, basically, to trust adults or mistrust them? How does he show this?
- Does he go easily to any adult, or only to specific people?
- Does he seem to need to be physically close to the teacher at all times; does he just need to have her in sight; is he indifferent?
- Does he seem comfortable and friendly with adults; clinging; demanding; anxious; placating; defiant; different at different times; and/or with different people?
- Does he seek adults out for comfort, or avoid being comforted by them?
- Does he ask their help? When and how? How does he react to being limited? How does he ask to *be* limited? Does he spend a lot of time watching adults?
- Are his ways of relating to adults age-appropriate; precocious; immature?

8. **Play activities**

   ◻ What activities does she get involved in? How are they begun; what course do they run; what does she go to next?

   ◻ Does she play for a long time at something, or play briefly at one thing after another? Does she play briefly in some activities and with prolonged absorption in others? Are there activities she avoids?

   ◻ What does she seem to be getting out of an activity: the sociability of being with other children; sensory pleasure; a sense of mastery or problem solving; a sense of creative expression of ideas and feelings? What aspects of an activity seem especially frustrating or especially pleasurable to her?

   ◻ Does the tempo of her play remain even; does it speed up; slow down? When?

   ◻ Does she prefer to be alone when she plays: never, always, sometimes? Under what circumstances?

   ◻ Does she express fantasy in her play verbally; gesturally; through creative media? What kinds of roles does she enjoy taking in dramatic play (baby, mother, father, dog)?

   ◻ Does she seem to feel more comfortable playing indoors or outdoors? Does she like to confine her play to a narrow area in space, or does she prefer to expand over a large area?

   ◻ Are there times when she abruptly stops playing? When and why? What does she do then?

   ◻ Does she try new things? Show curiosity about her environment, equipment, people? Does she have special skills?

APPENDIX B

SUGGESTED ITEMS TO LOOK FOR IN OBSERVING A PLAY MATERIAL OR ACTIVITY[1]

Item 1: Which Children Gravitate to This Play Material or Activity?

- Is there any similarity between them (all boys, all girls, both boys and girls, all quiet)?
- Which children seem to avoid this play area? Is there any similarity among that group?
- Is this an activity or material that some children avoid but like to watch others participating in?

Item 2: How Do Different Children Use the Same Material or Activity?

- Do different children seem to be getting different things out of it, or do most of the children seem to be getting something similar from it?
- How do children of different ages play with the same materials or engage in the same activities?
- Do boys and girls use it differently, or in much the same way?

Item 3: Why Would This Material or Activity Be Made Available to Young Children?

- What are its built-in possibilities for creative expressions, problem-solving, or sensory enjoyment?

[1]*Source*: Adapted from Carbonara, N. T. (1961). *Techniques for observing normal child behavior*. Pittsburgh, PA: University of Pittsburgh Press. Reprinted with permission of the University of Pittsburgh Press.

📖 What are its built-in frustrations (e.g., blocks fall over, computer screens go blank)?

📖 How much self-control is necessary to use the material or activity for constructive purposes? Do some children or particular age groups have difficulty with this self-control?

📖 Is this a material or activity that seems to promote a lot of socializing among the children?

📖 Does this material seem to induce more solitary play?

📖 Is it better adapted to play between only two children?

Item 4: How Do Children Affect One Another When They Are Sharing a Material or Activity?

📖 Who begins the play?

📖 Who suggests changes?

📖 How is it ended?

📖 What kinds of problems come up that need to be solved if the play is to continue constructively?

Item 5: What Is the Teacher's Role In Relation to This Material or Activity?

📖 Does he simply make it available?

📖 Does she make suggestions?

📖 Does she step in and structure it quite actively?

📖 Does he completely direct it?

📖 What features of the material or activity would account for her decision to act in this manner?

APPENDIX C

SELECTED OBSERVATION FORMS USED IN THIS TEXTBOOK

You will find, in this appendix, a blank copy of most of the observation forms in this textbook. Consider using the forms that will best help you get a good clear view of a child's development or progress. Some of the forms can help you assess specific aspects of your own professional development or teaching practices. Here is a list of all the forms in this appendix:

- Anecdotal Record: Format
- Checklist: Guidelines for Writing Anecdotal Records
- Running Record Observation: Format
- Hand Washing Checklist
- Participation Checklist
- Example: Forced Choice Rating Scale (Cleanup)
- Example: Numerical Rating Scale (Cleanup)
- Example: Graphic Rating Scale (Cleanup)
- Checklist: Organize Portfolios Well: Develop a Good System
- Checklist: How_____Exhibits Stress
- Who, What, When, Where, Why: Five Questions About Behavior
- Checklist: Timeline for Assessment (Sample)
- Checklist: Memory Development in Early Childhood
- Checklist: How Children Express Anger
- Checklist: Causes of Anger in Early Childhood Classrooms
- Graphic Rating Scale: How_____Manages Anger
- Social Attributes Checklist
- Checklist: Characteristics of Abused or Neglected Children
- Checklist: What Can I Do to Minimize the Stress of Moving for a Child?
- Self-Reflection Planning Sheet
- Rating Scale: Conflict Resolution Skills
- Checklist: Self-Reflection Action Plan on Conflict Resolution
- Checklist: Self-Reflection Family Involvement

Permission is granted by the publisher to reproduce these observation forms.

Suggested format for recording anecdotal records—Part one is for context; part two for the anecdote; part three for reflecting/commenting

Anecdotal Record

Goal for this observation:

Setting: **Date/day:**   **Time of day:**

Basic activity:

Focus child: **Others involved:**_____

The Anecdote:

Reflection/Comment/Interpretation:

Checklist: Guidelines for Writing Anecdotal Records

Use these criteria for analyzing an anecdotal record. Check the appropriate box next to each numbered statement. Write comments that will help in your analysis.

	Met	Not met	Comment
1. Develop an observation plan	_____	_____	_____
2. Record the anecdote as soon as possible after it happens	_____	_____	_____
3. Describe the context in which the incident occurs	_____	_____	_____
4. Write useful notes about the activity. Notes are in separate section of form	_____	_____	_____
5. Exact words recorded in writing dialogue/in quote marks. Paraphrased remarks not in quote marks	_____	_____	_____
6. Information about how others responded to speaker's words or actions	_____	_____	_____
7. Written in proper order: Describe setting, then action, then how incident ended	_____	_____	_____
8. Complete enough in data recorded to get clear idea of event. Written objectively	_____	_____	_____
9. Interpreted carefully (interpretations in body of anecdote in brackets; most interpretation done in separate section)	_____	_____	_____

Running Record Observation: Format

Focus:_____

Date:_____

Context/Background Comments	Intensive Observation	Reflection/Comments

Hand Washing Checklist

Do a health check by observing children's willingness to wash hands properly. Write children's names at top of chart. Read descriptors in left column; place a check mark under a child's name if s/he demonstrates each ability. May also be used for a single child.

Children's Names:

Proper hand
washing technique

Washes hands
before preparing food

Washes hands
before eating

Washes hands
after using tissue

Washes hands
after using toilet

Washes hands
after painting, etc.

Washes hands
at other times

Washes hands
voluntarily 90%
of the time

Summary:

Participation Checklist

Get a picture of which children are participating in which centers. Discover which centers are used most frequently and which are not used much at all. Print each child's name in the left column. Write center names across the top as the sample center shows. Check if a child works in that center; leave blank if not.

Date: _____

Areas/Centers in This Classroom

	Writing	Science	_____	_____	_____	_____

Child's Name

_____	_____	_____	_____	_____	_____	_____
_____	_____	_____	_____	_____	_____	_____
_____	_____	_____	_____	_____	_____	_____
_____	_____	_____	_____	_____	_____	_____
_____	_____	_____	_____	_____	_____	_____

Summary Comments Based on This Observation:

Example: Forced Choice Rating Scale (Cleanup)

Child's Name:
Date:
Circle One: indoors/outside (playground)

Circle one phrase from this list describing child's participation in cleanup:
- blocks efforts to clean up
- does not stop playing unless
  teacher (T) makes a firm request
- does not participate
- cleans up only with supervision from T
- cleans up without supervision from T

Example: Numerical Rating Scale (Cleanup)

Child's Name:
Date:
Circle One: indoors/outside (playground)

Circle the number of the phrase describing child's participation in cleanup.
1. blocks efforts to clean up
2. does not stop playing unless
   teacher (T) makes firm request
3. does not participate
4. cleans up only with T supervision
5. cleans up without T supervision

Example: Graphic Rating Scale (Cleanup)

Child's Name:
Date:
Circle One: Indoors/outside (playground)

Rate child on each of the following by marking appropriate spot on line next to each numbered phrase.

	Always	Often*	Occasionally**	Seldom***	Never

Never
1. blocks efforts to clean up
2. does not stop playing unless
   teacher (T) requests firmly
3. does not participate
4. cleans up only with T supervision
5. cleans up w/o T supervision

*Often: at least four times for period observed
**Occasionally: two or three times for period observed
***Seldom: only one time for period observed

Checklist: Organize Portfolios Well:
Develop a Good System

❑   **Use a simple, uncomplicated system to organize materials**
   Choose ordinary inexpensive folders or boxes (children can decorate)
   Clearly label each child's folder or box
   Use a straightforward filing system (line up boxes/folders alphabetically by
      child's last name)

❑   **Date every work sample and observation**
   Write date on each item, in upper right corner (date is then visible when filed)
   Tells reader when item was created

❑   **Place items in chronological order in the portfolio**
   Older items in front; more recent items behind older ones
   Saves a teacher's valuable time
   Enables teacher to assess development and progress without additional
      sorting

❑   **Place all items from similar categories together,** for example
   Easel painting samples from beginning, middle, end of school year
   Photographs of playdough products
   Writing samples (filed chronologically)

❑   **File all items promptly**
   Avoid letting things pile up
   Consider filing items immediately, or
   File at end of each day
   Children can file a work sample after teacher has dated it

Checklist: How _____ Exhibits Stress

Children can show stress in a number of ways. Check any boxes that pertain to this child and give a brief explanation for each choice.

Date:_____

❑   **This child's reactions to stress seem to be passive**
Excessive fatigue
Withdrawing and putting head on table or desk
Excessive fears

Explanation:

❑   **This child's reactions to stress seem to be more active, with behaviors that involve only the child**
Nail biting
Manipulating one's hands or mouth
Repetitive body movements

Explanation:

❑   **This child's reactions to stress seem to show up when s/he interacts with others**
Stuttering
Bullying, threatening, or hurting others
Nervous, inappropriate laughter

Explanation:

❑   **This child's reactions to stress seem to show up as s/he works with objects**
Excessive squeezing or tapping of pencils, markers, crayons
Clumsy or fumbling behavior

Explanation:

Who, What, When, Where, Why:

Five Questions About Behavior

- *Who* was involved in this behavior or interaction?

- *What* happened?

- *When* does the behavior typically occur, or when did the behavior occur?

- *Where* did the behavior occur?

- *Why* did this behavior happen?

Checklist: Timeline for Assessment (Sample)
Early Childhood Classes: Oaklawn School

Sept. 1–14	_____Social Attributes Checklist (Existing/Ready-made)
	_____Williams's Motor Development Checklist (Existing/Ready-made)
	_____Explain concept of portfolios to children and parents
	_____Portfolio items as appropriate: writing samples from all children
Sept. 15–30	_____Portfolio items as appropriate: art samples for each child
	_____Anecdotal or running records for 1/3 of the class
Oct.1–15	_____Math skills checklist (all children)
	_____Portfolio items or other checklists as appropriate for each child
	_____Anecdotal or running records for 1/3 of the class
Oct.16–31	_____Social Attributes Checklist
	_____Anecdotal or running records for 1/3 of the class
	_____Begin Project Spectrum Motor Development Assessment Obstacle Course
	_____Portfolio items as appropriate; writing samples
	_____Review portfolios for 1/2 of the class
Nov. 1–15	_____Portfolio items as appropriate
	_____Review portfolios for other half of the class
	_____Math Skills Checklist
Nov. 15–Dec. 10	_____Portfolio items as appropriate
	_____District administers standardized test for motor skills to all early childhood classes
	_____Emotional development checklist: two parts
	_____Rating Scale: How _____ Manages Anger
Dec. 27–Jan. 8	_____Holidays (work on observational reports and portfolios)
	_____Consolidate observational data for each child: write reports
	_____When school starts up again: Portfolio Review & Reflection
	_____Work with each child to review portfolio's contents
	_____Organize for parent conferences
	_____Write helpful comments for parents as appropriate
Jan. 12–14	_____Parent conferences
	_____Portfolios: midyear observational report/analysis of children's work samples

A checklist/timeline: observation and assessment in Mr. Nellis's school for first semester. Mr. Nellis uses this checklist to track assessment activities. He has also made a notation of each item in his day planner.

This is an example of a timeline/checklist that the focus teacher in this text used during one semester. Consider making a similar timeline for yourself to keep your assessment plan on track.

Checklist: Memory Development in Early Childhood

Child's Name/Age:
Date:

Birth to approximately 5 months
_____ Recognizes familiar objects; *habituates to*—becomes accustomed to or bored with—a stimulus, such as a toy put in front of him several times
_____ Can recall a memory but must get a *cue or reminder*

5 months to 1 year (5 to 12 months)
_____ Recognizes objects after seeing them only a few times
_____ Remembers an object for several weeks (Fagan, 1984)
_____ Actively recalls (needs fewer cues) events from the recent past

12 to 36 months (1 year to 3 years old)
_____ After about age 2, recalls events that happened quite some time before
_____ Occasionally tells about the memory in the form of a story
_____ 3-year-olds recall events from 1 or 2 years before

4 years to 12 years (all of the above plus . . .)
_____ 4-year-olds can recognize an array (group) of items
_____ 4-year-olds recall only 3 or 4 of a group of 12 items
_____ Third-graders able to recognize all of an array of 12 items
_____ Third-graders can recall about 8 of the items

Comment:

CHECKLIST: HOW CHILDREN EXPRESS ANGER

Observe how this child reacts to anger-arousing situations. Check *Yes* if s/he expresses anger as described in that method. Check *No* if the child does not express anger that way. Observe over a period of at least several days.
Child's name and age:_____

- **Venting.** Expressing anger through facial expressions, crying, sulking, or complaining; "blowing off steam."
  _____Yes   _____No
  Comments:

- **Active resistance.** Physically or verbally defends position, self-esteem, or possessions in nonaggressive ways.
  _____Yes   _____No
  Comments:

- **Express dislike.** Tells offender that he or she cannot play or is not liked.
  _____Yes   _____No
  Comments:

- **Aggressive revenge.** Physically or verbally retaliates against the provocateur with no other purpose evident—name calling, pinching, hitting, or threatening.
  _____Yes   _____No
  Comments:

- **Avoidance.** Attempts to escape from or evade the offender.
  _____Yes   _____No
  Comments:

- **Adult-seeking.** Tells an adult about an incident or looks for comfort from adult.
  _____Yes   _____No
  Comments:

Checklist: Causes of Anger in Early Childhood Classrooms

Observe this child reacting to social interactions that typically arouse anger. Check *Yes* if the child reacts with anger; check *No* if s/he does not; check *Not observed* if you have not yet observed the child's reactions to this type of interaction. Write brief comments.

Child's name and age:_____

CONFLICT OVER POSSESSIONS.   Someone takes or destroys focus child's property or invades child's space.

___Yes   ___No   ___Not observed

Comment/Date:

PHYSICAL ASSAULT.   Something done to a child's body, such as pushing or hitting.

___Yes   ___No   ___Not observed

Comment/Date:

VERBAL ASSAULT.   Taunting, teasing, insults, or degrading or demeaning statements.

___Yes   ___No   ___Not observed

Comments/Date:

REJECTION: Other children either ignore or refuse to allow a child to play. Rejection by adults is one of the classic forms of emotional child abuse.

___Yes   ___No   ___Not observed

Comment/Date:

ISSUES OF COMPLIANCE.   Someone asks or forces a child to do something that he does not want to do. Almost all anger over issues of compliance occur between an adult and a child.

___Yes   ___No   ___Not observed

Comment/Date:

Graphic Rating Scale: How _____ Manages Anger

Reflecting on your observations of this child, rate how she or he manages the emotion of anger. For each statement, choose the rating that best describes this child and circle the appropriate spot on the scale. Write a brief narrative in the *Comment* section. Use this information when you write your observation report of this child's development.

Child's Name:

Date:

	Always	Often	Occasionally	Seldom	Never
Uses words appropriately to express anger					
Strikes out when angry					
Name calling when upset					
Expresses anger appropriately toward teachers					
Expresses anger appropriately toward other children					
Generates word labels for frustration and anger					

Comment:

Social Attributes Checklist

Child's Name: _____

Date:

Observation # Circle one: 1   2   3   4

I. INDIVIDUAL ATTRIBUTES

The child:

_____ Is *usually* in a positive mood

_____ Is not *excessively* dependent on the teacher, assistant, or other adults

_____ Usually comes to the program or setting willingly

_____ Usually copes with rebuffs adequately

_____ Shows the capacity to empathize

_____ Has positive relationships with one or two peers; shows capacity to really care about them, miss them if they are absent

_____ Displays the capacity for humor

_____ Does not seem to be acutely lonely

SOCIAL SKILLS ATTRIBUTES

The child *usually:*

_____ Approaches others positively

_____ Expresses wishes and preferences clearly; gives reasons for actions and positions

_____ Asserts own rights and needs appropriately

_____ Is not easily intimidated by bullies

_____ Expresses frustrations and anger effectively and without escalating disagreements or harming others

_____ Gains access to ongoing groups at play and work

_____ Enters ongoing discussion on the subject; makes relevant contributions to ongoing activities

_____ Takes turns fairly easily

_____ Shows interest in others; exchanges information with and requests information from others appropriately

_____ Negotiates and compromises with others appropriately

_____ Does not draw inappropriate attention to self

_____ Accepts and enjoys peers and adults of ethnic groups other than his or her own

_____ Interacts nonverbally with other children with smiles, waves, nods, and so forth

PEER RELATIONSHIP ATTRIBUTES

The child:

_____ Is usually accepted versus neglected or rejected by other children

_____ Is sometimes invited by other children to join them in play, friendship, and work

_____ Is named by other children as someone they are friends with or like to play and work with

This is from an ERIC DIGEST. You may duplicate it without permission but must give credit to the developers. McClellan & Katz (2001, March)

**Checklist:
Characteristics of Abused or Neglected Children**

❑ Seem old for their age

❑ Lack ability to play

❑ Temper tantrums beyond that expected for age and stage of development

❑ Negative self-esteem—child behaves in a way that tells us that he does not feel competent or in control or that he is not worthy of the attention of others

❑ Withdrawal—can, but does not always indicate abuse

❑ Chronic aggression or overt hostility against peers, animals, adults, themselves

❑ Passive watchfulness—an excessive amount

❑ Compulsivity or efforts to control some small aspect of their lives

❑ Fearful of failure

❑ Difficulty listening to or carrying out instructions

❑ Difficulty organizing thoughts, conceptualizing, and verbalizing

❑ Regression to an earlier stage of development—bedwetting, thumbsucking, baby talk

❑ Poor social skills

❑ Extreme shyness

❑ Steal or hoard food

❑ Little or no empathy for others

**Checklist: What Can I Do to Minimize
the Stress of Moving for a Child?**

❑ Obtain the child's file and read it carefully. Follow school policy on contacting the previous teacher for clarification on any issues.

❑ Do a home visit if your school encourages teachers to make home visits.

❑ Familiarize the child and family with the new school. Invite them to come to school for a tour so that the new school is not so new on the child's first day.

❑ Make sure that the child and his family know the schedule in your room. Give them a handout of your schedule and encourage parents to talk about their child's new schedule.

❑ Create a space for a new child by preparing a locker or cubby, cot for napping, and any other individualized area or material. Create her space before she arrives.

❑ Take a new group picture with the new child included. Do this on the first day that the new child enters your room.

❑ Walk through your classroom's and center or school's routines, such as bathroom, snack, or lunch, getting on the bus, waiting for parents.

❑ Take your class through the fire safety drill so that *everyone,* including the new child, knows the procedure.

❑ Ask the child to tell you about how the new routines are different from or similar to those in her old school.

❑ Talk with the child and find out what he likes to do in school.

❑ Include the child in activities of his new room at his pace.

❑ Request that other children in the class act as guides for the new class member. Be specific in your requests: "Joe, please walk with Robert to the lunchroom. He will be sitting next to you, and I thought that you could show him how lunch is served in our school."

❑ Be sure that every child wears a nametag so that a new class member can get to know names.

❑ Read a book about moving with the child or with the class.

❑ Listen carefully for the feelings that the new class member has about moving. Acknowledge the feelings, and avoid commanding him to feel differently.

Self-Reflection Planning Sheet

<u>**I am (or we are) working on these goals**</u>:

<u>**To reach these goals I/we will**</u>:

Rating Scale: Conflict Resolution Skills

Child's Name:_____

Date:_____

First, does this child seem to understand how to resolve conflicts? Yes   No

Second, how does this child use conflict resolution skills? Place an "X" on the line at the spot indicating the child's ability to use conflict resolution skills.

	Always	Often	Occasionally	Seldom	Never
1. uses appropriate conflict resolution skills					
2. uses inappropriate conflict resolution skills					
3. uses conflict resolution skills only if T firmly requests					
4. uses conflict resolution skills only with T guidance					
5. uses conflict resolution skills without teacher guidance					

Recommendation for helping this child:

Checklist: Self-Reflection
Action Plan on Conflict Resolution

❑ Rate each child's ability to solve conflicts (use teacher-made rating scale)

❑ Invite guidance counselor to do three sessions on conflict resolution

❑ Use the "thinking puppets" to reinforce guidance counselor's lessons

❑ Read story about children who resolve a conflict to class

❑ Make poster on how to solve problems; hang on wall near group area

❑ Give on-the-spot guidance to children about resolving conflict

❑ Remind children about how to resolve conflict

❑ Remind children about negotiation

❑ Designate a special spot in our classroom for resolving conflicts

❑ Rate my classroom in 6 weeks on how we have changed in conflict resolution

Reflection:

**Checklist: Self-Reflection
Family Involvement**

Keep track of how you are communicating information about each child to his or her parent(s) monthly. List family names; check *Yes* when you've made contact. Under the last column, indicate the method that you used: e-mail, phone, face-to-face, mail, electronic mailing list, other. Briefly note the nature of your comment about each child.

Month: (indicate month)_____

Have I communicated with each family this month about their child's development and progress?

Family Name	Yes	No	Comment about their child:
_____	_____	_____	_____
_____	_____	_____	_____
_____	_____	_____	_____
_____	_____	_____	_____
_____	_____	_____	_____
_____	_____	_____	_____
_____	_____	_____	_____
_____	_____	_____	_____
_____	_____	_____	_____
_____	_____	_____	_____
_____	_____	_____	_____
_____	_____	_____	_____
_____	_____	_____	_____
_____	_____	_____	_____
_____	_____	_____	_____
_____	_____	_____	_____
_____	_____	_____	_____
_____	_____	_____	_____

Reflection:

Name Index

Subject Index